&See, Know & Serve

Praise for *See, Know & Serve*

Churches know that the forms and traditions of the past no longer resonate with many today. Yet mere rejection is inadequate. This book offers a positive alternative in which the church exists for mission—not as a program but as a disposition to bless people other than themselves. Bandy also offers tools to understand and respond to the complex realities of the lives of people within the reach of your congregation.

—Lovett H. Weems Jr., distinguished professor of church leadership and director, Lewis Center for Church Leadership, Wesley Theological Seminary, Washington, DC

Demographic analysis and psychographics sound arcane until you learn that marketers have used them for years to learn more about you and your family. Then they sound slick and corporate. They are neither. In this book Tom Bandy builds from decades of work with churches and faith-based nonprofits to unlock their potential for ministry. His theological reflections offer a framework and process for learning how to use this data to bless the people in your mission field. They offer a springboard for creative and spirit-filled ministries.

—Cory Sparks, director, Louisiana Association of Nonprofit Organizations

Other Books from Tom G. Bandy and Abingdon Press

Kicking Habits: Welcome Relief for Addicted Churches
Growing Spiritual Redwoods (with Bill Easum)
Moving Off the Map: A Field Guide to Changing the Congregation
Christian Chaos: Revolutionizing the Congregation
Coaching Change: Breaking Down Resistance, Building Up Hope
Roadrunner: The Body in Motion
Fragile Hope: Your Church in 2020
Mission Mover: Beyond Education for Church Leadership
Uncommon Lectionary: Opening the Bible for Seekers and Disciples
Why Should I Believe You? Rediscovering Clergy Credibility
95 Questions to Shape the Future of Your Church

See, Know & Serve

The People Within Your Reach

THOMAS G. BANDY

Abingdon Press

Nashville

SEE, KNOW & SERVE THE PEOPLE WITHIN YOUR REACH

This book is printed on acid-free paper.

Library of Congress Cataloging-in-Publication Data

Bandy, Thomas G., 1950–
  See, know & serve the people within your reach / Thomas G. Bandy.
    pages cm
  Includes bibliographical references.
    ISBN 978-1-4267-7417-1 (book - pbk. / trade binding; soft black : alk. paper) 1. Mission of the church.   2. Christian leadership.   3. Pastoral theology. 4. Church renewal.   5. Christianity and culture.   6. Christianity—21st century.   I. Title.   II. Title: See, know and serve the people within your reach.
  BV601.8B36 2013
  253—dc23

13 14 15 16 17 18 19 20 21 22—10 9 8 7 6 5 4 3 2 1
MANUFACTURED IN THE UNITED STATES OF AMERICA

To my wife, Lynne, whose patience and optimism sustains me as I travel and whose own experience as a pastor has helped me test and refine the observations of this book.

I have become all things to all people, that I might by all means save some. I do it all for the sake of the gospel, so that I may share in its blessings. (1 Corinthians 9:22b-23)

Contents

Contents

Foreword

by Chuck Salter

Recently, I have suffered with a fair amount of eyestrain at the end of a workday. Initially I blamed it on the size of my computer monitor so I replaced it with a 32" flat screen! As a last resort, I went to have my eyes examined and was surprised by two discoveries. First, it had been three years since my last complete exam. Where did all the time go? Second, my vision had changed enough that I wasn't seeing well close up. I was missing the details that I didn't know I was missing. I had enough vision to see the big picture, but it was a strain to see the details, and the *details* made all the difference.

Many church leaders are aware of changes taking place around them, but only at a distance, at a rather abstract level. They see the big picture, but the details of change elude them. May I suggest that it's nearly impossible to see even the people within our reach when we have a blurry field of vision?

This book is about seeing and *serving* the people who are in and around your church—the people your church is uniquely called to serve. You may think you know them, but you probably don't—even if you have reviewed demographic data for your neighborhood. In my experience, many leaders read demographic reports and are overwhelmed by the data and confused about what to do. Others simply review the reports, sort the data, filter the data in some creative way, and then make small tactical adjustments. I have heard other church leaders proclaim, "We have done our demographics," assuming that one eight-page report generated every few years will reveal a complete understanding of the people in that area.

What is true is that more than forty-one million households have moved in the United States over the past twelve months, and our communities continue to become more and more diverse. Look around you. Do you *really* know your church's neighbors? Or do you know who you *think* they are, based on old assumptions, limited demographic information, or outdated research?

As the world around us is always changing, so is the demographic information. How would you react if you logged on to a website and found three-year-old information, or even month-old information? Most of us would find that irritating at best. We might disregard the website entirely because we know that the information is outdated and probably irrelevant. The world is changing so rapidly that no single report by any demographic provider, no individual map regardless of how colorful or compelling it is, no strategic study or process is sufficient for answering all of our missional questions. One question logically often leads to another. In the twenty-first century, we cannot see clearly how to serve the people around us without an ongoing discovery process. A simple, static demographic study generated once every five years will not cut it anymore.

As a church leader, you must begin to see the details. The most useful demographic research tools provide lenses of discovery, which provide a way to see more clearly the current and future realities of the people who live within your church's reach. These lenses reveal nuanced information about the actual human needs in the place where God has called your church to serve. And let's be clear: This is not about the numbers...it's about location—*where God has placed you today*—and it's about the real human needs present in the households where the church serves. This is not about generating a demographic report to include in an annual review of existing church ministries. It's about becoming a blessing and doing what we are called to do, where we are called to do it. Along with my partners we founded Mission-Insite, a church demographic system built to equip churches to gather and utilize this type of research, which we call "location intelligence," to provide close-up views of the people in your area. Tom has worked with us in this effort. MissionInsite delivers lifestyle information provided by Experian, specifically MOSAIC USA Household Portraits. MOSAIC USA is one of several national segmentation systems that provide detailed consumer-based information for household types in your community.

The world and all its communities are changing. People and families no longer fall into a few neat categories—as if they ever did. Our assumptions about people are too often based on outdated realities or shallow information. Churches give birth to vitally relevant ministry when they focus their passion and mission upon blessing the people who live within their reach. *But how can we bless people we really don't know?* The tools are available, and churches should be using them. Tom Bandy shows us why and how.

Chuck Salter
President
MissionInsite
www.MissionInsite.com

Part
1

Introduction

The transition between Christendom and post-Christendom is still unfolding at different speeds, with unique twists, in diverse contexts. Some regions and publics are transitioning faster and some slower. Each culture experiences special and often unexpected implications. This is why standardizing ministry practices, or replicating "best practices" from one church to another, has been so unsuccessful in growing God's mission.

Christian leaders often talk about the gap between "church" and "culture." We imagine two ships passing in the night. "Church" is one ship, and "culture" is the other. It's not that simple! A more accurate metaphor is that even in the crowded shipping lanes of the emerging post-Christendom world, when religions of all kinds are carrying exotic cargos to foreign destinations, *flotillas* of churches are managing to pass *hundreds* of microcultures without even getting into hailing distance of one another.

The great debate in this transition period has been between relevancy and integrity. The debate has unfolded *as if* these represented two extremes of a polarity. It assumes that those who try to be relevant must necessarily sacrifice integrity, and those who try to preserve integrity inevitably sacrifice relevance. Church leaders scramble to find the right balance. Chaos ensues.

Starting with the apostolic experience of the "Mission to the Gentiles," and repeated often in the history of missionary churches, we see that *relevance* and *integrity* are not either/or choices. It is possible to be both relevant *and* faithful to the integrity of Christian faith and the import of Christian practice. How is this possible?

3

First, it is possible to be both relevant *and* faithful because the Holy Spirit simultaneously employs *and* shatters all cultural forms. God can use anything—literally anything—as a vehicle for the Gospel. However, God will not allow *anything*—literally *anything*—to usurp the preeminence of the Gospel.

This means that God can use any cultural form for hospitality, worship, education, small groups, and outreach. God can use any cultural form of property, symbolism, or technology; or any cultural form of financial management, fund-raising, or administration; or any cultural form of communication. God can also use any individual, shaped by any cultural experience, to lead any church, in any context. God can use anything!

On the other hand, this also means that God will shatter, break, discard, and throw out any cultural form that attempts to supplant the gospel as the raison d'être (reason for being) of a church. There can be no sacred forms. There can be no sacred food groups to serve in hospitality; no sacred music, musical instruments, artistic expressions, languages, or ceremonies; no sacred programs, curricula, or educational methodologies; no sacred locations, properties, or technologies; no sacred stewardship strategies and administrative structures; no sacred communication vehicles. Not even the leader can be "sacred" in himself or herself. Nothing is sacred by God. If a cultural form mediates the incarnation of God, well and good; if it overtly or even inadvertently claims to be God, it will be rejected.

The test of this principle has often been worship. Christian leaders in the transition time from Christendom to post-Christendom have hotly debated (and occasionally resorted to fisticuffs), arguing about "good worship." The ancients would remind us that the only good worship is worship that reveals God incarnate. If it does that, it's good…even if it entails rap music and holy laughter. If it doesn't do that, it's not only inappropriate but sinful…even if it entails plainsong and expository preaching.

Among the majority of Christian churches in the world, the real test of this principle is Eucharist or Mass. Debates rage in the period of transition between east and west, young and old, innovators and classicists, cathedrals and battlefields over the relevance and integrity

4

of Holy Communion. The ancients would remind us that the essence of Eucharist is the regular experience of the real presence of Christ. If Christ is *really with us,* exactly how that came about doesn't really matter.

Usually, when I say things like that, alarms ring and stress increases among the audience. Surely I must be implying that old traditions and beloved practices are obsolete! Yet if you listen carefully, I am saying nothing of the kind. If any given practice of Holy Communion *works,* by all means keep doing it! If a particular public experiences the real presence of Christ in some traditional way, praise the Lord! I am also saying that what works for one public, in one context, at one time, may not work for another public, in another context, at another time. Even the public that once was blessed with the real presence of Christ may change over time and urgently need to experience Christ in fresh ways.

And the publics *are changing!* Populations are migrating. Communities are evolving. Lifestyle segments are diversifying. If you blink, it's different.

It is possible to be both relevant *and* faithful because we now have more objective ways to track the changing expectations of the publics surrounding a church. The apostles and their mission teams relied on their personal intuition to figure out what would work best in order to bless the Philippians, the Ephesians, the Romans, the Iberians, and eventually the Nova Scotians, the Iowans, and the San Franciscans. That worked, partly because they were good listeners and keen observers, but mainly because life spans were shorter and most people stayed put. The same intuition today leads only to personal bias. It spawns hidden agendas, subtle manipulations, and ideological crusades. It tempts controlling and charismatic individuals to shape the church around themselves.

Today we have sophisticated, and remarkably accurate, demographic research methodologies with which to understand publics and target missions. We can explore in detail more than seventy distinct lifestyle segments in the United States and Canada alone, and many more distinct groups in Australia, Europe, Africa, Asia, and the Pacific Rim. The data in this information age are accumulating exponentially and systematically. Computers not only enhance our intuition but also challenge our preconceptions and critique our motivations. Christian leaders can now design mission, and if asked why they choose one tactic over another, the response does not have to be "Trust me!" Individual intuition is grounded in objective research.

This does not mean that intuition is unimportant. Even when all the data have been collected and sifted, there is no substitute for listening and observing in the mission field. Much qualitative data will only be gathered in person and interpreted through experience. The very filters we use to sift and interpret information (including the filters I describe here) are going to evolve and change.

Research and development is not a "plug and play" process. It is not automated. The human factor and the Spirit factor are still there. Church leaders cannot just run the computer, print out a report, implement a program, and watch the church grow or the mission field change without once leaving the office, kneeling in prayer, or breaking a sweat.

Nevertheless, strategic planning today is a great deal more objective than it was for the ancients. We don't need to just rely on the opinion of the most charismatic leader, hunker down for weeks of church council discussions, close our eyes and hope for the best, or even open our eyes and fear the worst. We have information. We have methods to retrieve and sort that information. We have objective ways to make strategic plans, manage risk, learn from failures, and never give up trying to bless the explosion of diversity that is the way of our world.

Tom Bandy, 2013

1. The Mission Attitude

The emergence of the "global village" has made daily living more complicated than ever before. The creative and destructive interaction of publics with each other changes local and world affairs faster than ever. One result of the emerging multicultural reality is that demographic research has expanded dramatically in the last half century. Research is increasingly detailed, constantly updated, accessible to the average person as well as corporations, and urgent for all sectors of society.

Nevertheless, I find that local, regional, and national churches are either indifferent or befuddled by demographic research. Churches purchase expensive research packages for their postal code and subscribe to search engines, but they rarely do anything with this information. Research into demographic trends and lifestyle preferences rarely figures in their annual strategic planning. Staff leaders are poorly trained to navigate the engine or interpret the data. This is in marked contrast to other sectors (government, business, law, education, social service, health care, and even the military) that use demographic research effectively to market effectively, plan strategically, and shape policy.

Why is the church surprisingly slow to undertake demographic research? I think there are two reasons, and both result from the lingering vestiges of Christendom.

First, the church persists in approaching mission *as a subject*. It is an abstraction and an intellectual exercise. The church spends so much time thinking about mission (negotiating mission, explaining mission, debating about mission, justifying mission, and reconciling mission with other religions and ideological agendas) that leaders are exhausted and overly cautious, and very little mission gets done.

Mission is not a subject, but an attitude. It is a disposition to bless people other than ourselves. It is the opposite of self-centeredness. Mission is a stance toward the world that is fundamentally compassionate. It prioritizes the needs of "the other" above the needs of "the member." The common attitude of Christendom is that "first-mile giving" addresses the needs of the church, and "second-mile giving" addresses the needs of the world. The mission attitude is just the opposite. The priority of compassion is for the stranger to grace, and those who have already experienced grace are content with whatever is left over.

Second, the church persists in doing mission *as a program*. It is something church representatives are deployed to accomplish. The church raises money to pay somebody else to do mission (professionals and missionaries, agencies and denominations). Church members, therefore, are always at arm's length from mission. It is how churches spend *a portion* of their resources, a *percentage* of their money, and *a proportion* of their time.

Mission is not a program, but a habit. This disposition to bless people other than ourselves is so automatic that Christians are often not even conscious that they have made room for the stranger. It is built into the routine of daily living. It is like a software platform that is hidden from view, but provides the format in which every other program operates. Because mission is a habit, the intuitive choice is always self-sacrifice, even in the most risky situations. Count on it! Regardless of context or culture, and regardless of demographic diversity or lifestyle orientation, the Christian will instinctively behave lovingly, patiently, kindly, and peaceably, with goodness, generosity, and justice.

The mission attitude means that the challenge to bless others is never an "if" but a "how." It is the mission attitude that drives any religious organization to do demographic research in the first place. Demographic research is extraordinarily pragmatic. It is an imprecise methodology that reveals what works. It is imprecise because "what works" is constantly changing. Researchers must pay attention, and practitioners must be ready to adapt on short notice. If anything, demographic research encourages "bottom-up" thinking rather than the "top-down" thinking familiar to Christendom. Theologians want to start with universal principles and defend sacred strategies for personnel, property, and procedure. Missionaries want to start with basic needs and uncover public expectations, and then innovate tactics that, in themselves, are never sacred at all. As I often say in workshops, *all that matters is the Gospel, and everything else is tactics.*

I have discovered that ambiguity about mission is itself related to the experience of different demographic groups. Certain groups do not get very far learning how to use a demographic search engine and become quickly confused interpreting demographic data. I can see the participants (clergy or lay) becoming impatient with the methodologies and puzzled by the detailed information about diverse publics. Why bother? Why *must* they acquire new skills that they never learned in seminary? Why *should* they reflect on the nuances of age, culture, relationships, occupations, educations, worldviews, and perspectives on seemingly small matters of media, recreation, personal debt management, and other details of everyday living? Inevitably, within about thirty minutes of the workshop, someone asks, *What exactly is mission?*

The demographic makeup of groups asking about the meaning of mission is remarkably consistent. These are almost always relatively affluent, educated, professional men and women over forty-five years old, of western European descent, whose family has lived in Western Europe, England, Canada, the United States, Australia, or New Zealand for at least three generations. On the other hand, the question almost never arises among groups composed of relatively poor, modestly educated, laboring men and women under forty-five years old, of non-Western European descent, whose family has immigrated to a new place within the past two generations. There is a sense in which contemporary Christians who have grown up in a world shaped by the church have been struck with a kind of "spiritual amnesia." They have forgotten the meaning of mission. They have been privileged for so long, and have assumed such a posture of entitlement, that they have no sense of what it would mean to *receive* mission, and therefore they have no sense of what it really means to *participate* in mission.

9

Demographic research, for some Christian organizations, is a tiresome and pointless exercise. They subscribe to demographic search engines but fail to hire, train, and deploy leaders to use it effectively. They download printed demographic reports but fail to integrate them into strategic planning. The search engine remains idle, and the report collects dust, because so many church groups do their planning "top down" to prioritize internal institutional concerns. If personnel and property claim 95 percent of a church budget, and program and outreach receive barely 5 percent of a budget, why bother to do demographic research?

Demographic research, for other Christian organizations, is an exciting and poignant adventure. They not only subscribe to search engines but also train leaders to use them. They not only download printed reports but also incorporate them into annual evaluation and strategic planning. These churches do their planning "bottom up" to prioritize external mission concerns. They have found creative ways to minimize personnel and property costs, so that budgets for program and outreach are greatly increased. Demographic research is absolutely urgent.

The surge in demographic research among churches parallels the rise of church planting, church transformation, parachurch outreach, faith-based nonprofit organizational development, microphilanthropies, multisite ministries, house churches, and fresh expressions of the Holy Spirit.

What is mission? *Mission is what happens whenever the blessings of God intersect with human needs.* The diagram below is my latest attempt to describe the mission attitude that prompts church leaders to engage demographic research.

This diagram is not intended to be a *theology* of mission. It is simply intended to describe *the phenomenon* of mission. It explains to confused Christians and outside observers *why* Christians feel urgent about mission, and *how* mission-driven Christians link demographic research with strategic planning.

It all begins with an actual experience of God's redemptive grace, and the awareness that God's desire to bless the world is universal, constant, and surprisingly personal. God's blessing is like the benefits of nature. Jesus says, "Love your enemies and pray for those who persecute you, so that you may be children of your Father in heaven; for he makes his sun rise on the evil and on the good, and sends rain on the righteous and on the unrighteous" (Matthew 5:44-45). God's mission is to redeem, reunite, renew the world; use whatever incomplete metaphor you like.

Yet God's blessing is more personal than this. God calls you *by name*; God knows the number of hairs on your head; God epitomizes self-sacrifice, going far beyond reasonable behavior, and to the extremes of human endurance, to do whatever it takes to "rescue" each and every human being. The mission attitude is connected with experiences of incarnation. As people instinctively "reach up" to find hope in the midst of hopelessness, they can experience God's touch "reaching down" to bless them at the precise point of their need.

The list identified in this diagram exemplifies, but does not exhaust, the multiple ways people experience hopelessness. The mission attitude identifies with people who are trapped by self-destructive habits or oppressive contexts from which there seems no escape. To be "mission minded" is to experience a "heartburst" of compassion for those who are broken and yearning for healing, those who are lost and yearning for guidance, those who are anxious and yearning for assurance, those who are lonely and yearning for meaningful intimacy, and those who are victims and yearning for justice. Again, this is very personal. One cannot be sensitive to the needs of others without being aware of one's own neediness, and one cannot risk intervention without some confidence of divine help.

Similarly, the list identified in this diagram exemplifies, but does not exhaust, the multiple ways in which God's love is revealed to bring hope. The mission attitude celebrates the grace that liberates the trapped, giving them a fresh start and a new life. To be mission minded is to anticipate the power of God to heal the broken, guide the lost, keep promises to reassure the anxious, model perfect relationships, and vindicate the abused. This, too, is very personal. One cannot give what one has not received, and one cannot anticipate what one has not previously experienced in some way.

Incarnational Experience
The New Being
The Healer
The Spiritual Guide
The Promise Keeper
The Perfect Human
The Vindicator

Spiritual Yearning
The Trapped
The Broken
The Lost
The Anxious
The Lonely
The Victimized

Core Values and Beliefs

Leadership Organization
Hospitality   Worship
Small Groups   Education
Technology Communication Finance
Outreach

Mission Mix
Community, Change of Heart, Social Action

The Primary Mission Field
Demographic Trends   Lifestyle Segments   Heartburst Affinities

The same mission attitude that experiences hope and empathizes with hopelessness regards the organized church as one agent that connects the real presence of God with the spiritual yearning of real people. Churches vary. Even congregations of the same denomination have distinct identities shaped by nuances of core values and beliefs. God's grace is like the sun, shining on the just and the unjust, and the church is like a lens held up between sun and earth. It refracts and concentrates the light on a particular spot on the ground. Two things happen:

- First, the church *magnifies* that spot on the ground. That is the "primary mission field" of any given church. Demographic research reveals the trends, lifestyle segments, microcultures, and affinities that exist and evolve within the church's primary sphere of influence.

- Second, the church *intensifies* the light to warm, illumine, and even burn or purify that spot on the ground. In other words, the "primary mission field" is *different* because the church is active in its midst. Things change. Life is improved. Communities are shaped to be healthier, safer, and vital.

The church exists to impact the community, or communities, that surround it. The goal of mission is really not to generate *faith*. It is to generate *hope*. Faith may come later, and it may take forms that are different from that of the church itself. The goal of mission is to give faith a chance. The church rescues the community from hopelessness and gives people a reason to endure, persist, anticipate, and eventually overcome the challenges that beset them.

There are three elements to mission in any primary mission field: preservation of positive tradition, change of heart, and social action.[1] Every church is a unique blend of all three mission motivations.

- **Positive Tradition** is all about the urgency to maintain the institutional church:

  Caring and mutual support among church members

  Welcoming the diversity of the public and expanding membership

  Preserving a theological, denominational, or local tradition

  Cultivating a specific taste for the arts and an atmosphere of goodwill

  Honoring the benefits of membership

13

- **Change of Heart** is all about the urgency to transform lives and reshape lifestyles:

  Healing broken lives

  Convincing people about Christian faith

  Embedding confidence and hope for personal redemption

  Living a more fruitful or blessed life

  Discovering a fulfilling, personal destiny

- **Social Action** is all about the necessities of living and vindicating helpless or oppressed people:

  Obtaining the basics of food, clothing, and shelter

  Living in safety, respect, and peace

  Nurturing healthy intimacy and family relationships

  Protecting human rights and intervening to rescue victims

  Liberating the full potential of every human being

All of these mission motivations are applied to the primary mission field in different ways. The methods and goals are shaped by the unique expectations of the publics within any given mission field.

Only now does a mission-minded church pay attention to the issues of personnel, program, and resources. Nothing is assumed about the structure or ministries of a church. Everything is adjustable and adaptable. A mission-minded church is remarkably pragmatic. It is clear about outcomes to bless the surrounding publics in particular ways and is prepared to make whatever adjustments are necessary to accomplish those outcomes. Church members will initiate new creative ideas, constantly improve ongoing programs, and readily terminate even the most historic or beloved strategies if they are ineffective.[2]

The adjustable strategies of a church that are shaped by the expectations of the mission field encompass much of what Christendom might once have considered "sacred." Even leadership is matched to the needs and expectations of the mission field, rather than the needs and expectations of the parent denomination. Hospitality, worship, education, small groups, and outreach are all adjusted to address the emerging needs of the mission field. Even the location and facility floor plan, the technologies and the financial management strategy, and the internal and external methods of advertising and communication are "up for grabs." As we all know, the content, message, methods, and structures that were relevant just one hundred years ago are often irrelevant today, and whatever adjustments the church makes today might become irrelevant in just ten years. Other things endure. Conviction about essential values and beliefs, clarity about outcomes, and adaptability in everything else is as crucial to the post-Christendom church as it was to the pre-Christendom church of the apostolic age.

It really is imperative that church leaders approach demographic research with the right attitude. The goal is not really to *attract* people to the church, but to *bless* people beyond the church. Even more than this, the goal is to bless people so that they, in turn, bless still more people. It is the cascade effect of mission that not only accelerates church growth but also impacts the world locally and globally. If leaders study demographics solely for the purpose of what they can do *to people*, then their analysis will be limited to a quick study of the community every ten years. However, when leaders study demographics to discover what they can do *with* people, *through* people, and *alongside* people, then their analysis continues on a daily basis. Demographic research helps the church mature members, equip leaders, and collaborate with partners to reshape society.

The "Mission to the Gentiles" illustrates very well the mission motivation for demographic research. Paul and his team did instinctively what today's church leaders are doing intentionally and with ever-greater sophistication. It is the strategy of blessing the world one microculture at a time. Paul's team innovated mission in one city and then moved on to the next. What worked in Ephesus may not work in Philippi. Paul is always having a vision, a "heartburst," for some Macedonian (or other identifiable, describable demographic) for which he stakes everything to bless in a particular way. In Corinth, he breaks tradition to open a house church next door to the established institution. He persists despite criticism because "one night the Lord said to Paul in a vision, 'Do not be afraid, but speak and do not be silent; for I am with you, and no one will lay a hand on you to harm you, for there are many in this city who are my people'" (Acts 18:9-10).

Demographic research can help an organization with marketing, but it will do much more *if church leaders want to do it.* Leaders must be properly motivated to do demographic research and have clear goals in mind. Consider this a spiritual exercise. It is like a long-distance runner mentally focusing, physically stretching, and preparing himself or herself for the big race. It is a race against despair, and the prize is hope.

2. A Brief History of Applied Demographics

"There is the *right* way; there is the *wrong* way; and then there is the *way that works*." That simple phrase captures the shift in strategic planning from the old Christendom world to the new post-Christendom world. It is a return to the ancient mission philosophy of St. Paul, who wrote: "I have become all things to all people, that I might by all means save some. I do it all for the sake of the gospel, so that I may share in its blessings" (1 Corinthians 9:22b-23).

In the Christendom years, strategies for congregational life and mission in North America were defined by denominations or traditions and imposed on all publics without much regard for context and culture. This made sense through the first half of the twentieth century. North America was remarkably homogeneous. Strategic plans and tactical applications could be standardized across all sectors (public education, business, municipal government, health care, and social services).

However, diversity has accelerated exponentially through the latter half of the twentieth century and the start of the twenty-first. It is driven by migrations of people, mobility of workforce, instant communication, global networks, and volatile economies. Remote communities in northern Canada are watching television programs and advertising from urban centers like Detroit and Atlanta. Once, a new generation appeared every thirty years. Now, a new generation appears every ten years, and a new affinity group or microculture emerges, thrives, morphs, or disappears in a matter of days.

Church planners and planters have come a very long way in the five decades since the collapse of Christendom. In the scramble to contextualize ministry, church leaders have gone through several phases.

The "Generation Gap" Phase

Age-based planning was most popular in the late 1960s and '70s as the *builders* and *silents* sought to understand their *boomer* children and grandchildren, and then later as everyone sought to adapt ministry for the *buster* grandchildren and great-grandchildren (otherwise known as "Gen Y"). New "generations" have been coming so fast, however, that planners soon regretted having started so late in the alphabet.

"Generation gap" thinking introduced the comparative terminology of "traditional" versus "contemporary" styles. However, the very term "contemporary" has come to mean so many different things, to so many different publics, that it is now useless to describe any particular ministry tactic. Age alone is no longer helpful to determine relevant ministry applications.

For example, the additional worship service was often called the "Youth Service," complete with guitars, drums, dance, drama, and new music. Yet by the next decade, church leaders were observing eighty-year-olds in the "youth service" and a growing number of twentysomethings in the "traditional" service. Age was no longer the key factor.

The "Degree of Urbanization" Phase

Economic and transportation changes in the late 1970s and 1980s encouraged planners to categorize regions as urban core, urban, and exurban, suburban, small town, rural, and remote. Denominations designated staff portfolios for "rural" or "urban" ministries. Ministries in each context were stereotypically different from those of other contexts. Further economic shifts and the emergence of the Internet have so blurred these distinctions that they are much less useful.

"Urbanization" thinking defined any given mission field by geographical or physical boundaries: rivers, railroads, interstate highways, city thoroughfares. People are now bursting those boundaries, prompted by new retail strategies and social media. They will now travel the equivalent time or distance to reach a spiritual destination as they will customarily do to reach employment, shopping, or recreational needs.

For example, church leaders assumed that parking for an additional worship service would be adequate because each service would essentially serve the same neighborhood. Yet by the next decade, people were driving from the country to the city and from the city to the country, bypassing innumerable churches of the same brand name, in order to reach the spiritual destination that would meet their needs. Suddenly, adequate parking became an urgent crisis.

The "Ethnic Ministry" Phase

Ethnic sensitivity was most popular in the late 1980s and 1990s, as socioeconomic reform movements reshaped ministries. Denominations designated new departments for "Ethnic Ministry." Leaders realized that expectations for ministry among African-Americans differed from the expectations of those of Western European descent. The burgeoning Hispanic population stretched this sensitivity further, especially as the nuances between "Caribbean," "Mexican," and "South American" became more noticeable. Immigration from East Asia, Southeast Asia, and China stretched such sensitivity to the limit of effectiveness.[1]

The blur of ethnic identity among subsequent generations living in North America, and the emergence of a strong and diverse African-American middle class, has undermined the usefulness of "ethnic" thinking. The U.S. Census has been forced to introduce a whole new category for multicultural identity. What was once "affirmative action" has become another form of stereotyping because too many people no longer "fit" the ministry applications once associated with a given ethnic group.

For example, that additional worship service always assumed that everyone in the sanctuary spoke the same first language and enjoyed similar foods for post-worship refreshments. Yet by the next decade, worship required bilingual speakers or efficient translators, words to the liturgy and music needed to be published in multiple versions, and refreshments had to be expanded to several distinct serving stations.

The "Best Practices" Phase

Basic demographic information about age, race, marriage and family structure, income, occupation, education, and so on became less and less effective for strategic planning in any sector. Church leaders then shifted their attention away from demographics to study the "best practices" of thriving churches. Successful churches offered continuing education for clergy and lay leaders for new worship styles, educational methods, and outreach programs.[2]

The strategy assumed that, while generations and ethnic groups might vary from region to region, community needs and dynamics in a particular neighborhood, town, or census tract would be relatively consistent. One could categorize people not only by age and national origin but also by language, phase of life, income, occupation, marital status, and educational achievement. Basic skills and tactics would also remain constant and needed to be adjusted only slightly to be adapted to a different place.

Unfortunately, the very tactic that worked in one context did not work in another, no matter how skillfully leaders were trained. At best, this strategy taught principles of leadership, techniques to listen and observe the mission field, and theological perspectives to adapt programs while maintaining integrity. The direct transfer of tactics from one context to another, however, rarely worked. Common language, life stages, income, occupation, marital status, and educational achievement simply were not enough to build a reliably effective ministry strategy for hospitality, worship, Christian education, small-group affinity, and outreach. Nor were demographic traits sufficient to motivate property renovations, design fund-raising strategies, or even develop new communication techniques.

For example, church leaders assumed that they could borrow worship designs and resources from other churches and repeat the formula with the same success. Yet in less than a decade, they realized that what worked in Chicago or Kansas City wouldn't fly in Boston or Seattle.

The diversification of worship by time, style, and technique failed, and leaders had to find a way to diversify worship for spiritual need and mission purpose.

The Church Planting and Multisite Ministry Phase

In the first decades of the new millennium, churches leaders are shifting their attention to the multiplication of smaller, contextually sensitive communities of faith. They are less likely to imitate "best practices" of ministry and more likely to innovate fresh tactics to address very specific spiritual needs. Whether the goal of mission is to heal the broken, guide the lost, befriend the loner, share hope with the desperate, resurrect the addict, rescue the abused, or explore the mysteries of God, churches are shaping themselves around a single-minded purpose to reach a particular public.

The church planting and multisite movement may partially be motivated by frustration with the resistance of established churches to change. More positively, it is motivated by the need to be effective in a time of limited resources and to get measurable results in taking people deeper and further in Christ. The hallmarks of this movement include the following:

- The unity of social action and faith sharing
- The priority of leadership development over program management
- The urgency to move with the mission field
- The local methodology of relational evangelism
- The global networking of digital communication
- The desire to stake everything in order to get close to God

Church planting and multisite strategies are often misunderstood by surviving Christendom as yet one more technique to "attract" seekers to "adopt" established church traditions and practices. At best, however, church planting and multisite ministry has precisely the opposite intention. They "engage" seekers to "customize" whatever spiritual disciplines are best suited to do justice, love kindness, and walk humbly with God. Whether or not they gather, grow, and go in traditional patterns of "churchiness" is neither here nor there.

The Complexity of the Mission Field Today

The very definition of a "mission field" has changed dramatically in just the past hundred years. It was once defined by the town limits; specific neighborhoods demarked by streets, avenues, railroad tracks, or expressways, within which people presumably walked to shop, work, and worship; and zones for postal deliveries and free phone calls. Internet, satellite television, mobile cell phones, commuting workforces, shopping malls, interstate highways, and the availability of personal transportation have changed all that.

People are not only moving about more freely, but they are moving about more frequently, and they are doing so both as individuals and as mass migrations. I am often struck by the fact that church members often seem blind to what is going on around them. In many urban and small town consultations, I discover that most church members own their own homes and have lived ten to fifteen years (or more) in the same location. The people around the church, however, often rent their homes and move every three to five years. When you consider that it takes up to eight years or more for a resident to join an established church, acquire disciplines of stewardship, and eventually take leadership in a church, it is not surprising that churches are smaller, poorer, and aging in the leadership core. Mobility alone is taking its toll on institutional sustainability.

Mobility alone is not the only reason the mission field is complex today. Homogeneity is giving way to heterogeneity in even rural and remote regions of North America. In other words, diversity is the new normal. Society is subdividing in more and more ways all the time. Whether this is a "fracture" or a "nuance," and whether it leads to upheaval or adjustment, is hard to predict.

The very terminology that we once used constantly in the planning process has dropped out of common use among organizations in most sectors. The church, unfortunately, lags behind:

- **Economic Class**: The language of class struggle helped intellectuals define the revolutions that toppled the privileged hierarchies and challenged the bourgeoisie in the first half of the twentieth century. Today, the boundaries of "lower class," "middle class," and "upper class" are so blurred, and the issues of social unrest are so complex, that economic labels have become almost meaningless.

- **Black and White**: The language of color helped social reformers shape the civil rights movement in North America in the 1960s and 1970s. In the new millennium, mass migrations of eastern and southern European populations and the diversification of African-American generations that have claimed professional and political leadership have made this terminology inadequate.

- **Literate and Illiterate**: The measurement of reading capacity helped educators establish benchmarks for intellectual development from the invention of the printing press to the multiplication of universities. Since the advent of television, Internet, cinema, and animation, however, intelligent communication has diversified through alternative symbol systems. Great communicators can have small vocabularies and no grammar; reading can be replaced by sounds, images, and activities; and the size of a library is no longer a clue to the genius of a mind.

- **Young and Old**: When institutional membership and career ladders measured church and personal growth, it made sense to target just three or four generations with programs and technologies. The "youth" were still the future of the church, empty nesters were still the core of volunteers, and seniors were still the source of financial stability. Today, society is divided among people who never grow up, people who never get old, and people who never stop learning. Mission effectiveness and team relationships combine to make the capacity for cross-generational cooperation the measure of success.

- **Married and Single:** The pattern of life used to be that males and females courted, married, settled down, raised families, remained loyal, and thanked God for predictability. Churches facilitated the process. It is still common for established church memberships to include disproportiontately large numbers of married couples, heterosexual singles, and traditional family units compared to the actual proportions in the surrounding community. The new normal is that males and females (of all ages) experiment with relationships, delay marriage, remain mobile, plan parenthood, reserve commitment, and thank God for new opportunities. Few people are married or single. They are something in between and other.

- **Northeast, West Coast, Deep South, Midwest:** Regional stereotypes once provided a means to classify populations and build communication. Now they are more likely used to distort understanding and promote judgment. The average length of residency is shrinking, and people are as likely to relocate across the country as they are across town. The search for jobs, relationships, healthy environments, affordable housing, and recreational opportunities has created a national community of displaced persons.

- **Urban, Suburban, Rural:** As economic and racial stratifications have waned, so also have the residential boundaries that were once so clear been blurred. This is particularly true in the four great metropolitan regions that cross state and national boundaries (Northeast, Great Lakes, Gulf Coast, and Southwest). Inter-city travel, urban core revival, and home office productivity have blurred the boundaries. Satellite communication, costly commuting, and rising housing prices have forced the issue.

- **Religious and Nonreligious**: In the long era of Christendom, it made sense to classify people as "churched" or "unchurched." In the brief interlude of secularity following the world wars to the 1980s, it made sense to classify people as "religious" and "nonreligious." Religions could be subdivided into a limited number of optional movements and sects, and contrasted with rationalists. Now the secular city has given way to the pagan world. There are countless spiritualities and superstitions, in addition to traditional religions and venerable sects, and even rationalism has become a form of faith.

Churches still tend to cling to old terminology that applied to simpler times. This has handicapped strategic planning because it has kept church leaders inside an ever-shrinking box of tactical options and discouraged experimentation and creativity.

Ancient maps of the world defined a region of the known world and then described the unknown world beyond with the anxious phrase *There be dragons!* Today, the world that can be adequately described using familiar terminology has become very small...and the dangerous region has grown large. It's dangerous not only because it is evolving but also because it is transforming in unpredictable, and therefore uncontrollable, ways. The categories, terminologies, and analytical "shorthand" that we used to use won't work.

This dangerous world is difficult to navigate for all organizations, but particularly for churches. Most organizations are based on *products*. They study demographics because they need to position their "products" in the marketplace. Certainly it is true that the church also has a "product" of sorts. The church wants to position Christian faith so that it competes in the spiritual marketplace that has suddenly become so competitive. In the old modern secular world, the church could just declare a belief system, and it would stand out like a bright-colored light in the midst of the grayscale of contemporary skepticism. In the postmodern pagan world of competing spiritualities, just as in the postmodern consumer world of digital auctions, it is much harder to stand out, attract attention, and be relevant. To that extent, the church also studies demographics in order to compete.

Yet this dangerous, unpredictable world poses an even greater challenge to churches than it does to many other organizations. Ultimately, the church is not based on *products*. It is based on *relationships*. Postmodern people are less interested in consuming church programs, and more interested in relating to a community of faith and to a living God. They are less interested in "the truth" and more interested in "truing." This is a process in which truth is a mystery beyond any distinct rationalization of it, so that truth emerges in different ways, at different times, in different situations. What do you do when "truth" is no longer a noun, but a verb? You do what premodern, preliterate, preinstitutional Christians did. You don't cozy up on the couch and read a book. You cozy up with other people and experiment with life.

The hard part for the church is that the institutional alliances that once helped define truth aren't as helpful anymore. This includes denominational networks, publishing houses, missionary agencies, professional clergy associations, seminaries, and various historical societies. Today, if you hang out with just those groups long term, you find yourself increasingly alienated and irrelevant in the mission field. You may end up feeling helpless or self-righteous, but either way, the sustainability of your church organization is doubtful. That's why the postmodern world is also a post-Christendom world.

Churches are finding companionship in unlikely places. They are "hanging out" with different kinds of people. Finding those compatible partners, however, can be risky. It is part of an expanding cross-cultural danger zone in which it is hard to tell whether some strange animal or plant species is an herbivore or a carnivore. Here are some of the surprising companions with whom church leaders are now chasing truth:

- Christ-centered Christians are finding they have more in common with non-church-going seekers than with regu-

lar church members. They can talk more freely and profoundly about incarnation in the coffee shop than in the
seminary.

- Mission-driven church boards are finding they have
  more in common with tradespeople, small business entrepreneurs, and executive managers than with teachers, nurses, and middle managers. They can manage risk
  and empower teams more effectively over early-morning
  breakfast than in late-night meetings.

- Pastors are learning more relevant skills in hospitality,
  communication, education, cell groups, fund-raising,
  and technology from community colleges, restaurateurs,
  and business colleges than from theological colleges.
  They can learn more through apprenticeships and webi-
  nars than pastors' conventions.

- Outreach teams are networking with microcharities,
  faith-based for-profits, and military and diplomatic
  corps, rather than philanthropic societies, corporations,
  and government committees. They can be more influential through inside conversations rather than outside
  protests.

- Church members are befriending other cultures, in their
  own languages, during midweek, rather than chatting
  with their own kind, in a private code, on Sundays. They
  can give and take more healing, guidance, intimacy, justice, addiction intervention, and hope outside the "sacred
  time clock."

There are dangers in this. The broadening postmodern wilderness
is a dangerous place. The boundary between relevance and accommodation is often blurry. Seemingly compatible partners can suddenly become abusive, dictatorial bullies. Benign clients and friendly folks can
suddenly become aggressive litigation adversaries. Credibility that has
taken years to build up can disappear overnight by a thoughtless action

or an ill-chosen word.[3] Yet this is the risk Jesus himself took when he ate with sinners, fraternized with despised Samaritans, spoke kindly to occupying Romans, recruited tax collectors, forgave prostitutes, and generally mingled with all of the lifestyle segments of Palestine.

The Christian movement in the postmodern, post-Christendom world is becoming ever more creative, but it also faces urgent challenges in a spiritually yearning, institutionally alienated mission field. Skeptical publics have many questions about leadership integrity and ministry relevance. Christian organizations increasingly ask questions about population shifts, organizational sustainability, leadership succession, mission targets, and program development.

The diversity, cultural sensitivity, and innovation of "fresh expressions" of Christian experience today are often compared to the rich tapestry of the Christian movement in the apostolic age. Two keys factors account for the acceleration of the Christian movement and the impact of Christianity on surrounding society, then and now:

- First, the Christian movement requires a whole new method to acquire, train, evaluate, and deploy leaders. These leaders are trained as entrepreneurs, rather than managers, and as mentors rather than chaplains.[4] They are less interested in preserving a heritage, and more sensitive to the needs and aspirations of the local mission field. They are not trying to attract people to a foreign tradition, but to bless people through indigenous methods.

- Second, the Christian movement therefore requires more detailed information about seeker sensitivity. Christian leaders need to be trained to survey the mission field and analyze each microculture within it. Christian communities are clear about the essentials of Christian behavior and faith, but they are extraordinarily flexible to match leaders with expectant publics, focus the message directly on the spiritual needs of the moment, and adapt ministries to the preferences of each culture.

The broad demographic categories of age, race, language, family status, income, education, and occupation are less and less helpful. Understanding lifestyle segments, and their expectations for ministry, is increasingly important.

Consider, for example, Paul's habit of acquiring protégés from each context on his travels, mentoring them in the essentials of faith and adaptive methods of community building, and then deploying them to travel and repeat the process. It all reveals an uncanny ability to relate quickly and intimately with men and women of any culture, communicating the Gospel in any manner that they can readily understand.

Thus, for example, Paul encounters Prisca (or "Priscilla") and Aquila and includes them in his team. They are so significant that Paul says they "risked their necks for my life," and that all the Gentile churches should thank them (Romans 16:4). They are deployed to develop house churches in Corinth and Rome, and they appear in the home of Onesiphorus (2 Timothy 4:19). Aquila and Prisca in turn find Apollos in Ephesus and mentor him more accurately in the "Way of God" (Acts 18:26). Apollos in turn develops communities of faith in Achaia and passes through the house church of Titus (Titus 3:13). The identification of Paul's teammates with indigenous publics is so keen that it threatens to undermine the meaning of baptism. Paul complains that Christians are identifying with the messenger rather than the message (1 Corinthians 1:12).

> What then is Apollos? What is Paul? Servants through whom you came to believe, as the Lord assigned to each. I planted, Apollos watered, but God gave the growth. (1 Corinthians 3:5-6)

The mission to the Gentiles takes extreme measures to resist top-down standardization of community-building tactics, and its innovative tactics clearly alarm the head office in Jerusalem. They have to establish boundaries within which Paul and company are free to innovate, but beyond which they cannot go (Acts 15:28-29).

3. Progressive Lenses of Research

Church leaders analyze the mission field in the same way that astronomers study the solar system or biologists study an organism. The telescope or microscope uses progressive lenses. Greater magnification reveals more detail, but less relationship with contiguous bodies. Lesser magnification reveals more dynamic relationships, but less detail. Both are important to understand not only the inner workings of an object but also the interactions of an object with other objects.

Imagine, then, that you are investigating a community as a distant object in the galaxy, or as a complex organism in the natural environment. The naked eye is not enough to understand the object of your interest, just as your individual opinion isn't enough to understand a community. I often use the words "community" and "mission field" interchangeably, and later I will describe just how strategic planners define the boundaries of their inquiry. Right now, it is important to understand why a "community" becomes a "mission field" when the person looking through the lenses is a Christian.

There is a difference in purposefulness. The scientist explores an object or organism to *know* it better. The demographer explores a community in order to help government, business, and other sectors *use* it more effectively. But a Christian explores a mission field in order to *bless* it more abundantly. A community becomes a mission field because the goal of the researcher is not to get something out of it but to give something to it.

Remember the two basic properties of a lens that I described earlier. A lens *magnifies* the spot and also *intensifies* the light. Christians not only seek to magnify, explore, and understand the region of research. They want to warm, illumine, and improve the life of the publics within the region of research. Each progressive lens helps the church empathize more profoundly and bless more effectively. That's a mission field.

Pure Demographics

The first level of magnification provides the broadest insight into any given community. This is pure demographics. It is most useful to understand the most powerful forces that shape a community and the largest trends that may determine future obstacles and opportunities for any public organization (corporations, governments, social services, educational institutions, churches, and so on). We study the following:

• Age	• Parenthood
• Gender	• Educational Level
• Race	• Occupation
• National Origin	• Mobility
• Language	• Home Ownership
• Phase of Life	• Income and Debt
• Marriage Status	• Generosity
• Household Occupancy	• Religion

In Canada, we can study religious affiliation directly with the national census, but in the United States, we must study religious sensibilities indirectly by tracking philanthropic giving or entertainment preferences, or use denominational or nonprofit research.

The insights from this first magnification of analysis focus our attention, but they always beg for more detailed information. For example, let me list the *most frequent insights* that surprise church leaders as they study the mission field with this lens. These have emerged from my church consultations across the continental United States and Canada. This layer of analysis challenges many of the hidden assumptions of churches.

Average Age

We all hear that North America is aging, but most church people are surprised that the average age in their mission field is often between thirty-two and thirty-eight years old. It can occasionally be much lower or higher, depending on the economic boom or bust of a community. For example, it is lower in Fort McMurray, Alberta, where they are developing the "oil sands," and higher in Watertown, New York, where they have downsized the military base. The average age, however, is often around thirty-two to thirty-eight years old and projected to climb to about thirty-four to forty in ten years.

Most church people I meet are surprised that this is so low. After all, the average age in many churches is often between sixty-two and seventy-eight. The members mainly associate with people their own age and assume that "everybody is older." It makes good strategic sense for the church (or any community organization) to develop tactics that would be more relevant to the average age of the community, and that is the challenge.

On the other hand, some church people I meet are surprised that the average age is so high. Church people often live in the illusion that "the youth are the future of their church" and are dismayed that they aren't there. Not only are there fewer of them (especially teenagers, as we shall see) but also many of them have relocated to seek employment.

Regardless of the direction of their surprise, this level of analysis forces church leaders to think again about their strategic plan. What, exactly, will have to change in order to design a church that is relevant to the real average age of the community?

Gender

The proportion of men and women in most communities is roughly equal. That may not seem like a particularly shocking insight, until you consider how gender is a factor in church strategic planning.

First, the *membership* of many churches today is disproportionately female. Worship services are often designed with them in mind, providing awesome moments of silent meditation, quiet lyrical music, and children's stories. Men, especially men under fifty-five who are not yet grandfathers, are often distracted, bored, and disinterested. How do churches connect with men, who represent half the mission field?

Second, the *leadership* of many churches today is disproportionately male. Boards are often preoccupied with property maintenance and financial management, and dominated by successful business leaders who are also most frequently male. Women, especially those working in educational, social service, and health care sectors, are often frustrated. How do churches empower women, who represent half the mission field, in leadership?

Race and National Origin

Theoretically, we all know that our communities are becoming more multicultural. Analysis of the demographic trends in our own mission field suddenly makes the theory concrete. The Caucasian population is generally declining. The African, Hispanic, and Asian populations are generally growing. Immigration and birth rates will probably make the Caucasian population a *minority* in the next ten to twenty years in most communities.

Yet most churches in North America have grown as homogeneous communities, predominantly of a single race or culture. The churches may be white or black; Chinese, Korean, or Philippine; Romanian, Russian, or Greek; or associated with any number of national origins. Yet they do not reflect the cultural diversity of the community.

The problem, of course, is that the racial and national stereotypes from another century no longer apply in a world of migration, mobility, and instant communication. Probably they never did apply, but churches *thought they did*, and today they can no longer even *think* that way. Second generations are shaping and merging with a new culture. Today, especially among people under forty-five, behaving inclusively, respecting other cultures, and having multicultural friendships are a primary sign of credibility. How will churches embrace the blatantly multicultural community?

Language

One result of the emerging multicultural world is that English is not the only language spoken in most communities. The second language,

34

however, may be surprising. In Canada, the real second language in many communities outside Quebec is a dialect of Chinese, rather than French. On the West Coast of the United States, the second language may be Spanish (with a Mexican or Philippine accent), or a language from Southeast Asia. On the East Coast, the second language may be Russian or an eastern European language, Spanish with a Cuban accent, or Portuguese with a Brazilian accent. On the Gulf Coast, the second language may be Creole or French (with a Haitian accent). In Newfoundland, it may be Naskapi, Montagnais, or an English dialect largely incomprehensible to most people who speak English.

The challenge for churches, however, is not that everybody needs to speak English, but that church members need to speak a second language. Identity, integrity, and individuality are increasingly contingent on language; and respect, inclusivity, and clear communication are more urgent for church ministries. As the fulcrum of the global economy shifts away from Europe to the east and south, the ability to become bilingual is one of the great challenges of the English-speaking world (and the Christian movement within it).

Phase of Life

Demographic research groups people according to stages or "phases" of life. These groupings are chronological, and they isolate the key life issue in the life cycle:

- Ages zero to four are primarily concerned with nurture before formal schooling begins.

- Ages five to nineteen are primarily concerned with formal schooling.

- Ages twenty to twenty-four are primarily concerned with starting college or careers.

- Ages twenty-five to thirty-four are primarily concerned with relationships and young families.

- Ages thirty-five to fifty-four are primarily concerned with raising older children and adjusting to empty nests.

- Ages fifty-five to sixty-four are primarily concerned with enriching and enjoying life as singles or couples.

- Ages sixty-five and over are primarily concerned with investing time and talent in retirement.

There may be other ways to do it, but the point is that our demographic analysis can trace the basic life cycle from birth to death.

There are several common trends that often challenge church planners. Again, these may not be universal, but they certainly are frequent:

1. The phase of life primarily concerned with nurture before formal schooling (zero to four) is growing again. This mini-boom is an opportunity for many nonprofit day care facilities. The bigger challenge for churches, however, is how to improve their church nurseries, provide better accessibility for young mothers, and make their Sunday morning experience family friendly for infants and toddlers.

2. The phase of life primarily concerned with college and careers (twenty to twenty-four) is scattering. This is a huge challenge for churches located near colleges and universities. The power of the Internet and better public transportation allow students to explore better options for housing that are farther away. It is getting even harder for churches to connect with this lifestyle segment.

3. The phases of life primarily concerned with empty nests (thirty-five to fifty-four) and enrichment (fifty-five to sixty-four) are relocating from the suburbs to small towns and downtowns. People in these stages of life are often the mainstay of volunteers and board leaders for churches, but many are moving farther from the city to find peace and quiet, or deeper into the city to take advantage of cultural opportunities.

Although churches need to connect with people in an earlier phase of life, the fact is that the growing publics most likely to be interested in the church are still over fifty-five.

Marriage Status

We all know that the institution of marriage has been in flux for some time. Young adults tend to marry later in life; more people (even seniors) opt to live together without a wedding; adults change partners more often and without guilt. The proportion of people identified as married, in contrast with single, never married, separated, divorced, and widowed, varies considerably between mission fields. However, marriage rates in general are declining significantly, especially among adults aged twenty-five to thirty-four, and especially in the northeast and southwest United States. Married couples now represent only about 48 percent of the population in the United States.[1]

Meanwhile, most churches identify themselves as "family churches" and often expect adult members to be in traditional married relationships or (if widowed) have had a valued experience of marriage. Churches that once emphasized marriage counseling and marriage enrichment and gave only minor attention to singles are now challenged to reverse that priority. Moreover, the category of "single" is more complicated than ever before.

Household Occupancy

A common pattern in many communities is that household growth is slower than population growth. In other words, more people are living in the same single-family dwelling. This may mean that young adults in low-paying jobs are forced to live with their parents, that multiple generations are living under the same roof, that immigrants are finding room for extended families, or that financially challenged homeowners are forced to rent space. Population density, with all its related stresses, is becoming more important than population size in many communities.

This contrasts sharply with the experience of many established local churches. Church members who own homes comprise a much higher percentage than do members who rent, and church members often have significantly more personal space than what is normal in the community. Church members tend to assume a degree of household stability that is not true for many non-church members. When members complain that newcomers don't bring sufficient food for the potluck supper or are unwilling to host a small group in their homes, they may need to become more sensitive to the stress levels of the community.

Parenthood

The birthrate in the United States has been declining for about twelve years, down 17 percent per thousand people since 1990. About one-third of the births are to unmarried women, and the number of infants with low birth weights is increasing.[2] Similar trends are true for Canada.[3] These facts usually lead researchers to discuss how immigration is maintaining or growing the population in both countries, challenging health care networks to provide better prenatal support, and challenging churches to provide better counseling services for single-parent mothers.

The biggest wakeup call for churches, however, is that the assumption that "the youth are the future of the church" is being seriously challenged. Not only are there fewer youth but also they are less likely to participate in a monocultural church. The key to church growth probably does not lie with "youth," but rather with adults closer to the average age of the community (which, as we saw earlier, is probably ages thirty-two to thirty-eight). However, it is precisely the age group between twenty and forty-five that is often the missing generations in churches today.

Parenting, of course, remains a big issue in most communities. Children and youth are finding their own ways to build relationships and have fun, but parents need more help nurturing mental and emotional health. The challenge for many churches is to shift their children and youth ministry strategies from "babysitting" while the parents are away, to "partnering" as parents struggle to stay connected with their children. Fun, fellowship, and Bible study is less relevant than health, intimacy, and outreach.

Educational Level

There are a number of standard levels of education: early and late elementary, high school, some college or professional training, basic university, and graduate school. It is not surprising that each mission field has different proportions in each category. Identity with a lifestyle segment probably influences the educational level achieved, and the educational level achieved contributes to mobility among lifestyle segments. That's not a surprise either.

What is a surprise to many churches is that even well-educated people have less background knowledge in history, religion, literature, and other liberal arts subjects than their parents or grandparents did. That affects liturgy, preaching, music appreciation, and Bible study. If leaders cannot assume basic knowledge, then worship design might fly over the heads of many participants.

Global competitiveness is nudging public education systems to stream children and youth in specific directions at an earlier age, and increasingly toward pure and applied sciences, mathematics, and engineering. These are all good fields, but they tend to limit "truth" to what is empirical and verifiable. Churches tend to communicate "truth" through metaphor (poetry, visual art, and story), and the nuances may escape even well-educated people.

Occupation

Occupations may be defined any number of ways, and there is not a direct connection between occupation and church participation. There might be a connection, however, between occupation and decision-making habits. People in occupations related to business management, office administration, production, and transport, for example, might be more results driven and favor top-down organizational models. People in occupations related to education, health care, personal services, and even retail might be more process driven and favor consensus organizational models.

I don't want to exaggerate these tendencies. Today, in all occupations, there is tremendous change in decision-making habits and organizational management. Even the military values team training more than ever. However, as I consult with churches, I often notice a pattern.

Churches that make decisions through consensus (with larger bureaucracies, task management models, and clarity about process policies) often attract board members from education, health care, and social services. Churches that make decisions through delegation of authority and responsibility (with empowered teams, policy governance models, and clarity about ends policies) often attract board members from business, administration, and professional specialties.

My perception is that established churches often use organizational models that haven't changed much since the nineteenth century (top-down, overlapping committees, representative councils, and so on). Their decision makers tend to be older and enter board leadership only after years of membership in the church. Meanwhile, new churches, growing churches, and multisite churches often use more contemporary organizational models (bottom-up, team-based, visionary board, and so on). Their decision makers tend to be younger and enter board leadership faster.

Mobility

There are several aspects of mobility especially relevant to church development. Many churches established before the 1950s assumed that members would walk or take public transportation a relatively short distance to worship. That is one reason why parking is often limited. Even in the postwar period of suburban sprawl, churches were still built for neighborhoods, though residents by then commuted longer distances to work.

- Commute time: The average commute time to work can be anything from under fifteen minutes in some small towns, to over an hour in congested cities. The important thing for church planners is that every new traffic light or changed traffic pattern creates an additional deterrent for impatient people to attend church for worship and meetings.

- Mode of transportation: Until recently, options for public transportation throughout North America have decreased or deteriorated. Most people travel by car, and this makes parking one of the big church growth challenges for many established churches.

- Vehicle occupancy: It is common to see the occupancy rate at 1 to 1.5. People are making more effort to carpool to work, but not to travel to worship or church meetings. The challenge for parking is complicated further by the congestion while dropping off seniors, young families, or disabled persons at the church door. Churches are reserving spaces for those with disabilities, expecting mothers, and visitors. They may even build covered entrances or initiate valet parking as part of hospitality.

North American habits of mobility have challenged churches originally designed as neighborhood centers. Churches that cannot afford to acquire parking may be forced to relocate or electronically link multiple sites of ministry.

Home Ownership

Data about home ownership that are very useful to municipal governments, retail developers, and boards of education may not be relevant to church planners. I have discovered in my consultations, however, that comparing the proportion of homeowners and renters in the community to the proportion of the same among church members can be very instructive. Data gathered regarding new home construction and resale of homes can also be helpful.

First, the proportion of homeowners to renters can be an important indicator of the stability of the community. More renters suggests the tenure of residence is lower and people are moving in and out more frequently. Indeed, the average tenure of residency in a community is often just three to five years, especially in population growth areas that are primarily building "starter" homes for young families.

The church, by contrast, is often an island of stability in a sea of change. The majority of members may have resided in their homes for ten to fifteen years and fail to empathize with the unstable lives of newcomers. They assume membership assimilation can take five years or more, but by that time many people have come and gone. Many young families and transient adults will not think it worthwhile to connect with a church because they know they will move again soon.

Second, homeowners and renters may have different perspectives on financial management and different priorities for budget development. So also will families in starter homes that are considered just "stepping-stones" to their preferred locations and residences. The more transient families and adults seek one-to-one coaching to develop an overall family financial plan on Christian principles. They care less about heritage protection or property costs, and more about program relevance.

The church, by contrast, often includes a majority of homeowners in longtime residence who prefer low-key stewardship programs that raise money through letters of solicitation, newsletters, and financial updates in the Sunday bulletin. They are apt to prioritize budgets for building maintenance, organ repairs, stained-glass windows, and other signs of permanency.

Income

Demographic researchers can gather considerable data about income and debt in any given community, and of course the story can vary from place to place. There are three common patterns, however, that are often surprising to church leaders:

1. The gap between the very poor and the very rich is often growing.
2. Incomes for people currently above the poverty line are actually improving despite recessions.
3. The greatest financial growth is among people who already have incomes of $100,000 or more.

The reason that this is particularly interesting for churches is that many members of established churches tend to fall into the second category. They are people currently living above the poverty line, and their incomes are actually *increasing*. I am not saying this is universally true in every church, but it is a common pattern in many churches. What does this mean?

First, I see a common trend that churches claim poverty and over-look wealth. Church members often *claim* to be poor in order to justify low or decreasing percentage giving, when *in fact* their incomes are generally stable or growing. Church members protest budget increases and yet still have the disposable income to take vacations, buy new cars, and indulge their hobbies. Ironically, churches often deny that people with high incomes exist in the community or assume that wealthy people would not be interested in the church. They rarely approach potential donors for philanthropic giving, even though demographic research proves that giving to philanthropic causes is on the rise.

Second, I see a common trend that churches expect all missions and ministries to be self-supporting. This includes forms of outreach, seeker-sensitive worship, hospitality, and so on. In other words, ministries and missions should financially break even (or make a profit) primarily from user fees (or the donations of participants) combined with subsidies from denominations or outside agencies. If a ministry or mission "loses money," church people usually assume that they should not have to pay for it.

It is notoriously difficult to gather personal financial information from church members. Yet the habits seem clear. Established churches tend to claim their incomes are worse than they really are and tend to avoid asking wealthy people for money. This combined habit places outreach ministries of all kinds chronically at risk.

Debt

Demographic research can compare the asset-debt ratio of any local community to that of the state as a whole. I have been struck by the fact that this ratio is so often declared "average" even in difficult economic times. Some communities clearly have "above average" debt compared to assets (particularly upscale subdivisions where homeowners overreached their financial potential and suffered later). Personally, I have yet to consult in a community where assets are "above average" over debt, although I know they exist. It raises a question about what "state average" really means, and given the economic crises of our time, it appears that what is "average" today would have been unthinkable to our parents or grandparents.

Churches are no less challenged than the average citizen in trying to determine what "manageable debt" might look like. A few churches refuse to have any debt at all, but that means in order to grow they must insist on strong disciplines of tithing from church members and aggressively seek grants, memorials, or other financial gifts from philanthropic entrepreneurs who are excited about their big, bold vision. Most churches have lower expectations. Although there is a lingering question about whether such churches can financially survive in the post-Christendom world, there remains for them the challenge to determine "manageable debt."

The rule used to be that debt retirement should never exceed about 22 percent of a church annual budget. I think there is every indication that that percentage is going down as the national economy slows down. Moreover, churches with fewer than two hundred in worship (surely 80 percent or more of the churches in North America) will keep debt retirement lower than churches with higher attendance, because their financial viability depends too much on a handful of good givers.

Generosity

Demographic research can provide helpful benchmarks regarding charitable giving in any mission field. These benchmarks identify giving not only to religious organizations but also to public television and radio, health and university institutions, nonprofit and political organizations, and other social agencies. Research often compares the philanthropy of a mission field to the state average by indicating the percentage of people contributing $200 or more.

Although charitable giving for church members is often confidential, many churches provide a breakdown of how many members contribute specific dollars each year. The most obvious goal for some churches is simply to match the percentage of church members who give $200 or more to the church with the percentage of the surrounding community. However, because most philanthropically minded people actually divide their giving among multiple recipients, more and more churches are broadening their Christian financial coaching to help members develop a "mission portfolio" of philanthropic invest-ing tailored to their personal interests. Overall, this increases financial generosity to the church.

Religion

I think that religion is one of the weakest areas of demographic research, and perhaps the *least* helpful for churches. The United States census intentionally does not gather data about participation in reli-gious organizations. Although Canada does, the research is usually fil-tered through classic Christendom definitions of "Catholic" and "Prot-estant" churches and used to inform the school systems that receive public funding. Both census databases generally ignore the ferment of spiritualities emerging today.

The priority of research in multicultural and post-Christendom North America is really to track major religious groups. This research is pursued most often by nongovernmental organizations. Education, health care, social services, public services, and businesses are inter-ested in emerging and declining religious groups because their mores, languages, and expectations influence classroom curricula, hospital ser-vices, language tutoring, food management, and so many other things.

Demographic research alone does not really help churches that are trying to connect with the largest and fastest-growing category of people in North America. I call them the "Spiritually Yearning, Insti-tutionally Alienated" public. I use the acronym SYiA to describe their attitude toward organized religion in general ("See Ya Later!").[4] These may be frustrated or abused church dropouts, generations that never participated in organized religion in the first place, or second- and third-generation immigrants who stepped away from religion in order to blend with culture.

This, then, is the *first level* of research. I call it "pure demographics." At one time, these filters of research were the only filters used, and stra-tegic planners in all sectors simply relied on this level of perception to make decisions. Today it is helpful, but insufficient. All of this research raises as many questions as it answers. The community, or the "mission field" from the church's point of view, is more complicated than this.

Lifestyle Segments

The second progressive lens goes beyond pure demographics to explore more closely the daily behavior and habits of groups of people ("publics") within the mission field.

Basic demographic categories alone are no longer adequate for effective strategic planning. There was a time when organizations made decisions, developed products, implemented programs, and created advertising specifically for groups of people defined by pure demographics, but no longer. These categories are certainly not irrelevant, but by themselves they are no longer sufficient for strategic planning. Not only is there enormous diversity of behavior and attitude in each category, but blends and permutations among categories are constantly changing. This is why the "lifestyle segment" is a more profound and detailed insight into subgroups of people, and why sensitivity to lifestyle segments has replaced basic demographic categories as the key to strategic planning.

Consider, for example, the following quandaries that are regularly confounding church leaders as they plan for the future. None of these quandaries can be resolved simply by pigeonholing people in general categories:

- Clergy know they can't be all things to all people, but they can't figure out exactly what they need to become, and for whom, next year.

- "Radical hospitality" for one group of people is "basic" to another, and refreshments currently served on Sunday morning are "cheap" to one person and "extravagant" to another.

- Seniors are attending worship services supposedly aimed at youth, and young adults are attending services supposedly aimed at mature adults.

- Sunday school curricula that work well in one church fail in another church, but the churches are of the same denomination, of the same demographic makeup, and just two blocks from each other.

- Men are keenly interested in educational programs labeled "Women's Studies," and gay, lesbian, and transgendered people are looking for hybrid curricula.

- French, Mandarin, and Creole speakers are desperate to preserve their languages but eager to learn about uniquely American or Canadian history and cultural mores.

- Small groups for new parents include traditional and nontraditional couples raising children who are their own, adopted from other cultures, or merged from several relationships into a single new household; the "parents" may be aged fourteen to sixty-five.

- The outreach agendas of nonprofit groups that use the church building have no connection with the outreach passions of the actual members of the church.

- The building needs to be renovated, and the capital campaign has to be launched, but nobody can agree on what technologies need to be included in the budget and engineering designs.

- Annual giving to the church is less than the average giving to charitable organizations by people in the zip code, but the Finance Committee doesn't know what to do about it.

- The church is on the corner, by the bus stop, at a major intersection, and nobody in the neighborhood knows or cares that it exists.

All these quandaries can be resolved only by a close examination of lifestyle segments to interpret expectations for spiritual leadership, relevant ministries, meaningful symbols, useful technologies, effective communications, and so on. None of these quandaries can be resolved by basic demographic information alone; by stereotypes about age, race, or culture; or by untested assumptions about education levels, learning methods, personal relationships, and occupational habits.

The segmentation of publics into distinct "lifestyle portraits" is a better way to understand what daily life is really like in the areas defined by the church as the "mission field." People may be self-conscious of their age, race, relative affluence, occupations, relationships, and so on, but they actually live in the context of peer groups that share particular social attitudes, rely on particular media, and behave in particular ways. Those data are collected in myriad ways, by tracking spending habits, recreational priorities, group memberships, and so on.

We can now draw more than seventy distinct "portraits" of lifestyle segments that behave in certain predictable ways. That number will likely grow as society continues to diversify. The "portrait" of these life-style groups reveals that specific groups of people shop in certain stores, enjoy *these* recreational activities rather than *those*, live together in distinct neighborhoods, gravitate toward selected activities, learn new things in distinctive methodologies, and share common social needs. They share unique worldviews, attitudes, and perspectives. Key social issues, personal anxieties, and spiritual questions have higher, average, or lower priority for some, compared to other people in their province or state. All this guides marketing and business practice, shapes public policy and social services, and constantly revises the strategic plans of school boards and curricula for universities.

Awareness of lifestyle portraits is also very important for churches. One size no longer fits all. One strategy no longer works everywhere. Each lifestyle segment has distinct expectations for leadership priorities, hospitality choices, worship options, educational methods, small-group practices, and outreach emphases. When strategic planners are sensitive to the lifestyle segments within their primary or targeted mission field, churches can focus ministries with much greater effectiveness.

A church in exurban south Florida, for example, may have a completely different strategy for ministry than a church in urban Illinois or suburban Pennsylvania does. Yet they may all be churches of the same denomination. A century ago, a visitor could attend each one, and the churches would be so similar that he or she would feel "right at home." Today, they are so dissimilar in tactics that a visitor only gradually realizes the churches belong to the same denomination. They are all so different, and yet, through time and association, it becomes clear that they all basically behave and believe in the same way.

The exurban church in south Florida may welcome guests with five layers of trained greeters and have multiple choices in health food, herbal tea, and sugar substitutes. The worship is presentational and performance driven; the music is classical jazz; the sermon delivers three points, based on three Scriptures, following the Christian year. Sunday school is age based and classroom style, and it uses curricula from the denominational publishing house. Midweek ministries include recovery groups for prescription drug abusers and Bible studies. Outreach is a K-12 Christian school, and they send mission teams to Africa.

In the church in south Florida, they may raise money the old-fashioned way (fall campaigns and every-member visitations). They may hate video but love "surround sound." The new sanctuary has a steeple on top, but everybody gets e-mail.

Meanwhile, a church of the same denomination in a stagnant satellite city of Chicago only welcomes guests at the front door with untrained families (with children) and smiling disabled veterans in wheelchairs at the side doors. They may deliberately serve basic coffee and tea in big steel urns, with creamer, sugar, and donuts. That's it. The worship is interactive and exuberant. They sing Christmas carols *before* Christmas. The sermon follows themes of practical lifestyle struggles. Healing prayer and Holy Communion are offered every week. Sunday school teaches the great Bible studies through crafts, cartoons, and puppets. Small-group affinities are based on sports and hobbies. Outreach is a food bank and a neighborhood watch on Halloween.

In small-city Illinois, the church may raise money through tithing and donations to its many public services. The church was formerly a supermarket and was renovated to have great sight lines to the video screens (even though it has lousy acoustics).

Meanwhile, a church of the same denomination in the northern suburbs of Philadelphia may welcome guests in the parking lot, escort them to the Welcome Center, and give free plush toys to the kids and free flash drives to the teenagers (with the URL of the church on them). They may buy their coffee in bulk from Starbucks and have espresso makers in the narthex. Worship starts out with praise and heavy metal and includes an "intermission," when newcomers are personally introduced to the pastor and members can refill their insulated travel mugs. When they return, there is forty minutes of Bible-based teaching about the ethical dilemmas of postmodern living, but no offering. There may be a state-of-the-art nursery and cross-generational, topical discussion groups. Outreach may be a Family Christian Counseling Center and regular mission trips to rehab houses in New Orleans.

In suburban Philadelphia, this mainstream church may raise money through preauthorized bank withdrawals and Christian family financial planning seminars. The stewardship campaign is in late April to help people spend their tax refunds on a personalized mission investment portfolio. Yes, the sanctuary has a steeple on top, but people sit in comfortable cathedral chairs in the round. There is high-quality video and audio . . . and one LCD screen is tuned to CNN online throughout the entire worship service. They may even provide cash machines in the vestibule because their visitors don't carry cash and the church can't afford to accept credit cards.

The metaphor "lifestyle portrait" is apt. These descriptions try to capture in a single image a living, changing, unique being. A great portrait not only paints the subject in a context, surrounded by scenes and symbols that would be familiar, but also captures the facial expression, fashion statement, poise, and general attitude toward life of the real person. A portrait reveals the subject's personal priorities and prejudices and suggests the kinds of recreations, relationships, activities, and work that this person might do after sitting for the painter.

Moreover, a great portrait elicits empathy or antipathy from the observer. This may be less important for a business, government, board of education, or medical practice, which permit greater objectivity about people. People are, after all, merely customers, citizens, students, and clients who can be quantified by statistics and valued as potential financial income. Indeed, one of the persistent criticisms of the church growth movement is that the study of generations, ethnic groups, and neighborhood demographic diversity treats Christian mission as if it were a business amassing wealth. Understanding a lifestyle segment, however, is like viewing a portrait. One is moved to really care what happens to this individual or to this peculiar public.

I call this earnest compassion a "heartburst." One's heart does not burst for a demographic category. The poor and wealthy, the young and old, singles and married couples, families, blue- and white-collar workers, the uneducated or well educated are all categories that include enormous diversity of likeable and unlikeable people. Even the people assigned to those categories are uncomfortable with the stereotype. Young people, for example, do not associate with one another just because they are young, and may not like one another despite their similarity in age. Because of this, the era of the single, large Sunday evening youth group is long over as a successful strategy of youth ministry for most churches.

Instead, the lifestyle segment clusters people together the way they do it themselves in real life. Each lifestyle segment tends to live in proximity to one another, eat in certain kinds of restaurants, shop in certain kinds of stores, enjoy certain kinds of entertainment, drive certain kinds of cars (with specific sorts of accessories), and so on. They also tend to share certain kinds of needs and have certain kinds of expectations for a church.

The term "church shopping" only partly describes why newcomers may visit a church, return many times, and eventually join the membership. Lifestyle segment research reveals why different publics connect with any particular ministry, and the "urgent search" that may connect them with the mission of a congregation. The era of "religious dilettantism" is ending. People connect with a church, particular church leaders, and worship, educational, small-group, or outreach opportunities because they can address their unique spiritual and social compulsions in ways that are user friendly.

Of course, the lifestyle segments that comprise the primary mission field of a church are a moving target. They are constantly growing, declining, changing, mutating, and evolving. In the same way, a portrait is only a snapshot of a life in progress. The artist should really repaint a portrait many times to capture the dynamic of life itself, much like reality television follows an individual every second and records his or her words and actions. That might be inconvenient for the portrait painter, but today it is actually possible to monitor the development of a lifestyle segment. Not only is research updated constantly by governments, better business bureaus, real estate developers, and shopping mall franchisers but every purchase with a credit card and investment choice from low risk to high risk can be pooled, sorted, and analyzed. That is the potential of the sophisticated search engines of today.

The challenge of lifestyle segment research is that we can now generate *too much data!* We need filters through which to sift information, sorting out what is essential to know for Christian mission, and what is not. The filters that are useful for a business, board of education, or health care service may not be useful for churches. And we already know that the filters used even fifty years ago at the end of Christendom are no longer useful in the post-Christendom and post-secular world. The next section of this book lays out an entirely new "filtering system" to shape relevant ministries for emerging lifestyle segments.

Psychographics

The third "progressive lens" gives us an even more detailed, more highly nuanced insight into the publics that make up the primary mission field of a church. Psychographic research explores the attitudes, social perspectives, worldviews, and values of various publics living proximate to each other. These insights are more instructive for retail businesses, social service providers, and other organizations dealing directly with the public, and which are more vulnerable to shifting public opinion.

Psychographic information is sometimes included in the previous category of lifestyle segment research. Indeed, psychographic information is combined with demographic information to focus changing lifestyle segments every few years. I separate these categories here, however, because I think it is more helpful to church leaders trying to understand their mission field:

- First, psychographic research *for churches* is not done through complicated surveys, but through face-to-face interviews. There really is no substitute for experience, constant dialogue, and "leg work." People act and react on the spur of the moment, and the unrehearsed words or spontaneous deeds reveal the real truth about their prejudices, habits, and assumptions regardless of how they completed a survey.

- Second, psychographic research can test the insights from the previous two progressive lenses. The conclusions we draw from demographic trends and lifestyle segments can be put to the test right here, right now, to see if our assumptions are true.

If a pastor really wants to understand the shifting attitudes of the public, he or she simply must leave the office, mingle and mix, lurk and observe, and generally interact with real people beyond the church. Only then can the pastor preach effectively. Similarly, if a music director really wants to understand the shifting values of the public, he or she has to leave the choir room and circulate among the bars, coffee shops, and night clubs; sample all the radio stations; track the top ten charts; and explore every musical genre. Only then can he or she understand what "contemporary music" is this week.

To understand the difference between demographic, lifestyle segment, and psychographic research, consider the precarious situation of automobile dealerships. Automobile sales are big businesses that drive the economies of entire cities. I read somewhere that in 2008 there were nearly eight hundred automobiles for every one thousand people in the United States, which is the largest proportion in any country. The number may well be higher today, but whatever it is, that's a lot of cars! People buy a car not for transportation, but as an expression of their personalities, a declaration of their personal values, and a sign of personal success. However, the profit margins for automobile dealerships are very narrow, and competition is very steep.

Psychographic research equips car sales personnel to anticipate the sale even before the customer has opened the negotiation. Have you noticed that sales representatives are always staring out the window when you drive up? They are not daydreaming. They are sizing you up for the sale. They have studied the psychographics. They can tell just by looking at you what kind of vehicle, with what kind of accessories, at what kind of price point, you are looking for:

- Compact, midsize, full size?
- Sedan, minivan, SUV, sport car, truck?
- Basic, loaded, luxury?
- Neutral colors, bright colors, fire stenciled on the hood?
- Sunroof, mag wheels, satellite radio, roof racks?
- Ski package, surf package, touring package, storage package, towing capacity?

The moment you as the customer begin to speak, the sales representative is learning more about your personal priorities and potential trade-offs. What is really important to you? What is expendable, and what is essential? Automobile dealers have all the options covered. They have researched their community, stocked up on what will most likely sell, and shipped what's left to another dealer in a different kind of community. This is why automobile sales representatives have a reputation for manipulation. They know how to tempt you. They have to know! Whether the dealership thrives or dies depends on their insight.

Here is an example of how church leaders add psychographic insight onto their previous research into pure demographics and lifestyle segments. In this example, church leaders in a saturated downtown "spiritual marketplace" wanted to make their church *radically relevant* in order to stand out from the fifty other churches (some in the same denomination as their own church) that were all struggling in the urban core. Here is what they gleaned from research:

Demographic Insight	Lifestyle Segment Insight	Psychographic Insight
Average age: forty-two	Three major publics downtown:	Key issues and questions:
Singles and empty nesters: ages twenty to thirty-one and fifty-eight to eighty-three	1) Quietly aging singles and couples, who shop at JC Penney, watch NASCAR races, drink flavored coffee, and listen to oldies and country music. They tend to be heavily insured and take lots of prescription drugs. Rarely read an entire book, but like magazines with short articles and pictures.	Relatively happy with life

Worried about violence and crime

Important to be well informed

Prefer quiet evenings at home

Good at fixing things

Not interested in other cultures |
| Highest education level: high school with some college and professional training | | |
| Primary languages: English and Spanish | 2) Struggling African-American families, with multiple generations under the same roof, who shop at thrift stores. The TV is on all day, and they listen to pop and hip-hop music. About half are unemployed at any given time. Bowling and basketball are favorite sports. They watch movies and rarely read. | Believe that "real men" don't cry

Religion is a private matter

Church is a support group

Like to stand out in a crowd

Find it hard to say no to kids

Children should express themselves

Take time from family to succeed |

Demographic Insight, cont.	Lifestyle Segment Insight, cont.	Psychographic Insight, cont.
Household incomes: declining numbers below poverty line; growing numbers with incomes between $25,000 and $55,000	3) Under age thirty-five singles and cross-cultural couples, in non-traditional relationships, living in old homes and apartments. They juggle several part-time jobs, socialize at night in bars and cafes, watch reality TV, and listen to punk, rock, and Latino music. They have high debt but upgrade cell phones and text constantly.	Better a boring job than no job at all
		Practical outlook on life
		Would like to start own business
Common occupations: food service, maintenance, health care, administration		Religion is a public matter
		Church is important
		Workaholic behavior
		Tend to be influenced by others
Declining young families		Live for today
		Have a keen sense of adventure
Larger households		Interested in other cultures
		Time is more important than money
		Friends more important than family
		Religion is the reason for wars
		Church is boring

This information is invaluable to the church. The first thing the church realized is what the automobile industry discovered long ago. One size does not fit all. The church is going to have to offer multiple options in everything from worship style, to refreshments after church, to outreach ministries. This information will help the pastor to focus preaching, the music director to choose music and instrumentations, the small-group leaders to focus affinities, the Sunday school director to adjust media and curricula, and the outreach committee to plan off-site interventions.

Large corporations, political parties, and universities with research grants may be able to do extensive public surveys to identify attitudes and social preferences, but this is beyond the means of most churches. Moreover, churches would be right to question their accuracy. Most lifestyle segments by far *don't like surveys.* Aside from invasion of privacy, the multiple choices for each question rarely express participants' true feelings at the moment of the survey, much less their true feelings ten minutes later. Is there a better way? Yes, there are two basic ways to gather more accurate psychographic information, without alienating the public.

The first method is the focus group. A focus group is a small group of perhaps five to twelve people who have been specifically invited to participate in a conversation. Churches focus on a particular target public that they want to research. For example, an older church may want to target young families, and specifically dual-career parents with preschool or elementary-age children. Obviously, the best focus group will include representatives of the target public who are relatively inactive or not represented in the current membership.

How do you know whom to invite? Usually, a church approaches a young family somewhat active in the church, or connected with grandparents active in the church, and asks for help in forming a focus group among neighbors, work associates, or friends they know. The church promises to pay for babysitting and for dinner at the best restaurant in town, provided participants sit with two representatives of the church over dinner and let them ask friendly questions about their likes and dislikes. The church may well send them the topic they want to discuss, or even send them a dozen questions they want to raise. No surprises. No manipulations. No membership or committee recruitment. No hints about financial donations.

Focus groups are usually done in clusters of at least three. In this example, there may be three such groups. The church may want to design each group a bit differently for comparison purposes. One group, for example, might be single-parent young families; another group might be young families with preschool children only. Make sure that the topics are the same and the basic questions are the same. This facilitates better comparisons as you reflect on the results.

Focus groups become a strategic habit with growing churches. Every year, these churches deploy different focus group strategies among people who are involved in significant ministries, or who might be involved in new initiatives. Attitudes, worldviews, and social perspectives change. In order to adjust everything and anything (hospitality, worship design, Christian education, small groups, outreach, fund-raising strategies, technology upgrades, and communication media), churches are as constant with focus groups as retail businesses, hospitals, and charitable organizations are.

The second method to gather psychographic information is through strategies of intentional observation. To paraphrase Sherlock Holmes: *most churches see, but do not observe.* Growing churches deploy leaders to observe the behavior patterns of distinct publics and overhear their conversations. This should not be a violation of privacy. It is simply an intentional strategy to deploy leaders in any gathering of people, within the church or beyond the church, to keep their eyes and ears open. Shut up, and listen!

Intentional observation requires preparation and follow-up. The preparation usually comes from reflection about lifestyle-segment and demographic-trend research. Observers have a list of assumptions or perceptions that they want to test. In other words, they are looking and listening for specific things. They do this intentionally in several gatherings. The follow-up is usually some kind of log or journal in which they record their insights (without any names) about attitudes and preferences that are more common.

For example, a church may want to test attitudes toward worship among empty-nest adults who have sufficient disposable incomes to travel a lot. Presumably, this gives them an opportunity to experience different kinds of worship in different contexts. What do they think? What do they like and dislike? What do they find profound or shallow? The church deliberately deploys leaders (alone or in pairs) with a mental list of questions or assumptions they want to test. They attend the church couples club meeting, hang around upscale coffeehouses, attend a cocktail party in the neighborhood, mingle at the office party, and seek out opportunities to be around fellow empty nesters even while on vacation. When they go home, they take fifteen minutes to write down their insights. What surprised them? What assumptions were confirmed? What assumptions were challenged?

Church members are notoriously opinionated about the cultures and experiences around them, but they are often inaccurate or even dead wrong in their assumptions. Consider, for example, a common assumption in traditional churches that seniors are computer illiterate, don't use e-mail, and hate video screens in worship. Psychographic research through focus groups and intentional observation often revealed that by 2012, seniors in most lifestyle segments were surprisingly computer savvy, used e-mail constantly, and preferred video screens so that they could read the words of the liturgy, stop struggling to hold heavy hymnbooks, and look up to sing louder. The seniors who continue the old habits are the minority who happen to be inside church, but they do not actually represent the majority of seniors out there in the mission field.

Psychographic research is all about immersion in the surrounding cultures—the opposite of immersion in the churchy culture. Demographic research may reveal trends that shape church budget priorities, and lifestyle segment research may reveal challenges that shape programs, but psychographic research will help focus preaching topics, small-group affinities or book studies, outreach strategies, and the intercessory prayers of the congregation. In other words, psychographic research reveals the *motivations* of people that prompt their actions. It reveals how people actually apply church "products" (for example, programs, sermons, fellowships, and resources) to their daily living.

Heartburst Affinities

Most businesses have three progressive lenses in their organizational microscope to analyze the marketplace: pure demographics, lifestyle segments, and psychographics. The church, however, has a fourth lens because, for the Christian community, the "marketplace" is really a "mission field." The church's goal is not to make a profit from the world, but to give blessings to the world. Its goal is not to carve out a bigger market share, but to participate in the one realm of God. Therefore, the church goes beyond psychographics to look even deeper into the spiritual yearnings of the public to discover how specifically, right now and right here, the church can bless people.

Churches have a *mission attitude* that is different from the attitudes of secular organizations. I have always defined this mission attitude as *the passion and call to transform and empower a peculiar public.*[5] It is a "passion" because the church is highly motivated and can get quite emotional from the love they bear toward particular groups of people in need. It is a "call" because they are willing to go out of their own comfort zones to do what they personally dislike, and associate with people they may ordinarily avoid, from the love they bear toward God. Their goal is to "transform" people by liberating them from self-destructive habits they chronically deny and to "empower" people to become all God promises for them to be. They expand this mission strategically one microculture at a time, as they discern the peculiar needs and yearnings of each public they encounter.

This discernment of a peculiar public, motivated by love of people and love of God, and guided by a desire to transform and empower, is what I call a "heartburst." It is the fourth lens through which churches examine the surrounding mission field (or spiritual marketplace).

St. Paul would probably say that the ultimate question for Christian mission is "Who is your Macedonian?" In Acts 16, the mission to Philippi begins with the vision of a Macedonian appearing in a dream. The Macedonian is a describable, definable, demographic group, probably encompassing several lifestyle segments (some of which include middle-class businesswomen like Lydia), who have specific perspectives about society, religion, success, friendships, and other things. Most important, some of them have spiritual needs that drive them to the riverside, which Paul discovers is the place of prayer. Paul and his companions not only risk dangerous seas to get to where the Macedonian lives, but they also clearly take the time and trouble to figure out who the Macedonians are and what motivates them to look for God.

Although spiritual yearnings are unique to every individual, there are patterns. I define six specific patterns. You may define more, and the patterns in your mission field may differ from the patterns in the mission field in another country, state, county, city, small town, or neighborhood. Each church will probably define its filter of analysis a little differently. Here is the filter I have found most helpful as I consult with churches.[6]

Progressive lenses highlight progressive questions as the church shifts its focus from "marketplace" to "mission field." At first, you answer the question "What are the trends?" Your mind is all curiosity. Then you go deeper and ask, "Who exactly *are* these people?" Your heart begins to empathize. Next, you ask, "What are they thinking?" Your instinct is to start a dialogue. Finally, you get to the heart of the matter and ask, "What blessing are they seeking?" Now your heart begins to burst.

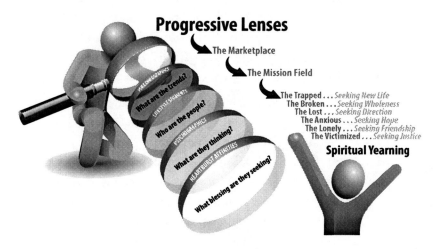

Progressive Lenses

The Marketplace
The Mission Field

The Trapped . . . *Seeking New Life*
The Broken . . . *Seeking Wholeness*
The Lost . . . *Seeking Direction*
The Anxious . . . *Seeking Hope*
The Lonely . . . *Seeking Friendship*
The Victimized . . . *Seeking Justice*
Spiritual Yearning

What are the trends?
Who are the people?
What are they thinking?
What blessing are they seeking?

DEMOGRAPHICS
LIFESTYLE SEGMENTS
PSYCHOGRAPHICS
HEARTBURST AFFINITIES

Research is hard work. Leaders pore over seemingly endless statistics, spend hours brooding over lifestyle descriptions, and ponder the significance of group perspectives and attitudes. Eventually, organizational leaders will wonder what the point is. In the business world, the point is profits. In the church world, the point is blessing. Yet for both, the key word is *relevance*. Unless you are "relevant" (that is, applicable, appropriate, apt, congruous, fitting, germane, pertinent, suitable, or significant), you will neither sell products nor channel Christ.

I have already identified these on the chart in the first chapter of this book, when I described a basic theology of demographic research. Each spiritual yearning is tied to a distinct experience of the real presence of God (or incarnation of Christ). God has a response for each spiritual yearning, and this response provides the clue to how a church can bless the Macedonian in its midst.

- People who are trapped are bound by circumstances or compulsions beyond their control. This might include crushing poverty, oppressive authorities, and chronic addictions. People particularly seek new life or a fresh start. God's grace is experienced as the intervention of a Higher Power that can liberate from oppression or turn life around. A church might bless the trapped by establishing food and housing co-ops, multiplying 12-step programs, or offering political advocacy.

- People who are broken are beset by physical, mental, or emotional illness, or suffering broken relationships. This might include chronic disease, debilitating stress, or marriage and family breakdowns. People particularly seek wholeness. God's grace is experienced as healing that can restore health, balance, and intimacy. A church might bless the broken by establishing medical and counseling clinics, marriage enrichment programs, or parish nurse ministries.

- People who are lost are unclear about moral behavior, aimless about purpose, or lacking motivation. This might include confusion over career, frustration with materialism, or sociopathic behavior. People particularly seek direction or advice. God's grace is experienced as guidance. A church might bless the lost through topical worship services, mentoring relationships, vocational counseling, or ethical instruction.

- People who are anxious are often depressed, fearful, or withdrawn. They might see conspiracies everywhere, or experience panic over global and international crises, or despair for a lost utopian dream. People particularly seek hope and confidence. God's grace is experienced as promise-keeping. A church might multiply opportunities for personal service and outreach, focus on volunteer empowerment, or provide guided meditation.

- People who are lonely often feel isolated, unloved, or forgotten. They may have relocated to a new environment, experienced the death of family members, feel unappreciated at home or work, or struggle to make friends. People particularly seek safe, healthy intimacy. God's grace is experienced as acceptance, empathy, and perfect companionship. A church might multiply fellowship opportunities, expand small affinity groups, or train lay visitors.

- People who are victimized are abused, denigrated, or manipulated. This might include sexual, spousal, or elder abuse; bullying or stalking; prejudice or bigotry; or criminal actions. People particularly seek justice, vindication, and restored self-esteem. God's grace is experienced as vindication and rescue. A church might establish legal aid services, advocacy programs, protest marches, or shelters.

Researchers learn that some lifestyle segments may be more at risk in one or more of these spiritual needs than others. The very affluent and the very poor, for example, are more vulnerable to addictions; third-generation immigrants may be more vulnerable to feeling lost; upwardly mobile young couples may be more vulnerable to broken marriages. Spiritual needs may change over time. Older families with teenagers may have a primary spiritual yearning for guidance and direction. Empty nesters may feel particularly anxious and seek hope. Seniors may experience acute loneliness and seek friendships.

This fourth lens of research requires tactics similar to those of the investigation of psychographics. Some might say that it is a form of psychographic research, but clearly the listening that is required is multidimensional. Prayer and listening to God are as vital as listening to the public, and often God speaks through the voices and behaviors of the public.

Focus groups are valuable but are often shaped differently. The affinity of the participants is not a demographic or lifestyle similarity that they share (such as age, phase of life, and tenure of residence). People who gather around these more superficial similarities may not have the confidence to share their deeper personal issues or spiritual questions. Instead, the focus group affinity may be that participants are all first-time visitors to a church, or that they are all participants in an outreach ministry of the church, or that they are all active in a community charity. The least helpful focus group is one in which the participants are all currently active church members, because they are likely to reinforce what is already happening inside the church institution rather than give insight into community issues.

One of the most effective focus groups is a gathering of people who connect with the *church building*, even though they do not connect with the *church fellowship*. Most churches rent or donate space to community groups through the week. Numerous people connect with the building through Boy or Girl Scouts, exercise and diet support groups, 12-step groups, wellness clinics, and so on. These are often people with a strong sense of spirituality, but for one reason or another, they fail to connect with the church as a faith community. They are often more open to participate in a focus group to share their perceptions about personal issues and spiritual questions out there in the community.

There are different forms of intentional listening that are particularly helpful. These all require disciplines for listening and observation of the public, but also spiritual disciplines of prayer, meditation, Bible study, and faith conversations between church leaders. None of these tactics should invade privacy. These are simply tactics to listen, observe, and pray intentionally for people other than ourselves.

Listening-Prayer Triads[7]

Threesomes of church leaders covenant for several weeks to listen and pray for the public. Each week, they gather as a triad to pray for guidance and read Scripture (often from Luke-Acts) and then go to any place the public gathers, such as food courts, sports arenas, and shopping malls. They do not speak with anyone but simply spend an hour or more listening to conversations and observing behavior. Then they return to an individual home, debrief, and pray aloud for strangers. This is repeated for several weeks, while listening in different public places. Insights are often shared in preaching and intercessory prayer on Sunday. Deploy multiple triads. A good benchmark for a congregation is to deploy one triad for every twenty regular worshipers. For example, several triads observe various forms of borderline child abuse in discount stores, shopping malls, and sports arenas. Abuse includes slapping crying babies, exaggerated verbal berating of young children by parents, and other excessive measures of discipline. These are not extreme enough to report to police, but a pattern of parenting dysfunction is emerging. This suggests spiritual issues about "lost" parents and "victimized" children. The church initiates parenting classes and children's rights advocacy in the coming years.

Prayer Walks

Church leaders invest a few hours, over several weeks, to walk through neighborhoods that are proximate to the church, but in which they rarely spend time. This is best done in pairs. They do not speak with anyone. They may take notes of their insights. Their notes are divided into three categories:

- *The agony I see.* Note the pain, stress, anger, frustration, despair, or other negative emotions or actions revealed around you.

- *The blessing I long to give.* Focus the gift or response that you long to provide, whether or not it is in your personal power to give it.

- *The message I long to share.* In a few simple words, identify the single most important message of hope that might effectively improve a stranger's well-being.

Prayer walk partners return home to debrief and pray for strangers. Their insights may be shared with strategic planning retreats or board evaluation processes for the church. For example, several teams walk a street in the urban core with mixed retail and apartment housing. They notice the number of singles on the street, the number of bars on the corners, and the sex shops and magazine stalls selling the extreme literature. They suspect that if they had the courage to walk at night, they might see signs of alcoholism and prostitution. All this suggests spiritual issues about people who are "trapped," "broken," and "lonely." The church initiates 12-step programs and healthy entertainment opportunities in the coming years.

Interviews

Individual church leaders (often board members) make annual appointments with social service and health care leaders, police and emergency services, real estate and retail developers, and local municipal planners. They are prepared with a list of open-ended questions to explore both negative and positive social trends in the community. They gather data and perspective about demographic and lifestyle segment change. They debrief with each other and discuss what this insight reveals about the personal circumstances and spiritual situations of the public.

For example, several board members have met with hospital CEOs, emergency room directors, and police chiefs and discovered that suicide attempts and traffic fatalities among relatively affluent males between twenty and thirty years old have been growing significantly over the last three years, since a major natural disaster affected the community. The board debriefs and prays about it. All this suggests spiritual issues about hopelessness and brokenness. The church starts free counseling services for post-trauma depression and reshapes Sunday worship to be highly inspirational.

Tactics such as these help church leaders go deeper than simple analysis of the surrounding publics. Now they are able to *synthesize* all that they have learned about demographic trends, lifestyle segment behavior patterns, psychographic attitudes, and spiritual needs. They have taken demographic research from "marketplace" to "mission field," and they are in a better position to do effective strategic planning.

4. Demographic Research and Planning

The primary mission field of a church is defined by the average time or distance required for people in the area to go to work and shop. This crucial bit of information can be obtained from the U.S. Census itself or from any demographic search engine. This is also the distance seekers are likely to travel in order to attend worship and participate in small groups and routine educational opportunities. And it is also the distance church members are likely to travel routinely to serve what they understand to be "their community."

There are extensions to this mission field. There may be seekers moving into a contiguous region bordering on the primary mission field who readily connect with the primary mission field because of lifestyle segment compatibilities. Similarly, there may be members who will occasionally travel beyond the primary mission field for a particular mission about which they are particularly passionate. In the old days, this led denominations to buy property, redeploy professionals, and found a new church. Today, this is more likely to lead a congregation to rent property, train and deploy mission teams, and multiply the sites for their expanding church to more than one location.

Multisite churches, or denominational franchises, tend to expand across compatible lifestyle segments. Think of the game of dominos. Each domino has two halves, each with a different number of dots. The game is played by matching one half-domino to another half-domino of the same number of dots, and then matching the other half-domino with a second half-domino in the same way. The central domino is a bridge between two others.

Lifestyle segments are more complex than dominos, but the planning principle is the same. Something about one lifestyle segment is compatible with a different one, and the church expands its reach by aligning those compatibilities. Once a new lifestyle segment is connected to the mission of the church, another aspect of that lifestyle segment can be used to make a connection with yet another lifestyle segment. The one thing you can't do easily is connect entirely incompatible lifestyle segments. You may have a heart to reach them with your core message, but it will take a more circuitous approach through lifestyle segment compatibilities to get there.

This metaphor reveals an important truth about demographic research and strategic planning. The seekers are the ends and the membership is the means—not the other way around. Yet the attitude of established churches often really is the other way around. For many established churches, the members are the ends and the seekers are the means. In other words, the only point in reaching additional lifestyle segments is to convert them into card-carrying, pledge-making members who will pay the bills and staff the committees of an institutional church. In that case, demographic research is severely restricted. It doesn't take long before the lifestyle segments who are members become too uncomfortable with the lifestyle segments who are seekers. Too much growth radically changes the tactics, and perhaps the identity, of the institutional church. Growing discomfort prompts church planners to actually slow down, and eventually stop, membership growth. This is why declining or stagnant churches are often indifferent to demographic research. Why bother to understand the people we really don't want to include in the first place?

This is the difference between an "attractional" church and an "externally focused" church. Attractional churches have only limited use for demographic research. They sift through the information, looking for that one golden nugget or tactic that will hook outsiders to institutional agendas, and discard everything else about that lifestyle segment as unimportant. Externally focused churches reverse this attitude. They explore every nuance of a lifestyle segment, looking for porous seams of social need or spiritual hunger that they can flood with rich blessings. Attractional churches remove the wealth of lifestyle segments for their own purposes. Externally focused churches enhance the health of lifestyle segments for their unique benefit.

The contrast is startling, and it is often revealed when I consult with churches about ministry applications for lifestyle segments. For example, the most common pattern among denominations is that a judicatory subscribes to a demographic information provider, but congregational leaders fail to use it or even attempt to understand it. One of my associates has the habit of advising, "Just play with the search engine! Just explore!" Yet that is just what these denominational and congregational leaders do not want to do. Why is it necessary? Why waste their time? There are a hundred needy church members to visit, and no time for prayer walks, listening triads, and focus groups. They ask the consultant simply to provide a printed report, the briefest of summaries, emphasizing one or two key tactics that will hook outsiders.

Recently, I consulted with a large downtown Protestant church in a large city. They had already done extensive survey *of church members* to complete a SWOT analysis of perceived strengths, weaknesses, opportunities, and threats. I provided the requested demographic summary and advice to adapt ministries to lifestyle segments currently underrepresented or unrepresented in the membership. Yet when I advised them to generate a number of focus groups among these church outsiders, they were surprised and alarmed. *Why? What good would that do? We've already surveyed the members!* Common marketing sense should have suggested that if an organization is failing to reach a particular public, then there must be a serious flaw in the perceptions of the members. Go to the source!

The remarkable thing is that the members of the Long Range Planning Committee were all senior management professionals. True, some were academics and health care providers, but others were successful corporate leaders. Why would they refuse to do for the church what they would automatically do in their business? The answer was that reaching nonparticipating publics was never the real goal of planning. Preserving the institutional heritage was the real goal of planning. Therefore, research was confined to the opinions of members and a few tactical nuggets sifted from demographic studies that would be least stressful for members to implement.

Strategic Planning

Demographic research is relevant in preparation for strategic planning, and also at every step on the way. All four lenses in demographic research are valuable. The context will dictate how frequently each lens of research is used.

For example, churches in fast-growing cities or regions will need to pay very close attention to all four lenses of research. The fastest-growing areas in the USA, Canada, and Australia at the time of writing are displayed in the table below.

United States	Canada	Australia
Austin, Texas	Toronto, Ontario	Sydney, New South Wales
Raleigh-Cary, North Carolina	Calgary-Edmonton, Alberta	Perth-Bunbury, Western Australia
Las Vegas, Nevada	Montreal, Quebec	Hervey Bay, Queensland
Riverside-San Bernardino, California	Ottawa-Gatineau	Brisbane and "Gold Coast," Queensland: Coolangatta-Mount Tamborine
Orlando, Florida	Barrie, Ontario	
Charlotte, North Carolina	"Golden Horseshoe," Ontario: Oshawa-Kitchener-Brantford	
Phoenix, Arizona		
Dallas-Fort Worth, Texas		

In fast-growing regions like these, pure demographics and lifestyle segments should be reviewed every year, and psychographic and "heartburst" research should be done through focus groups and listening strategies every six months. The same might be said in regions that are experiencing accelerated population decline. These often include former industrial regions like western and northern New York, USA, or Maritime regions in Canada. Since migration from remote and rural areas into small towns and cities has been a worldwide trend, churches in both contexts should do more frequent demographic research in order to prepare for strategic planning.

On the other hand, contexts that are not experiencing such significant population change may practice a different discipline of research. Communities in the U.S. Midwest and Canadian Prairie Provinces or around Adelaide, South Australia, and southern New South Wales may review pure demographics every five years, lifestyle segments every two years, and psychographics and "heartburst" research annually.

The goal of all strategic planning is to accelerate creative ideas, perfect ongoing programs, and terminate ineffective tactics, in order to accomplish the mission of the organization.[1] Church leaders always review the research from all four lenses of demographic research before evaluating the past year and planning for the next.

One of the great mistakes of inward-looking, traditional churches, which greatly accelerates decline, is that they ignore this necessity to evaluate and plan. They simply repeat the same programs and tactics, delaying the initiation of creative new ideas and failing to terminate ineffective tactics, under the false assumption that nothing has really changed. The only thing that causes them to alter a strategic plan is a crisis of internal resources (money or volunteers). This is no way to be about "God's business" to redeem the world!

Strategic planners in churches follow a clear and logical process in prioritizing any given idea, program, or tactic. Their thought proceeds from *foundational*, to *functional*, to *formal* considerations:

- Foundational (rationale and purpose)

   Why are we doing it?

   Who will benefit by it?

   What result will measure success?

- Functional (leadership and tactics)

  Which team will lead it?

  When will they do it?

  How will they do it?

  Where will they do it?

- Formal (cost and stress management)

  How much will it cost in money, morale, and organizational change?

  What are the stress points we can anticipate?

Demographic research informs every step. Churches that fail to do their research are like blind guides who follow a plan without knowing what they will encounter or how they will succeed. Churches that do their research are visionaries that see the goal, anticipate obstacles and opportunities, and get results.

I used examples to illustrate strategic planning steps in my book *Accelerate Your Church.*[2] In that book, I followed the planning process for a monthly healing service and weekly Bible study program, prayer ministry, and community food bank. Here, I will step back a bit and describe a not-so-hypothetical church that is not only growing in size and mission impact but also expanding its ministry to additional sites. The story illustrates the crucial significance of each demographic "lens" for strategic planning:

> This chapter of the life and mission of "New Hope Church" begins when the congregation of about 500 members hears their beloved pastor announce his retirement in nine months. The pastor had already wisely chosen a board of men and women with imagination, business sense, and an ability to interpret demographic research. They were already clear about the core values, bedrock beliefs, motivating vision to be "church of all nations," and mission to bless "strangers to grace." Now their first priority was to find the right pastor for the future.
>
> Research into pure demographics revealed that their urban/exurban mission field was changing dramatically. The African-American population was growing most, but other Hispanic and Southeast Asian groups were growing as well. The emerging lifestyle groups were an interesting mix, however. These lifestyle segments included more upwardly mobile black families; cross-cultural relationships; a combination of childless, dual-career

couples and multiple generation households; rising lower-middle class incomes; and a percentage higher than state average for administrators and professionals. Median education was rising, even though it was mainly specialized in business, education, health care, and government service. These people were technologically savvy, whether or not they could afford it, and moved to a different kind of music.

The retiring pastor had been an enabler, caregiver, and excellent CEO for the church. However, this was not the kind of leader that would be most appreciated by the emerging lifestyle segments. They were looking for a visionary and a discipler with additional skills in administration. The former pastor was an expository preacher. The new pastor needed to be a motivational speaker, who could confidently dialogue from pulpit or coffee cup with any seeker. The church chose a young African-American pastor who had apprenticed with a large church in another part of the city. He lived from a "mobile office"; preached with a "tablet"; phoned with an "android"; and talked via "blue tooth." His wife was a public school principal. Their spiritual discipline was humble, but visible.

Notice how this hypothetical church models the attributes of an externally focused church. Their demographic research leads them to choose a pastor who "fits" with the lifestyle segments of the mission field, rather than a pastor who "fits" with the lifestyle segments currently in the church. (The different kinds of leaders preferred by different lifestyle segments will be described shortly.) This flexibility is made possible by their clarity about identity and purpose. They will make sure the new pastor is in essential agreement with their values, beliefs, vision, and mission, but then they are open to adapt themselves to a pastor whose first priority is to accelerate growth and mission impact. This same combination of mission attitude and sensitivity to the mission field will be repeated as they acquire, train, evaluate, and occasionally redeploy all staff:

> New Hope Church now begins to plan the future. They understand, as most churches do, that God's mandate to the church is to multiply disciples who bless the world in the name of Christ. More specifically, however, they understand that a "disciple" is someone who has been *accepted* as they are; and then *changed* by grace, *matured* in faith, *focused* in personal mission, *equipped* to follow Christ, and *sent* to be a blessing. In order for that to happen, they know that the church needs to *resource* disciples with whatever money, tools, and skills might be required; and *manage* personnel and technology so that it is ready and effective when required. Demographic research informs their decisions each step of the way.

73

- *Hospitality:* Research into lifestyle segments, confirmed through focus groups, reveals that most people in the mission field value *multiple choices*. They feel most accepted and valued when the church provides trained greeters and ushers who are sensitive to their individual needs; and when refreshments are high quality, diverse, respectful of different tastes and health concerns, and provided before, during, and after worship. Previously the church deployed friendly, but untrained greeters. They served only coffee and tea from large steel urns and occasional donuts.

- *Worship:* The same research into lifestyle segments, confirmed through focus groups, reveals that two educational and caregiving worship services repeated twice each Sunday morning were not going to grow participation. The emerging lifestyle segments valued highly inspirational worship, with a strong practical, lifestyle coaching content. The church began to shift the traditional service to be more presentational and inspirational; and added a second service that was topical, informal, and participatory.

- *Education:* The classic Sunday school still had a future despite the changing mission field. Research, confirmed by interviews with public and private school teachers and principals, revealed that people still preferred age-based classes, in formal settings, studying a curriculum that was strongly Bible-based. However, the Sunday school needed to be "tech-ed up" with improved video, audio, and computerized resources.

- *Small Groups:* Research into psychographics, combined with listening-prayer triads, revealed key life issues, spiritual questions, and interests that would define future affinities for small groups. The previous lifestyle segments of the church had preferred rotated leaders with groups meeting at the church. However, the emerging lifestyle segments preferred designated and trained group leaders meeting in private homes.

- *Outreach:* Demographic research revealed that the "very poor" were actually decreasing in the mission field; and further lifestyle segment research, plus interviews with social service providers, revealed that outreach ministries oriented to daily survival were less urgent. The future concerns of the community had more to do with neighborhood safety and crime prevention; plus opportunities for career counseling, job placement, and tutoring; plus opportunities for relaxation and relationships.

All of these strategic moves would provoke some stress within the church. Old tactics would have to be terminated. New tactics, and new teams, would have to be created. The transition sought to preserve tactics that were still clearly meaningful and relevant to the present church members, while adding new tactics that could be meaningful and relevant to people beyond the church.

Notice how the church has used all four lenses of demographic research to initiate creative ideas, perfect ongoing programs, and terminate ineffective tactics. Unity about identity and clarity about purpose reduce the stress associated with change for longtime members. The strategic changes they introduce not only accelerate church growth but impact the mission field in positive ways unrelated to church membership. New Hope Church measures success by the numbers of volunteers released to bless the community, rather than the number of attendees attracted into membership.

New Hope Church begins yet another chapter of its life and mission when they redefine their primary mission field. This is a direct result of their ability to mature and equip disciples, who connect with more lifestyle segments, and experience more heartbursts for particular publics with unique needs. Originally the mission field was defined by a polygon bordered by major highways and a river on the expanding north side of the city. However, key lifestyle segments are beginning to migrate back into the urban core. Some are "pioneers" hoping to reclaim sustainable living in poor neighborhoods; and others are "cultural enthusiasts" hoping to enjoy the artistic and educational opportunities, and cultural diversity, of the downtown.

"Go with the flow!" New Hope Church begins to plan another site of ministry among compatible lifestyle segments in the urban core. They use lifestyle segment research to choose the leader of the new site. This time, the leader is defined by her strong spiritual accountability and proven executive management capabilities. They use pure demographic research to determine where to "headquarter" the new site of ministry, leasing a small corner strip mall at the center of current migration into the downtown.

Since the downtown is littered with dying churches and decaying church buildings, New Hope planners understand that a whole new strategy for ministry is needed. Once again, they do their research.

The lifestyle segments returning downtown have paradoxical preferences for "high tech" and "simple living." They also have eclectic tastes for a wide variety of food, entertainment, media, and recreation. Psychographic research reveals that they have many quality of life issues. They are interested in spirituality, but skeptical of organized religions. They are often lonely in a crowd, and crave safe, healthy, intimacy. They stay up late and sleep in on weekends. The church shapes the tactics of the new site of ministry accordingly:

- *Worship:* The church renovates strip mall space to create a "jazz club" environment, but upgrades audio and video capability. Worship is Monday night, highly informal, and books local Christian ensembles in various musical genres. A recording of the New Hope pastor's message is aired; and live Internet connects worshipers with other mission teams around the city for prayer concerns (like roving reporters on the evening news). Liturgy is nonexistent; prayers are spontaneous and intercessory. Refreshments are indigenous to the culture of the new site. Excellent coffee is free; participants can also order from a small list of wines and local beers.
- *Significant Conversations:* People come and go when the "headquarters" is open (Friday, Saturday, and Monday nights). Trained mentors are more important than programs. The site ministry leader equips and deploys volunteers to engage visitors in non-threatening, easy conversations about life, health, world issues, and personal problems. The only taboo topic is "politics." Trained volunteers may work as greeters, servers, or bartenders; or they may just mingle and chat when opportunities arise. The reputation in the community is that *a Good Time can be a God Time*…and the slogan is in big letters on the wall.
- *Short-term Learning Opportunities:* The weekly "programming" consists of an assorted "menu" of personal growth and educational opportunities. These range from guest speakers from city hall, the arts community, social service directors, local sports heroes, successful business entrepreneurs, and occasional global missionaries. The environment is Christian, although the presentations may not be explicitly religious. Dialogue is always a major piece of the program. Most are onetime events, and some are followed by small groups.

For the time being, that strategy achieves the initial goals of New Hope Church as they extend their primary mission field. They *may* hire additional staff and renovate another part of their strip mall space to provide professional services like counseling, legal aid, housing advice, health clinics, and so on. These future decisions will require more demographic research, and especially network conversations with other relevant organizations.

Notice that lifestyle segment research is particularly important to extend the primary mission field of a church in any particular direction. Research is always tested and refined through focus groups, networking, and listening techniques. Tactics are very indigenous to local culture and may take a church beyond its traditional comfort zones. In this example, New Hope Church does not actually read the Bible in worship, but relies on trained volunteers to be "living Bibles" who are able to refer to biblical stories or ideas without looking them up. Note that the church is willing to go so far as to obtain a liquor license from the city!

By this time, New Hope Church has grown in participation on two sites, and the challenges for technology management, fundraising, and communication have also grown exponentially. The good news is that the church can also use demographic research to meet these challenges.

- The nonecclesiastical look of the church "headquarters" in the strip mall is deliberate. The lifestyle segments they are trying to bless are distrustful of church overhead, but appreciate the sense of intersection between God and culture. Yet focus groups and listening tactics confirm that most of these people have a "Christendom" background. Therefore, visual symbols and background music are distinctively, and traditionally, Christian. New Hope avoids spiritual symbols that are "new age" or interreligious.

- The church uses enhanced audio and video technology, and has made the facility wireless. Yet they are aware that these lifestyle segments will not go too far. They want to set aside their cell phones and tablets to make eye contact and engage in old-fashioned conversations. They don't rely on Twitter, but use Facebook. They send e-mail, but set aside budget for printed newsletters also. They pay little attention to newspapers, browse the Internet occasionally, but are attracted to visual advertising on the street. So the church doesn't bother with newspaper ads, has only a modest interactive website, and installed a big, bright, LED video billboard on the property.

- The downtown demographic research is paradoxical. The home church mission field has more young families and large households, but the new site is very different. Here there are two extremes: childless singles and couples (many in nontraditional relationships); and childless, more affluent empty nesters (many in traditional relationships). Each group manages money (and charitable giving) in very different ways. This prompted the church to do two distinctly targeted fund-raising strategies. In November they encouraged the second group to give to New Hope Church as a first priority through direct mail, and offered a tax receipt. In April they provided the first group Christian investment counseling, so that they could develop personal portfolios to invest in worthwhile mission anywhere in the world, with any gift to the church as "second-mile giving."

New Hope Church is now poised to develop a second site of ministry on the east side of the city. The demographic trend there is clearly Hispanic, with first, second, and third generation immigration from Mexico and South America. They are already teaching Spanish to a core of leaders, and building conversations with both Catholic and Pentecostal churches in the area. As usual, the identity and purpose of New Hope Church will be consistent, but the strategies will be shaped and driven by demographic research.

When church strategic planners go about their work, it is helpful to know where the greatest leverage points are for church growth and mission impact. Each one of these leverage points is informed and guided by demographic research, using all four lenses of investigation. These leverage points can be organized using the same logical process of prioritization, and they can also be used for systemic assessment of the health and effectiveness of any congregation.[3]

Notice that New Hope Church accelerated church growth and expanded mission impact whenever it did any strategy related to certain key leverage points. Demographic research informed each decision.

Foundational Changes	Functional Changes	Formal Changes
Congregational Re-visioning	Radical Hospitality	Relocation
	Mission-Targeted Worship	Building and Renovation
Staff Change or Redeployment	Educational Methodologies	Technology Development
Leadership Training & Accountability	Small-Group Affinities	Fund-raising Potential
	Outreach Ministries	Realistic Stewardship
Organizational Streamlining	Other Program Expectations	Internal Communications
		External Marketing

New Hope Church uses demographic analysis as a means to focus externally on what is essential and avoid being sidetracked by internal squabbles.

Declining or plateaued churches are perpetually sidetracked by internal quarrels over tactics. This is because they research only the internal likes and dislikes of current members. Every decision becomes a political debate. Every strategic plan becomes a political compromise. Healthy and effective churches treat internal opinion surveys as secondary and emphasize external research about the mission field. That way, every decision is a declaration of priority. Every strategic plan becomes a pragmatic blueprint to implement whatever works to achieve specific results. In other words, poor demographic research is a clear sign that a church is, or soon will be, declining in size and less relevant in mission. Good demographic research is a clear sign that a church is, or soon will be, growing in size and more relevant in mission.

If we were to look at the organization of New Hope Church, we would see that they have set aside considerable budget for ongoing demographic research. The board spends almost no time micromanaging programs and properties, and a great deal of time networking with mission partners and community leaders. Staff leaders spend less and less time in their offices or visiting in member homes, and more and more time in the mission field and interacting with seekers and strangers to grace. Ministry teams (including teams for music, education, and small groups, as well as teams for fund-raising and marketing) intentionally deploy listening strategies through the year in order to be sensitive to the psychographic moods and spiritual undercurrents that constantly reshape the primary mission field. New Hope Church is *ultrasensitive* to the mission field.

Ministry Mapping

Church leaders today often use the word "mapping" instead of "strategic planning." In one of my previous books, I compared the planning process in the ever-changing postmodern world to a cartographer exploring unknown territory. Cartographers use research instruments to define elevation benchmarks, follow contours of land, and mark hazards like swamps and cliffs. They work from base camps, from which they send teams of surveyors, who can measure the risks and weigh the opportunities for future development.[4]

Today, sophisticated demographic research engines can create color-coded thematic maps that allow "Christian Cartographers" to do similar things by computer. Almost any given demographic, lifestyle, or psychographic detail can be highlighted and then projected for at least five years into the future. Trends can be compared to high or low benchmarks in the primary mission field. The contraction or expansion of microcultures can be traced across neighborhoods and communities, and the migrations of ethnic or lifestyle groups can be monitored over time. It is not just that churches can *follow* the mission field. They can now *anticipate* the mission field to a significant extent. A church can develop a site of ministry, or an event of ministry, *before* it is actually relevant to the extended mission field!

This is particularly helpful in church planting. Demographic research is not important simply to the acquisition and development of property. It is important to the design of any "event" of ministry at any place and time. It can guide the marketing strategy and identify the block groups and census tracts where specific ministry "events" might be most fruitful or engage the most willing volunteers. It can plot the best locations for a small group to form or target the public for any particular outreach project. Thematic mapping can follow the changing patterns of public behavior and even describe the mood and attitude of a particular neighborhood or region. It does not just describe reality; it scans for opportunity.

Unfortunately, popular use of the term "mapping" instead of "strategic planning" has created the illusion that anticipating the future is no longer disciplined work that requires training in specific tools. Topographical mapping is not done by untrained people wandering the woods. "Ministry mapping" is not done by earnest volunteers just walking about, sampling the food, and talking with people they pass on the street. There is remarkably little guesswork in demographic research. Once researchers have gone from the lens of pure demographics to lifestyle segments, their inferences are based on psychographic and heartburst research and so are very shrewd and well-calculated predictions.

Nevertheless, there is a good reason why leaders are using the terminology of "mapping" rather than "strategic planning." The phrase more accurately describes what we actually do when we try to anticipate change and focus the Gospel in the postmodern world of "speed, flux, and blur."[5] The degree of accuracy for strategic planning has dramatically shrunk from as much as ten years to as little as three. The best demographic resources don't go beyond five, and with greater caution in the major growth centers identified earlier. What, then, do planners actually do today?

Scanning

Scanning addresses the traditional strategic questions "Who?" "What?" and "How?" Demographic research (by computer and on foot) allows us to use microscopes with different lenses of magnification to understand who, exactly, is out there. We can then discover what exactly they are doing, or what they are running from, or what they are hoping for. We can even discover how they are going about it. We can learn what media they are choosing, what learning methodologies are most useful, what relationships are more or less encouraging, and many other life tactics that have become less or more of a priority for them.

As I said earlier, computerized thematic maps are the perfect example of how planners "scan" what the modern world calls a postal code, census tract, or block group, and what the postmodern world calls "the wilderness next door." Thematic maps can be generated using any demographic, lifestyle segment, or psychographic variable. Today, we can sit at a computer and discover where there is the highest concentration of families with preschool children, or individuals who feel the most lonely. Of course, for churches (and most nonprofit organizations) thematic mapping isn't enough. You have to send out explorers on foot to penetrate the wilderness and engage the indigenous population firsthand.

Plotting

Plotting addresses the traditional strategic questions "Where?" and "When?" Demographic research (by computer and on foot) also allows us to pinpoint the geographic locations where publics will gather, significant events will occur, communication will accelerate, and opportunities abound. We can plant or relocate a church property, plant a church or small group, or identify the next site of ministry, precisely where we expect specific people to gather. Most growing churches locate themselves somewhere that is already a "destination" for people to access shopping, entertainment, recreation, education, or employment. They are not located down neighborhood side streets and blocks from Main Street.

Obviously, knowing "where" to locate helps planners know "when" to locate. They can anticipate when their doors need to be open or closed, when to deploy volunteers on the ground and when to let them rest, when to worship and when not to worship, or when to have paid staff in residence and when to give them a day off.

Clearly, past assumptions about "sacred space" and "sacred time" are changing dramatically in the postmodern wilderness. Sacred space for Roman Catholics, the Orthodox, and Anglicans may still be consecrated or de-consecrated as strategic planning unfolds, but gone is the sentimental notion that any given facility or location is "sacred" simply by being historic. Sacred time for Protestants may still be associated with the preaching of the Word and the prayers of the people, but gone is the Christendom assumption that Sunday morning is the only or best opportunity to do it.

Projecting

Projecting addresses the traditional strategic questions "Why?" and "What is the measurable outcome?" Demographic research (by computer and on foot) forces us to be crystal clear about our motivations for undertaking this exploration of the postmodern wilderness. Why will we do this to ourselves? Why will we stake our lives, lifestyles, and livelihoods on a venture to reach strangers to grace? Clergy who are already struggling to maintain stable salaries and support families may well ask. Laity who are aging and having enough trouble already managing time and nurturing their strength may well ask.

Unfortunately, demographic research can only raise the urgent question. It cannot by itself provide the answer. Other organizations (political, corporate, educational, and so on) can more easily be motivated by a simple desire to sustain power, make profits, or compete as an institution. The church can't do that. It has a different sort of mission accountability. Churches need to discern God's call for the next five years, and not just the public drift of the next five years. One reason so many churches avoid demographic research is that it is just too uncomfortable. It challenges their very reason for existence.

Obviously, clarity about motivation provides clarity about results. Demographic research also forces churches to be crystal clear about how they intend to measure success. Most denominations have given up tracking mere membership or counting the number of baptisms as an effective means to measure success. There are other choices: worship attendance, repeat visitors, small-group participation and educational enrollment, volunteers in active service, faith communities planted, missions funded, and databases expanded. Growing churches go even farther, measuring stories of personal transformation, social justice achievements, reputation among community partners, and so on.

Once again, demographic research can raise the urgency to measure results, but it cannot by itself dictate what those measurable results should be. In the metaphor of "mapping," every strategy is weighed on a "doable-stretchable" continuum. Explorers in the postmodern wilderness measure risk by balancing what they think is "doable" and what they know will "stretch" their imaginations and resources. Demographic research can help you understand what is "doable," but it is up to you to figure out how far you want to be "stretched."

There is a certain "boardroom" mentality that is associated with strategic planning. In the Christendom era, denominational representatives, hierarchical leaders, and expert academics created effective plans far in advance. They planned a "lectionary" in three-year cycles, assuming that whatever Scriptures came up on any given week would be sufficient for the public to face the threats and surprises of the next six days. They had enough time to raise funds, create lengthy membership assimilation classes, develop lay and ordered leaders, and slowly upgrade technologies to minimize stress. In the post-Christendom era, that "boardroom" mentality has been replaced by "spiritual entrepreneurship." We see explorers huddled together or communicating by cell phone, innovating as they go, trying to keep several steps ahead of the chaos that is unfolding around them.

Earlier, I provided an illustration for demographics and strategic planning with New Hope Church. This may have impressed readers as an example of a fairly contemporary mega- or multisite church, but in truth it has more in common with modern, Christendom church planning than with postmodern, post-Christendom, intentional Christian communities. Therefore, New Hope Church found it most helpful to use a clear, but classic, form of strategic planning. Here is an example of the kind of church that would more likely choose ministry mapping:

> "The Servants of the Saints"[6] is a small group living communally in an urban apartment building in intentional Christian community. They practice individual and group spiritual disciplines and can best be described as a neo-monastic house church. They are not an official order of any church, and they include people from all Christian traditions. The individual participants all regularly partake of Eucharist (or Holy Communion) in nearby churches, and they have trusted relationships with various priests and ministers. However, they remain a distinct "pilgrim band" of believers dedicated to live spiritual lives and serve in the community.

The name they have chosen for their "pilgrim band" is significant. They particularly honour St. Rita (patron saint of "lost causes" and "the impossible" and "the lonely"); St. Juanita (patron saint of "forgotten people"); and St. Cecile (patron saint of "musicians"). Yes, most of the members of the group are musicians (active or retired), and their special "heartburst" is for anyone even remotely associated with the music business who is poor, addicted, divorced, and otherwise abandoned to his or her fate. "The Servants of the Saints" gather as a spiritual community or "pilgrim band." They do not consider themselves a church, but simply as a mutually supportive group of Christians placing themselves in service to a particular public.

> "The Servants of the Saints" have a big heart. Their prayer and service fill them with compassion to people without hope, and especially for musical people who have been abused in any way; or trapped by circumstances beyond their control; or struggle in earning a living; or are lonely, wounded, and suffering. At the urging of clergy friends, and with the generous financial support of an anonymous donor, they have decided to make themselves into a formal nonprofit organization, and initiate ministries across the city.

> • *Scanning:*
> They have a great calling, but no idea exactly who needs their services, what exactly they need, and how to deliver it. Demographic research can

help. They do a series of thematic maps of the city, tracking lifestyle segments that might be prone to suffer particular issues. Their scans reveal that there are several lifestyle segments that might be vulnerable to the issues that are their concern. At the time, they are using 2005 descriptions from Experian, and the search engine www.MissionInsite.com, and these segments include:

Minority Metro Communities

African-American Neighborhoods

Getting By

Southern Blues

Ethnic Urban Mix

They also track psychographic variables, and develop thematic maps to identify areas where the response is higher than state average. These variables include:

Music is an important part of my life

Like to pursue challenge, novelty, and change

Don't judge people by the way they live

Enjoy life and don't worry about the future

Feel very alone in the world

Don't want responsibility

Find that I am easily swayed by others

Their scan continues "on the ground" as they interview social service workers, representatives of the musicians union, local club owners, and emergency room nurses.

- *Plotting:*

Now that "The Servants of the Saints" understand who is out there, what their specific needs are at the moment, and how they might or might not meet those needs, they need to consider where and when to do ministry.

Their scans and interviews also revealed that these lifestyle segments tend to be concentrated in three regions of the downtown (one of which is their own neighborhood). They focus on two optimal locations. One is more residential, where they hope to develop a second Christian community offering short-term, cheap, safe, rental accommodations for transient musicians. The second is more commercial, where they hope to find a business partner willing to provide temporary jobs for musicians.

- *Projecting:*

Given their special heartburst, the "Servants of the Saints" are pretty clear about their motivations. The hard part is to focus measurable outcomes. Just what do they realistically expect to happen because of their initiatives? They dream about providing professional counseling, health clinics, and even legal aid, but none of that is really doable with their limited budget. They settle on four measurable goals:

1. Provide safe, short-term housing for transient musicians "in between" gigs;
2. Provide friendship, acceptance, and opportunities for safe friendship in their house;
3. Provide opportunities for musicians to earn some money and perform in local restaurants;
4. Collect tips to support down-and-out musicians from local bars and restaurants to raise awareness and help support the nonprofit.

The "Servants of the Saints" pursue these goals. They purchase a house with a large family room that they convert into housing for about twelve people per night; and members of their group rotate living there, cooking meals, and befriending the temporary tenants. They arrange with a sympathetic club owner to give a free meal and allow their musicians to perform Monday through Thursday, collecting whatever tips they can get. They arrange with a variety of clubs and hotels that provide live music to place a special "tip box" for the "Servants of the Saints" in their establishments.

The "Servants of the Saints" begin to establish their reputation in the community. Police, health care, and social workers begin to refer people to them; and the word spreads among musicians that they have sympathetic friends and advocates in the city. As the mission grows, so also interest in their Christian community grows. Eventually, a second "pilgrim band" oriented around the same spiritual disciplines is founded in another region of the city.

Demographics and Decision Making

If you have been paying close attention, you may have noticed that the decision-making process for the hypothetical Servants of the Saints is different from the process for New Hope Church. Indeed, it seems backwards. New Hope Church followed a more traditional process of strategic planning, and the Servants of the Saints followed a more entrepreneurial process of mission mapping. Which one is better?

Both decision-making processes can be effective. Your choice depends both on the demographic context and on the faith community.

If you are living in one of the fast-changing regions identified earlier in this chapter, it might be wiser to do ministry mapping. This is because business and residential patterns, social movement and attitudes, and city and health care systems are all shifting constantly. It is difficult to predict what things will be like beyond three to five years. The process of scanning, plotting, and projecting is going to be a constant routine. On the other hand, if you are living in one of the many other regions that are gradually evolving, relatively stable, or even slowly declining, then it might be wiser to do strategic planning. This is because development patterns, attitudes, and social systems are changing slowly. It is easier to predict what the mission field will be like more than five years ahead. Strategic planning can be updated annually.

If you are an established church, participating in a clear tradition or allied with a particular denomination, then your leaders are probably more familiar with traditional strategic planning. Established church leaders are usually more familiar with more bureaucratic organizations that go back one hundred years or more. They approach demographic research with assumptions about the Christendom world. On the other hand, if you are a church plant or innovative faith community, your leaders may actually be more comfortable with risk and familiar with start-up companies. New Christians or church pioneers are often more familiar with entrepreneurial businesses that have emerged in just the last twenty-five years. They approach demographic research with assumptions about the post-Christendom world.

The contrast can be explained by the following chart. Decision making generally follows a process that extends from the identity and purpose of an organization, through the policies for the organization, and finally to the action of an organization.[7]

	Christendom	Post-Christendom
	Modern	**Postmodern**
Identity	Command	Permission
Policy	Consistency	Experimentation
Action	Control	Partnership

The Christendom habit of decision making, exercised through established church or denominational traditions, begins with a management board that dictates the direction of the church at any given time. The board then makes sure that all strategic plans are consistent with church policies (or polity), maintains control over the personnel and tactics to avoid any breach in policy—and hopefully achieves results. This decision-making process requires maximum task management and minimum trust, and it works well when demographic change is relatively slow.

The post-Christendom habit of decision making, exercised through many church plants and alternative faith communities, begins with a predisposition of the board to give permission for innovation. Consensus is reserved for unity about common values, beliefs, vision, and mission ("DNA" for the organism of the body of Christ), but it is not extended to any standardized practices. Teams are given enormous flexibility to experiment with any practice that works to achieve mission results. Leaders are less concerned about centralized control and more intent to build partnerships with allied organizations and empowered volunteers. This decision-making process requires minimum task management and maximum trust, and it works best when demographic change is relatively swift.[8]

Both strategic planning and ministry mapping are effective, but the decision-making process behind the implementation of demographic insights is clearly shifting away from the old "command, consistency, and control" method to the new "permission, experimentation, and partnership" method. Even though many regions are relatively stable or experiencing only evolutionary change, the world still *feels* like a cultural wilderness. Nothing is what it once was. The only constant is change. The daily experience is unpredictability and anxiety.

The *feeling* that culture is now a wilderness and that life has become a jungle started about the same time as the emergence of the "global village" in the late 1970s. According to Wikipedia (no, not the "encyclopedia"!), the term originated with Marshall McLuhan in the 1960s and entered common usage by the 1980s with the rise of the Internet. A simple formula explains the impact on demographic research:

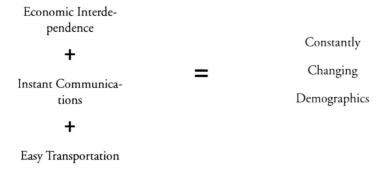

Economic Interde-
pendence

+

Instant Communica-
tions

+

Easy Transportation

=

Constantly

Changing

Demographics

Externally, publics are on the move. Internally, publics are morphing all the time. Relationally, publics are interacting differently with one another from one year, or even one month, to the next. Psychologically, publics are shifting attitudes and expectations with more information, less understanding, and deeper passion than ever before.

Part
2

5. Ministry Opportunities for Lifestyle Segments

I have described demographic research for churches in four "progressive lenses" of magnification: pure demographics, lifestyle segments, psychographics, and heartbursts. All have relevance, but perhaps the study of lifestyle segments is the most pertinent for all for church planning.

Currently, there are several demographic and lifestyle segment research tools in North America alone.[1] These offer concise summaries of seventy-plus lifestyle segments, providing insight into daily behavior, media preferences, attitudes and worldviews, relationships, and personal choices. The information is gathered from many government, business, education, social service, and health care sources.

Earlier, I said that these lifestyle insights create "portraits" of publics that capture their moods, motivations, aspirations, and spiritual yearnings. I could also say that lifestyle insights can be used to create "snapshots" of ever-evolving publics, capturing the ongoing evolutions and revolutions of their lives in a single "still" image. The "snapshot" metaphor underlines how publics are changing in a world of speed, flux, and blur. Every lifestyle segment seems a little "blurry" when you read the description. That's because it is actually not "standing still" but "on the move," weaving in and out, blending with its surroundings at one moment, and diverging from its surroundings the next.

Church planners have been handicapped in their analysis of lifestyle segments (whether as "portraits" or "snapshots") because they lack adequate filters through which to sift the information. I mentioned earlier in this book that our categories of thinking have become inadequate to assess the expectations of the cultural wilderness in which we find ourselves. For example:

- Churches think of leaders only as priests or preachers, or dictators or enablers, or impose institutional expectations that are antiquated and foreign to the largest and fastest-growing demographic in Western culture: the spiritually yearning, institutionally alienated public.

- Churches think of hospitality only in vague terms of "basic" or "radical," without clear ideas of what different publics might actually expect of a church host that considers itself "friendly."

- Churches characterize worship as "traditional" or "contemporary," even though these terms are relative among all seventy-plus lifestyle segments, and the many publics that are outside looking in use other classifications to find a "good church."

- Churches assume Christian education means "Sunday school," along with curricula and technologies that have been abandoned or radically modified by public and private educational institutions.

- Churches differentiate only between "large groups" (defined generically by age, gender, or marital status) and "small groups" (defined vaguely as groups that are not large and that study the Bible).

- Churches automatically associate outreach with missions that have to do with daily survival (food, clothing, and shelter), without realizing that most lifestyle segments have other urgent priorities.

- Churches quickly associate the legitimacy of a "church"

with property ownership; a facility with a steeple, pews, and pulpit; membership that implies financial obligations to pay for overhead; and communication tactics that stress oral communication and the printed word.

All these function as "filters" through which church planners have categorized what they assumed to be strategies for ministry appropriate to public expectations. It is clear that these "filters" are inadequate. Worse than that, these filters have become "sacred cows" used to criticize ecclesiastical competition or defend personal comfort zones.

The filters presented here originally emerged from my lifetime of ministry leadership among three denominations, and in multiple regions, contexts, and cultures in North America and Australia. I was licensed to preach in high school and have been engaged in the Christian movement ever since. This experience has included over 30 years of pastoral leadership, church planting, evangelism teams, national denominational leadership in three denominations and two countries, and another fifteen years consulting with churches across the cultural, denominational, and theological spectrum in the United States, Canada, and Australia. These applications have been tested and refined with numerous Christian leaders (ordained and lay) from diverse congregations, church plants, denominations, and agencies.

These filters are not scientific. They are not the result of controlled laboratory research and rigorous sociological analyses. Moreover, they are not "approved" by any denomination or Christian tradition. This is intentional. The more we live into the cultural wilderness, the more we must empower Christian leaders to "read" the spiritual expectations of seekers and other strangers to grace in unique ways. "Sacred cow" terminology is a straitjacket we can ill afford. By the time scientific research has verified that any given public expects *this* from a church, the public will have moved on and expect something else. Mission is an adventure. The mission field is a moving target. What we need are equipped leaders who can think on their feet and plan on the run, not manuals that require the world to pause for several weeks while leaders study what to look for.

I simply say that the filters described in the following pages are *useful.* These applications are *tendencies,* rather than *prescriptions.* Each lifestyle segment *tends to gravitate* toward certain kinds of leaders; *tends to appreciate* certain kinds of hospitality choices, worship emphases, educational methods, and small-group practices; and *tends to welcome or participate in* distinct outreach ministries. Each segment *tends to favor* certain kinds of facilities and technologies, *tends to manage money* in certain kinds of ways, and *tends to share and acquire* information through certain kinds of media.

This is a work in progress. I have already completely rewritten *Mission Impact*[2] to revise and upgrade it to the most recent and expanded 2010 lifestyle groups and segments defined by *Experian.* Even so, it does not presume to be comprehensive, nor does it pretend to describe every nuance of ministry in every context. It is simply intended as a guide to help you focus strategies that are relevant and engaging for the diverse publics in your mission field. Some applications may be wrong for your context, or require more precise refinement. Because lifestyle segments are evolving all the time, applications will also evolve.

- The primary use of these filters is to help you select and train leaders, design hospitality and worship, adjust educational strategies, focus affinities for small groups, and target outreach projects.

- The secondary use of these filters is to help you design advertising and marketing strategies, upgrade facilities and technologies, and multiply fund-raising opportunities.

Sometimes it is helpful to "reverse engineer" your ministry and outreach strategies by studying successful organizations in your mission field. Examine how retail stores, entertainment centers, restaurants, social services, and educational institutions develop space, program, and advertising and try to "guess" what lifestyle segments they are hoping to reach.

Examine your current ministry and mission strategies. You may not think that you are targeting specific lifestyle segments. Most churches live in the illusion that they are truly open, welcoming, and relevant to everybody. But just take a look at *who is there.* Who is actually *involved and who is not.* Suddenly you will discover that you do have a priority to reach certain lifestyle segments rather than others, although you may not want to admit it. The question is, is that sufficient? Will God be satisfied? Are you being faithful? Do you want to bless someone other than yourselves?

Church leaders often assume that regular listening strategies in your local context *supplement* generalizations about public perceptions and preferences about organized religion. In fact, it is just the reverse. Generalizations like these are intended only to *supplement your routine of local listening.* There is no substitute for actually engaging cultural diversity in your neighborhood, town, city, or region. No matter how sophisticated demographic search engines become, they cannot keep pace with instantaneous and significant convolutions of humanity, nor can they ultimately prescribe the exact tactics of organizational outreach that will work today and next week. Church leaders have to listen! In order to do this, they must escape the office, leave the building, exit their personal comfort zones, avoid the dependencies of their own church members, and mingle with strangers and seekers. There are several ways to do this:

- **Focus Groups:** Invite friends, neighbors, or work associates who seem to fit any given lifestyle segment to meet with you. If they will allow you to ask friendly, nonjudgmental questions, you will pay for lunch or dinner.

- **Network Interviews:** Schedule regular meetings with local mission partners (church and nonprofit agencies) to compare insights and evaluate the effectiveness of programs.

- **Cross-Sector Research:** Make appointments with senior management leaders in education, health care, social service, municipal planning, real estate, and retail business to discuss their perceptions of the marketplace, and ask to see their own marketing research.

- **Listening Teams:** Deploy board members and small-group leaders to regularly observe and listen in public places like malls, food courts, restaurants, department stores, sports arenas, and community events. Take notes and debrief.

- **Prayer Walks:** Deploy worship-design teams, musicians, outreach workers, and church members to walk prayerfully through selected neighborhoods, taking note of behavior patterns and human needs. Discuss the relevance of the core message of your church.

The generalizations about reaching lifestyle segments here are intended to *supplement* (not replace) these congregational habits that make every church sensitive to the changing diversity of people around them.

How often should you do this? Discover the average length of residency in your primary mission field and let that be your guide. Church members are often surprised to discover that the average length of residency in their area is a matter of a few years or even a few months. Growing churches will regularly paint a new "portrait," or take another snapshot, of each lifestyle segment in their mission field.

6. Leadership Alternatives

The credibility of clergy and program staff leaders depends on the passion and purposefulness of leaders relevant to the expectations of the lifestyle segments with whom, or among whom, they work. The *right* leader for *a particular* public is a unique blend of spirituality, spontaneity, skillfulness, and relational adaptability.

Credibility depends on four characteristics. Paid and unpaid leaders are hired (acquired), trained, evaluated, and fired (dismissed) for the same four consistent reasons: mission attitude, high integrity, skills or competencies, and teamwork. The mission attitude reveals a heart for the specific lifestyle segment to be blessed. The high integrity is the ability to immerse oneself in the segment's culture without compromising essential Christian values and beliefs (as defined by the congregation or specific Christian organization). The skills or the competencies allow leaders to engage with a target culture effectively. The teamwork is the ability to collaborate generously and effectively with other people.

This is a significant change from the days when professionalism and certification were all-important. In the past, clergy could be deployed in almost any demographic context because their leadership style matched the expectations of the institutional church. They were automatically respected because of their ordination and professional certification. Churches assumed that the public would be generous and make allowances for any shortcomings in attitude, integrity, skills, or teamwork. Yesterday, the mission field adapted to the leader; today, the leader adapts to the mission field.

Today, clergy must be deployed in any given demographic context because their leadership style *matches the expectations of the surrounding communities.* These "communities" are the lifestyle segments represented in different proportions, in diverse neighborhoods, behaving in unique ways. Obviously, it is much harder for clergy to gain credibility today than yesterday, because their reputation must be earned among a greater diversity of publics (some of whom may not even like each other very much).

Perhaps, if clergy cannot be all things to all people, they might at least be credible among the largest lifestyle segments represented in the postal code. But this, too, is hard to accomplish. Truly homogeneous churches are on the wane in North America. This is partly because only a limited number of people in any given lifestyle segment will still gravitate toward a church anyway, and if you stake the future of the church on just one segment, you may not pay the bills. This is mostly because in the emerging world of radical diversity, the very definition of "credibility" implies the ability to connect with multiple publics. The minister who connects with just one lifestyle segment is not credible even within that lifestyle segment.

Today the same lifestyle segment expectations for clergy are often extended toward church board members. Lay leaders of a church, and board members of a faith-based nonprofit, are also considered "spiritual leaders." There are more varieties of clergy, and the boundaries between paid and unpaid spiritual leadership are increasingly blurred.

Each lifestyle segment tends to gravitate toward certain kinds of leaders. In the spectrum of church life and mission today, there are at least seven distinct kinds of leaders. Any given lifestyle segment may value a wide variety of leadership characteristics, but usually at least *two leadership expectations dominate* the expectations of the mission field.

The first two kinds of leadership are the ones most commonly trained by seminaries of all traditions. This means that basic degree seminary programs may not be training leaders to be effective among more and more lifestyle segments. The deficiency may be addressed through field education, internships, and advanced training. This is a critical concern for large churches and denominations that find it difficult to provide staff for growing churches, multicultural churches, or newly planted churches.

Caregiver

This leader is usually ordained, with special training in pastoral care and counseling. He or she is expected to be very merciful and compassionate, a strong visitor in homes and institutions, and "on call" 24/7 for acute intervention and chronic personal support.

The Caregiver practices a "ministry of presence." Office hours are important. Health care ministries are a high priority. Credibility depends on a balanced personal and family lifestyle. If this leader is part of a strong sacramental tradition, he or she emphasizes the comfort of Eucharist, acceptance in the confessional, and last rites for the dying. The leader as caregiver prefers to work one-on-one, especially with people who are disadvantaged by age, physical, or mental limitations; or who are recovering from addictions or personal tragedies. The leader also may be a strong advocate for the poor (homeless, hungry, or unemployed). These leaders value the intimacy, mutual support, and informal accountability of small churches and small groups.

Lifestyle segments that prefer caregiving clergy also often prefer church boards that focus on task management. These boards are prone to micromanagement, and more oriented to "doing" than "planning." They tend to react very compassionately to emerging needs of members and adapt programs around emergencies and life cycles.

If we look ahead to the other categories of ministry, we discover that Caregiver leaders gravitate toward "caregiving" and "healing" worship alternatives, "survival" outreach emphases, and face-to-face communication strategies. They tend to be concerned about handicapped accessibility. Their desire to protect intimacy and emphasize human touch makes them cautious about technologies that seem to distance or separate people from one another (including fixed seating and video).

The lifestyle segments that prefer Caregiver leaders include many of the segments that were once the backbone of the institutional church in America. These include small-town and middle-class families, working rural families, and mature adult couples and singles. These can also include lower-income households, stable urban singles and couples, and families with young children. Many church facilities are located in areas where these lifestyle segments were once well represented. They may now be relatively minor lifestyle segments in the same area, although church members in this lifestyle segment will commute long distances back to the site to obtain the caregiving services of the leader.

Enabler

This leader is usually ordained, with strong professional skills in generational ministries, and is expected to be approachable. He or she is a facilitator for meetings and gatherings, is sensitive to lifecycle changes, and committed to local and denominational traditions. Enablers have reputations as being friendly, and often mingle with social service groups, educators, and civic leaders. They function most effectively in churches that already have strong visions and organizational structures. Enablers facilitate the aspirations of church members and are generally hesitant to impose their own vision, refer to their personal spiritual journey, or critique approved programs.

Enablers are especially competent in bureaucracies. They match individual talents with opportunities for service. They have a strong interest in personality typologies and spiritual gifts inventories. If these leaders are part of a strong consensus management institution, then they emphasize standardized liturgical practices and denominational policies. These leaders like to work collaboratively and ecumenically in educational and social programs. They enjoy interpersonal relationships but prefer to work in committees or groups. They are adept in conflict resolution and mediation, which makes them particularly effective in overcoming generation gaps, reconciling marriages, and healing congregational conflicts. Like the Caregivers, these leaders are very "hands-on" in leadership and have trouble delegating responsibility.

The lifestyle segments that prefer clergy as enablers also tend to prefer boards that function as representative councils. These boards tend to work top-down. They delegate responsibility, but not authority, and focus on overseeing committees, approving nominations and strategic plans, and coordinating activities. They work closely with enabling clergy to maintain peace and harmony.

Looking ahead, we discover that Enablers gravitate toward "educational" worship alternatives, curriculum-based small groups, and ecclesiastical architectures. They tend to favor large, generic groups for women, men, and youth, but they also lead small groups and Bible studies. The most comfortable technologies for these lifestyle segments tend to be the spoken word, print, and basic audio amplification. Enablers tend to take time for preparation and think long and hard about communication. Therefore, they tend to rely on slower media and spend more time at their desks.

The lifestyle segments that prefer Enabler leadership include many segments that resist high accountability for spiritual discipline and performance and emphasize unconditional acceptance and proper procedures. They may be white- or blue-collar and steadfastly conservative in their habits. Some segments are living well in the country, others are commuting from the suburbs, and others are living in smaller cities or stable urban neighborhoods. A wide variety of lifestyle segments connects with this kind of leader, from subsistence rural residents and hardy rural families, to successful small-town business leaders, to upscale suburbanites. Second- and third-generation, upwardly mobile Hispanic and Asian immigrants may connect well with this kind of leader.

Many church facilities are located in areas where these lifestyle segments are located. However, people are less likely to return to the church once they move away. They are more likely to "shop" for a church with an Enabler leader closer to home. Enabler leaders often help the church relocate to follow the migration of a lifestyle segment to a new geographical region. They are adept at merging and clustering churches under a single administration and common tradition. They are often perceived by the outside public as slow but earnest decision makers and consensus builders who seek the middle of the road and the common denominator.

CEO

This leader may not emerge from basic seminary training, but he or she often benefits from advanced seminary training and has a professional or academic doctoral degree. He or she is usually ordained, career clergy, or from a first career in senior corporate or nonprofit management. This leader has strong organizational skills with abilities to manage staff, multiply volunteers, and coordinate programs seven days a week. The CEO leader is very good at delegating responsibility, although he or she is sometimes challenged to delegate authority.

The CEO has strong interpersonal skills that are primarily applied to staff development, church boards and councils, and cooperative relationships with senior organizational leaders in other sectors. This leader works particularly well with corporate, small-business, and nonprofit leaders and tends to be impatient with the consensus management style of many denominations and educational institutions. This leader is adept at shaping policy and holding paid and unpaid staff accountable to policy. He or she is an excellent administrator and money manager and develops strong stewardship practices to support programs.

CEO leaders function best in an organization that already has a clear purpose and often help refine mission statements and make program adjustments relative to the changing mission field. They redevelop property and upgrade technology. They tend to be excellent communicators in public speaking and print. They may revise and update curricula. If they publish, it will often be on topics related to volunteer empowerment and leadership development. They tend to be driven by a quest for quality, emphasize performance and training, and evaluate success quantitatively. Although CEO leaders often have strong diplomatic skills, they tend to be available to members and the general public by appointment only.

The CEO thrives in a large, resource-size church environment. In an era of weaker denominations, underfunded social agencies, and theoretical theological studies, these leaders may promote church planting, outreach ministries, and practical workshops for clergy. They often evolve into middle or senior denominational leaders with supervisory roles. In an era of declining denominations, they easily transition to leadership in parachurch and nonprofit organizations. Looking ahead, we discover that CEO leaders gravitate toward multiple options for hospitality and worship, structured education and small groups with designated leaders, comprehensive stewardship programs, and utilitarian facilities.

The lifestyle segments that prefer CEO leadership tend to be of two kinds. The first are "high-achieving" people, who enjoy challenges, expect training, seize responsibility, and value accountability. New suburban families, affluent professionals, enterprising middle-class families, academic communities, families with older children, and even the very wealthy may be included in this mix. The second group of people may have lower self-esteem or critical needs that rely on high-quality programs for personal growth. This includes struggling urban households, minority metropolitan communities, and vulnerable city dwellers on the bottom rung of society.

Lifestyle segments that prefer CEO staff also tend to prefer church boards that are involved in long-range planning and community networking. These boards tend to focus more on policy governance than task management, and are more likely to delegate both responsibility and authority to committees or teams. Lifestyle segments in the second group above may be challenged to find board leaders with the self-esteem and skills necessary for leadership, and may rely on the pastor for more directive leadership.

Looking ahead, CEO leaders often manage repeatable educational and inspirational worship services that are high quality, performance oriented, and diversified by time of day and musical sophistication. Their churches are often large and diverse enough to favor multiple and healthy choices in worship. Christian education may include schools and academies on weekdays, although small-group affinities are often limited to Bible study and outreach. Outreach programs abound, often well funded by grants and led by specially trained staff.

CEO leaders often relocate facilities away from neighborhoods to major thoroughfares and intersections that provide easy access and parking. They may manage multiple sites of ministry and design facilities that are quite recognizable as a church but are designed to be multipurpose.

Visionary

These leaders may or may not be ordained but are definitely people of spiritual habits. Indeed, their primary reputation may be based on their spiritual insights, rather than their administrative skills. They are strong motivational speakers and have a reputation for guiding vocational discernment. Nevertheless, these leaders are strategic and long-term planners, with credibility across public sectors. Their greatest gift is their ability to see reality, discern truth, target injustice, or proclaim hope.

Visionary leaders are more concerned about the boldness, breadth, and power of a spiritual vision for a region, than about the small or large size of a church. If they lead a large church, they almost always have an executive minister on staff to oversee the details. If they lead a small church, they expect great spiritual discipline and entrepreneurship from individual members. They carefully define boundaries of shared values and beliefs and use an intuitive sense of alignment to vision as a primary method of accountability. They measure success more qualitatively than quantitatively.

Visionary leaders tend to have a strong artistic temperament. They tend to communicate with stories and metaphors, images and music, and even drama and dance. They can work with low or high technology but are very purposeful and never allow the media to become the message. Visionary leaders tend to be introverts and entrepreneurs, and they often find it difficult to pass leadership to a successor. The church may be less of an institution and more of a movement, and therefore it waxes and wanes according to the energy and direction of that leader.

These leaders tend to be more "maverick" in relation to their parent denomination, and many are independent of a denomination and blend Christian traditions. Their leadership crosses traditional social barriers of race, culture, gender, family structure, marriage, income, and occupation. They often cast big visions to reach an entire city and may speak at least two languages fluently.

The lifestyle segments that prefer visionary leadership are often younger minority or immigrant populations with a sense of powerlessness or successful early adopters with a global consciousness. Among the former group are many African-American segments, other minority groups, or multicultural households. These segments represent urban diversity, and many are just getting by. On the other hand, the second group may include wealthier entrepreneurs, enterprising couples, successful second generations of immigrants, and upwardly mobile sub-urbanites.

The lifestyle segments that gravitate toward visionary clergy tend to expect church board members to be externally focused and highly committed to the church. They often advocate public policy and set benchmarks for charitable giving; and they may have skills in demographic research, marketing, and fund-raising. They tend to be rigorous about aligning programs to mission, but flexible about tactics.

Looking ahead in ministry application categories, visionaries tend to emphasize inspirational and transformational worship, experiential learning methodologies, and affinity groups. Christian education is often merged with outreach to create action/reflection opportunities that combine social impact and personal growth. They often favor outreach ministries that explore interpersonal relationships, human potential, and human destiny.

Many church facilities are designed with nontraditional, non-denominational, external and internal symbols. Locations can vary. Visionary leaders may surround themselves in nature and exclude the world, or immerse themselves in multicultural environments. Their location, however, is never accidental or incidental, but purposeful and revealing in itself. Visionary leaders are often masters at multiple layers of communication, and they rely on the excitement of a big vision to motivate giving.

Discipler

These leaders may be ordained or not, but they must be people of great spiritual discipline and reputation. They are visionaries, but vision is often expressed in classic biblical words and metaphors. The "Great Commission" and the "Great Commandment" are particularly important, along with Old Testament visions to love God, do justice, and walk humbly with God. They are particularly passionate to multiply disciples and invest great energy to mature Christians and grow leaders. The marks of discipleship vary somewhat from leader to leader, but they generally include a personal and life-changing experience with Christ, spiritual habits and intense faith formation, discernment of personal mission, and dedication to some form of witness or service.

This leader focuses on leadership development, exercises constant accountability, and mobilizes teams consciously modeling the mission to the Gentiles. They are extremely adaptive to unique cultural contexts and are classic church planters who sometimes grow large churches (or multisite churches). They share a quest for quality like CEO leaders, and their cultural sensitivity may leave them vulnerable to criticisms of cultural accommodation. However, the true Discipler is primarily concerned about leadership development rather than program perfection. Disciplers stress learning through experience, problem solving, and spiritual growth. They tend to measure success in both quantitative and qualitative ways as they evaluate progress in spiritual maturity.

Discipler leaders are selective and intentional about relationships. They are less likely to attend denominational meetings and more likely to surround themselves with passionate, creative, and spiritually alive people from any church or sector. They rarely visit in hospitals or homes, and caregiving and counseling are not high among their priorities. They spend much of their time with a limited number of key leaders to mature and empower them to disciple others.

These leaders are considered to be "maverick" in their parent denomination and are not particularly concerned with the ideological or theological debates in denominational meetings. They are often non-denominational and do not easily fit stereotypes of "liberal" or "conservative." These leaders often value informality and coach people to merge lifestyle and spirituality, and they are less likely to favor classic liturgical worship and academic credentials.

The lifestyle segments that prefer Discipler leadership may be reasonably well off but dissatisfied with material things and passionate about personal growth. These segments may be dreamers and idealists, but they may also come from solid suburban life and have very stable careers. They are moderately conservative but believe in human potential and personal development. They may also be rather poor or marginalized but searching for self-confidence and eager to be upwardly mobile. These segments include African-American, Southeast Asian, and East Indian individuals and households, and other publics representing the ethnic urban mix of large cities.

The lifestyle segments that gravitate to Discipler clergy tend to expect church boards to focus on maintaining the integrity of the church, model ethical living, and set the pace of personal spiritual growth. Board members are often mentors, teachers, or small-group leaders in their own right. They are often visible in worship leadership and available to seekers before and after worship.

Looking ahead in ministry application categories, they tend to be extravagant when they plan hospitality and favor informal coaching worship based on topics or themes. Christian education may take many forms, but cross-generational affinity groups with well-trained leadership replace large groups with elected officers. They embrace any kind of outreach, provided it emerges from the spiritual growth of individuals or teams. They enhance communication and social networks with the latest technologies.

Many church facilities are designed with versatile yet comfortable conversation space. The church buildings tend to be located along urban beltways, providing easy access and parking. These leaders are particularly conscious of safety and confidentiality issues, and the physical environment intentionally reveals the core values and beliefs of the church.

Mentor

This leader is often nonordained and a person with penetrating intuition and high spiritual discipline. Like the Caregiver, the Mentor prefers one-on-one relationships. However, Mentors' intention is not to heal, comfort, or reassure. On the contrary, their intention is to mature, challenge, and stir holy discontent. Like Disciplers, Mentors are passionate about growing disciples. However, their intention is not to place others in a particular ministry role, but simply to guide them into a deeper experience of Christ.

This leader focuses on individuals or small groups to guide and shape spiritual life and intervenes to break addictions and focus personal mission. The Mentor often works in covenant relationships for time-limited periods with non-Christian seekers as well as Christian believers. They may use a variety of programs or spiritual exercises.

They often have a strong appreciation for ancient or historic disciplines of prayer, meditation, Bible study, and theological reflection. Mentors often adapt ancient monastic models to contemporary situations. This can be in urban core contexts or retreat settings that are linked to regular weekly worship.

The Mentor is more likely to maintain a connection with a theological tradition, or several theological traditions, than with a particular denominational institution. Mentors may come to ministry with backgrounds in psychotherapy or career counseling and may have advanced theological education. Alternatively, they may come to ministry through challenging life experiences in missionary work or the military. The church they lead is often intentionally small, with high expectations for membership, determined not to be sidetracked by unnecessary overhead expenses.

The lifestyle segments that prefer mentoring leadership are a rather eclectic mix, and the Mentor leader will have a background and lifestyle uniquely appropriate to each group. Credibility is not easily transferred, and the Mentor leader tends to stay anchored in a particular setting. In part, it is this continuity of presence that is part of covenant commitment. Many of these lifestyle segments are self-conscious about status, cultural roots, or specific traditions. Some have high priorities for the great outdoors, while others have high priorities for intellectual pursuits and military careers. These lifestyle segments tend to appreciate disciplined living, spiritual reflection, and intentional engagement with issues, problems, and cultures. Childless, affluent couples; unattached, mobile individuals; and university students often seek mentoring leadership.

What these lifestyle segments have in common is a sense of fragility or impermanency, an experience of living "in between" stages of life, or a lifestyle that is marginal or threatened by changing circumstances. That could, of course, include people in all lifestyle segments. However, these publics may feel more "at risk" in the world today. They long for "absolutes" but are more likely to express their longings in symbolic or metaphorical ways rather than in words and dogmas. These people may frequent religious bookstores but are likely to buy a talisman (devotional object, musical recording, icon, or image) rather than books.

Mentors tend to lead less institutional, but more intentional, Christian communities. The lifestyle segments that gravitate to a Mentor as leader are more interested in partnerships than organizations. The church "board" (if it can be called that) is really a handpicked core group of ardent disciples who invest themselves in mentoring others. They spend less time in administration or policy development and more time developing intimate spiritual relationships. The Mentor holds the core group to a very high standard of accountability.

Looking ahead to other ministry applications, these leaders tend to lead worship that is simple, mystical, and occasionally charismatic (transformational or coaching). "Preaching" is often very dialogical. The immanence and transcendence of God are very important and may be emphasized through sacraments or silence. Designated leaders guide small groups. Outreach tends to emphasize interpersonal relationships and explore human potential. The church often practices a kind of "reverse tithe," in which the individual member intentionally surrenders everything and expects God to return a tithe of resources for daily living.

There is no particular location or facility associated with this kind of leader. House churches are not uncommon. Their organizational center may resemble a monastic house that ensures security, confidentiality, and privacy. The location may be in rural, remote, or out-of-the-way locations, but it is often in urban core and multicultural settings. The location is frequently *in the midst of mission* and is often in surroundings that are ugly or dangerous. The mentoring community may well extend to web-based interaction through blogs and other social networks that limit access to a covenanted few.

Pilgrim

These leaders often have a "priestly" persona because they are quick to discern the sacred in ordinary events and participate in spiritual journeys or quests. They are very spiritually disciplined, practice rigorous accountability, and encourage sacrifice and simplicity. This leader shares a similar purpose with the Mentor but is much more mobile and cross-cultural. This leader also shares a passion for maturing Christians with the Discipler but is more likely to do this in action/reflection ways rather than progressive stages of training.

The Pilgrim leader is really part of a peer group of traveling companions who describe spiritual life as a journey. That journey may be theological, physical, and cross-cultural. The peer group may be physically together only at irregular intervals but remain in close communication through the Internet. They hold one another accountable to extreme spiritual habits, often deliberately modeling ancient pilgrimage practices. They share sensitivity for a common destination, in that members of the "pilgrim band" have a common goal of unity with God and alignment with God's purposes. Openness to the Spirit is perhaps the only real condition for belonging to the community.

The credibility of Pilgrim leaders is that they seem to be in a more advanced stage of spiritual awareness and clarity of purpose, and they are willing to guide others, provided they do not slow down or sidetrack the Pilgrim's progress. The Pilgrim leader measures success by proximity to God, rather than by programs developed, members acquired, or even leaders empowered. They have a clear and powerful mission attitude. Although they talk about "journey," they are very focused on "destination" and envision a final Utopian outcome for spiritual life (for example, the "City of God" or a "Return to Eden").

Pilgrim leaders are often interested in dialogue between traditions, cultures, and even religions. Their own career paths are often eclectic, with leadership experience in several sectors. This can even include military and civil service, public and private education, corporate business, environmental specializations, and law. These leaders combine an ascetic lifestyle with frequent hands-on service as they bless people along the way. The community that they foster is often small, frequently changing, and spiritually intense. They may establish a chain of mission outposts, travel from one to the other, and communicate frequently through the Web, a blog, text, and mobile phones.

The lifestyle segments that prefer a Pilgrim leader tend to encourage self-reliance. These publics often turn to elders with great experience, or to individuals with reputations for wisdom, to seek advice about life. They tend to be less attached to material things, closer to nature, or living in academic environments. Although such people may live in very poor or middle-class settings, they tend to be very optimistic and restless. People in these lifestyle segments may have changed careers, residences, and intimate relationships several times. They tend to be multicultural in their friendships, international in their travel, and prone to immerse themselves in whatever service project or cultural situation in which they find themselves.

Pilgrim leaders tend to surround themselves with a pilgrim band. They do not consider themselves a "board," nor are they regarded as such by the lifestyle segments that gravitate to a Pilgrim leader. They are colleagues who travel together to search for truth, collaborate in social service, and share spiritual disciplines, but separately participate in organizations in a time, place, and manner of their own choosing.

Looking ahead in ministry applications, Pilgrim leaders are very intentional about hospitality and rarely settle for the "basics." They are open to any worship alternative that expressly addresses the spiritual need of people they encounter on the way, but they gravitate toward "mission connectional" worship. Education methods are usually experiential rather than curricular, and they prefer to train designated leaders to guide small groups. Their sensitivity to the unique needs of publics around them makes them open to any form of outreach, but outreach usually will be short term or handed off to other established churches or nonprofit organizations.

Pilgrim leaders feel urgent about time but care less about space. They use any space that comes to hand for worship and teaching and may maintain elaborate interactive websites. Because there is little budget required to sustain an organization, and they often earn income from alternative employment, there is little emphasis on percentage-giving stewardship. However, there is a strong emphasis on lifestyle stewardship and complete surrender of material wealth and personal security to God's purpose.

7. Hospitality Alternatives

There are four basic kinds of hospitality among churches in North America, although within each category there are many variations customizing hospitality to ethnic and cultural expectations. "Hospitality" includes all ways the public is greeted, sheltered, nourished, connected to relationships, and introduced into congregational life before, during, between, and after worship services.

Some lifestyle segments may specially connect with two different kinds of hospitality, and even small churches may blend their strategy in a couple of ways. Large churches and multisite churches may offer very different hospitality ministries for each worship service or site.

Each lifestyle segment tends to gravitate toward certain kinds of hospitality tactics. This means that hospitality leaders (for example, greeters, ushers, and refreshment servers) are *conditioned* to behave in certain ways. Some of this "conditioning" is simply unconscious. Hospitality leaders behave in ways that seem "natural" to them. They simply mirror their own lifestyle segment experience at home, at work, and in other volunteer contexts. Some of this "conditioning" is intentional. Hospitality leaders are trained to act in ways that may seem exaggerated or foreign to them, but that are deliberately sensitive to *different* lifestyle segments of the surrounding community.

The hospitality alternatives described here are defined according to the expectations of *the community users*, rather than the preferences of *the church members*. In communities that are very homogeneous, community expectations and membership preferences are very similar and little training is required. However, even small-town and remote communities are more diverse than ever before, and urban contexts are quite complex. The contrast between community expectations and membership preferences can be very sharp.

This means that hospitality today is not something we do "naturally," but rather something we do "intentionally." It is hard work, just as every other ministry application (worship, education, outreach, and so on) is hard work. Church members who are used to "the basics" need to be trained to offer "multiple choices" and other alternatives, and some church members who are used to "multiple choices" need to be trained to be satisfied with "the basics."

The design of an appropriate hospitality strategy does not really depend on the *size* of a church. It depends on the degree of urgency to reach the surrounding community. Some small churches provide meager hospitality and claim this is due to their lack of resources. This is almost always false. Churches (small or large) provide meager hospitality due to their lack of desire to welcome outsiders. In order to be effective, all of the options below must reveal the sincerity, generosity, and abundant love of the church members for anyone who comes. Hospitality becomes *radical* when it ceases to be a ministry to the members and becomes a ministry to the mission field.

Every church will need to be sensitive to unique ethnic or microculture expectations. The most obvious issue is prejudice. Churches often consciously or unconsciously discriminate in every demographic category between insiders and outsiders (age, race, language, gender, education level, physical and mental abilities, income, and even occupation). *Radical* hospitality is ever more sensitive to our multicultural world.[1]

- *Body Language:* Different groups of people have different expectations regarding physical touching and gestures of affection; eye contact between men and women; odor and perfume; and fashion, jewelry, tattoos, and acceptable symbols.

- *Public Behavior:* Different groups have distinct habits about demonstrating respect, nurturing infants and disciplining children, interpersonal relationships, idioms and other verbal expressions, gift giving and special holidays, and superstitions and religious customs.

- *Food Consumption:* Groups not only differ over *what* can be eaten but also *how* it should be eaten. This includes food choices and taboos, eating utensils, environmental priorities, eating disorders, health choices, and addictions.

Do greeters shake hands or not? Do they physically touch one another or bow? Do they look into the eyes of female visitors, or would that be considered aggressive and intrusive? Are there foods to include or avoid? Which non-English phrases or words should be memorized, and in which language? Are there different expectations for each generation of ethnic immigrants, or for young adults, or for multicultural families? These questions can be answered only by local focus groups. The insights will lend nuance to each of the following hospitality alternatives.

As always, it is important to avoid making value judgments. These alternatives do not make one lifestyle segment better or worse, more or less sophisticated, or more or less authentic. People are simply different. The goal of hospitality is simply to reduce any possible barrier that might block Christian communication and create environments that encourage the greatest receptivity to the real presence of Christ.

The Basics

Many lifestyle segments expect only basic hospitality. There are many reasons for this. Some groups value worship but deliberately arrive at the last moment and leave at the earliest opportunity. They may prefer to initiate and deepen relationships in other ways and on other days. Other groups enjoy their friends and relatives but are extremely cautious among strangers and slow to develop relationships. Still other groups feel out of place in elaborate social settings and uncomfortable with too many social decisions.

Many of these lifestyle segments represent an older (perhaps even "old-fashioned") experience of the church. Older church buildings were really not designed for elaborate hospitality ministries. The narthex or gathering space before worship was extremely small (if it existed). The fellowship hall was downstairs beside an elaborate kitchen because Christendom churches expected members to gather in large groups and fellowship dinners during the week. Small groups frequently met in private homes.

These lifestyle segments include many lifestyle segments that have been stalwart participants in established churches. Their sense of belonging does not extend to demands for personal privilege. They are relatively content with their current situations, take people as they are, and ask only for respect and dignity. These lifestyle segments tend to be in small towns, working rural communities, urban cores, lower-middle to middle-class suburbs, and exurban regions with mixed housing and cultures.

Many of the lifestyle segments that prefer "the basics" grew up in homogeneous Christian communities in which interpersonal relationships unfolded at other times and in other places during the week. Sunday morning was primarily dedicated to building a relationship with God.

Hospitality teams may be untrained because the gap between community expectations and member preferences is very small and leaders do what comes naturally. If hospitality teams are deployed as an intentional outreach, they are trained to be sincere but behave with simplicity and reserve. Their Christian behavior speaks for them. They do not need to witness to faith, and they refrain from asking probing questions. They simply accept people as they are.

Hospitality tactics are simple. Veteran members greet people at the main door, but greeters are not stationed at other entrances (unless there are challenges for accessibility that require special assistance). Printed material is provided at the entrance to the sanctuary, but people seat themselves. People may or may not speak to each other in the sanctuary, depending on the mission orientation of worship, but there is an intentional time to greet one another or "pass the peace" in worship. Interventions to help people during worship (demonstrations of emotion, difficult children, and so on) are spontaneous. No one is stationed at the exits to say good-bye.

Visitors usually expect body language simply to be sincere. Any cultural gaffes are overcome as long as greeters are genuinely interested in a newcomer and readily apologize for any mistakes. If greeters and ushers occasionally seem cautious or distant, this is usually because they are being careful among strangers and unwilling to risk any demonstration of disrespect.

The refreshment center is located adjacent to the kitchen for easy service. There may be a few tables and folding chairs, but most people are expected to stand. There are two options for coffee (including decaffeinated), and both are brewed in large urns during worship. In the south, there will be iced tea. In Canada, there will be hot tea. Food may or may not be provided. Some lifestyle segments prefer occasional home-baked goods; most prefer packaged cookies or pastries. "Basic" foods also include food and utensils that are commonly used in the homes of families from the different ethnic groups immediately surrounding the church building. The service ware is often disposable.

There is usually just one serving station. People standing in line use this opportunity to engage in enthusiastic conversation. People tend to gather in friendship circles. The inclusion of visitors is facilitated by the pastor, or spontaneously by more extroverted personalities. No one is deployed to mingle and engage conversations intentionally. Refreshment servers are willing workers (usually women) whose primary purpose is to maintain service rather than talk with people.

Multiple Choices

This hospitality alternative is often described as "radical," especially by people who are most familiar with "the basics." The increasing diversity of the public has prompted many lifestyle segments to prefer "multiple choices" in how they are welcomed, how hospitality leaders mirror the diversity of the community, and how refreshments are served.

This is about more than just food variety. These lifestyle segments respect only a church that is welcoming to the real diversity of the public, and their decision to return to a church (or join a church) will depend more on what happens in the hospitality ministry than what happens later in worship or education. The lifestyle segments that value "multiple choices" are often groups that have grown distrustful of the institutional church. They need to see a clear demonstration of Christian behavior and faithfulness in the *spontaneity* of the church community, and this will encourage or discourage them from accepting the *rehearsed* (or formal) actions and words of the worship service. Hospitality is a way these lifestyle segments "check out" a church.

Therefore, the "multiple choice" hospitality alternative must be something that is done regularly, and not just for special occasions. It is the routine of the church. It is supported by expanded budgets for interior decorating, kitchen technology, specialized foods, and leadership coaching. Hospitality is not incidental to the worship and education pattern of Sunday morning, but of equal importance. These lifestyle segments value hospitality ministries as a crucial way to initiate and deepen friendships, and reality-check the integrity of a church.

These lifestyle segments include a cross section of income and education. It is not true that poor or poorly educated people are more likely to prefer basic hospitality, and it is not true that wealthy people or well-educated people are more likely to prefer "multiple choices." What is true is that these lifestyle segments "love to linger." They have strong motivations to visit with friends, make new friends, and make strangers feel welcome. These choices may be for food and drink, but they also may be to occupy their attention with an alternative video, a crafts table to explore, and different conversation partners to engage. With choices, they have a reason to linger.

Hospitality leaders usually are trained to empathize with the ethnic groups living around the church building. They speak key words in a second language and may dress with special sensitivity to the styles of other cultures. Greeters are often deployed as families representing multiple generations, and ushers are trained to demonstrate appropriate respect for seniors, new mothers, and women. Leaders are alert to the unique holidays of ethnic groups, recognize special symbols, and offer seeker-sensitive gifts to visitors.

The fact that so many lifestyle segments prefer "multiple choices" reveals both the importance of hospitality as a ministry and the hidden distrust of church institutions that has emerged in North America. People like choices because it softens the hard edges of institutionalism. It builds confidence that the institution really cares about their tastes, personalities, and health needs. Some of the lifestyle segments that prefer choices are also among the hardest to reach by established churches. These include affluent urban professionals and young independent cosmopolitans, university students, and busy suburban young families heavily invested in amateur sports. On the other end of the economic spectrum, it includes people who are just getting by, rural resource and agricultural laborers, and blue-collar shift workers.

Hospitality teams are selected because they have clear spiritual gifts, personal sensitivity to others, or extroverted personalities. They are trained not only to respond to visitors and members in culturally sensitive ways but also to model core values and share the basic beliefs of the church. Their role is not just to welcome people. They represent the church, kick-start spiritual reflection and conversation for Sunday morning, and guide people to ministry options on Sunday morning or midweek that might be beneficial to them. Hospitality teams often meet as a small affinity group for spiritual growth, mutual support, and ongoing coaching.

Hospitality teams are deployed in layers. Volunteers may be deployed outside to assist parking and escort visitors to the front doors in inclement weather. Greeters are stationed at every entrance. There is often a Welcome Center or booth near the main doors to the sanctuary or in the food court. Ushers may not only seat people but also provide wheelchair and stroller assistance and explain the use of audio, video, and Internet technologies.

Worshipers participate with a strong sense of expectancy for revealed grace. A team of caregivers may be deployed during worship to counsel and pray with individuals who become emotional. There is always a team of greeters in place during worship to receive latecomers. A prayer team is often deployed in an adjacent room. The same layers of hospitality are provided following worship to say good-bye and to invite people to return.

Refreshments are available before, during, and after worship. Because hospitality surrounds worship, there may not be a formal greeting time in worship. People are often encouraged to bring refreshments into the sanctuary, and in some contemporary worship centers, cup holders are provided.

The food court is usually located proximate to the worship center and on the same floor. The environment is tasteful, decorated with symbols of faith or images of church life and mission in ways that are empathetic with the cultural groups surrounding the church building. There are usually several comfortable seating areas for conversation. There are multiple serving stations, some of which may be designated for children or seniors. There is a rich variety of high-quality food and drink that has been selected with sensitivity to the dietary preferences of the publics being served. The church is usually committed to recycling.

Hospitality volunteers are also trained to mingle with people inside the food court. They intentionally connect with newcomers, especially shy visitors or people with special needs. They may be bilingual, or at least be able to express greetings in the indigenous languages of visitors. All hospitality volunteers are usually readily identifiable by a name tag, badge, or apparel.

The goal of the multiple-choice strategies is to encourage people to linger for at least twenty minutes before or after worship. The food encourages them to stay longer so that church leaders can build relationships, start significant conversations, and share vital information about spiritual growth and mission outreach.

Healthy Choices

As the North American population ages, people are becoming more conscious of healthy lifestyles. Many lifestyle segments expect the church to offer assistance to lead a balanced life and encourage healthy diets. Of course, healthy choices may well be included in the "multiple choice" alternative. Certain lifestyle segments, however, deliberately exclude what might be considered unhealthy options in order to advocate lifestyles that reduce anxiety, honor the environment, and prolong life.

These lifestyle segments may include wealthier and more discriminating groups of people (upscale suburbanites, status-conscious professionals, and busy suburban families looking to balance busy lives). They also include lifestyle segments with high priorities for health (young families, seniors, and country gentry). Lifestyle segments that live in multicultural environments and first- and second-generation immigrants may also prefer healthy choices.

Healthy choices involve more than food. These lifestyle segments also prefer environmentally friendly cups, tableware, and other accoutrements. They value natural light, relaxing environments, and soothing background music. And they appreciate sensitivity from any church leader they meet. All these represent deliberate lifestyle priorities about consumption that encourage physical, mental, and emotional well-being.

Hospitality teams intentionally mirror demographic diversity (age, race, gender, and even language) in order to celebrate healthy communities. Hospitality teams are selected not only according to spiritual gifts and friendly dispositions but also for their willingness to model or advocate holistic health. This implies a new level of training and ongoing coaching, as hospitality teams become a first line of evangelism and social advocacy. If they receive appropriate personal support, hospitality teams can include people with mental or learning disabilities, people with eating disorders, and people with other disabilities. They are coached to model core values and even talk about personal disciplines for health in which they participate. Hospitality often connects with outreach ministries that improve quality of life (including physical, emotional, relational, and spiritual health), and these missions figure prominently in worship.

In the "healthy choice" alternative, churches go to even greater lengths to adapt space and technology for the limitations of participants. Comfortable chairs replace pews; additional cushions are available for the elderly; additional space is provided for young mothers and the physically disabled. Audio and video technologies are enhanced, and hospitality teams are prepared to give special assistance to worshipers (refreshments, warmed baby formulas, diaper-changing services, and so on). These strategies are less about caregiving and more about including all people in healthy Christian community.

The food court strategy is similar to the "multiple choices" alternative. However, the foods are fresh, and healthy options for fruit and vegetables are emphasized. There may be assurances that fresh produce is grown locally and free of pesticides. Packaged foods may be served, but the ingredients and calorie content may be clearly listed. There are separate serving stations for sugar and sugar free.

The food court environment creates more comfortable conversation areas, easy accessibility, and additional technologies for wireless communication. Lighting, sound effects, natural plants, and other interior decorating eliminate the "institutional" feel of a classroom or multipurpose center. Some refreshment centers may resemble a garden atrium. Others may incorporate sophisticated visual art. These environments are easily used by small groups following worship or during the week, or for special musical or dramatic performances.

The goals for the hospitality strategy are also similar to those of the "multiple choices" alternative. Layers of ministry are still in place before, during, and after worship. Training may well be supplemented with ongoing coaching and prayer support. Hospitality may be connected to 12-step and other recovery groups that function in the context of the church, or meditation disciplines that combine physical exercise and reflection.

Takeout

A new hospitality alternative is emerging today, especially among church plants, outreach ministries, and innovative churches. Several things influence the rising demand for "takeout." Some lifestyle segments have limited budgets for food, or are unable to prepare food on weekends. Other lifestyle segments have extreme pressures on their time due to shift work, personal commitments, or family responsibilities.

These are very diverse lifestyle segments, but they all share a life experience that is either fast paced or unpredictable. They often rely on fast food or eat on the run, and they tend to communicate on the fly as well. Instant messages, whether leaving behind paper "hasty notes" or using services like Twitter, are part of their routine. This familiar habit has extended to the church.

Greeters and ushers are often younger and visibly model the respectful use of technology. They feel free to use cell phones before and after worship and may intentionally wear ear buds when greeting newcomers. However, they can politely remind worshipers to turn off cell phones during worship. They may use tablets to link with related websites during worship but politely encourage disuse of tablets and computers during post-worship conversations. The church often uses espresso makers for coffee, microwaves to warm food, and icemakers or coolers to provide specialty drinks.

The food court strategy is similar to the "multiple choice" alternative in providing options. The difference is that there are more serving stations, and more servers to pre-prepare refreshments, in order to reduce waiting. In addition, snacks are packaged or bagged to be taken away and eaten later. Often, an additional gift (prayer, meditation verse, devotional object, Bible, or other resource) is included in the package. Some people may partake of these gifts during a break at work or play, and for some the food contributes to their diet for the day.

Hospitality teams are trained to obtain contact information first and communicate in short bursts of intentional information. Any conversation upon entering or leaving the church is considered a *start* that can be followed up through other forms of social networking. The follow-up may be literally within minutes of departure using mobile phone applications. Hospitality may eventually extend to meeting visitors for coffee elsewhere during the week to build relationships. In this way, the hospitality team truly becomes a first line of evangelism or personal support.

It is important to emphasize that this kind of on-the-go communication is about developing a *relationship*. It is not about advertising programs, soliciting money or time, or uploading data about doctrine or ideology. Communication must be two-way, and hospitality team members must take the risk of being transparent about their own lives, questions, anxieties, and dreams.

The "takeout" alternative is often combined with an extensive small-group strategy. Small groups may meet immediately after worship, but more often they meet online or face-to-face through the week. Many of the same lifestyle segments that prefer "takeout" also gravitate toward small groups and mentoring relationships.

8. Mission-Targeted Worship Alternatives

Churches have offered multiple choices for worship for many years. At first, the choices were shaped by time and place. Then people could choose between simpler and more complex liturgies. In the latter half of the twentieth century, it became possible to choose between *styles* of worship (with traditional or contemporary technologies, instrumentations, and music). Today, lifestyle segments make choices about worship in a different way.

Christendom has faded, along with the popular habit of "church shopping." Going to worship is no longer a customary weekly practice or a high priority when people relocate. They are less likely to transfer membership and more likely to postpone, drop out, and find alternatives for private devotion or basic fellowship. People are much more *purposeful* when they come to worship. One might say seekers are *compelled* to worship for very particular reasons. Seekers come to worship knowing that the very act of worship attendance is countercultural. They are *driven* to worship in order to meet personal or spiritual needs *that they have been unable to address elsewhere.*

Even though people today are driven to spirituality by basic anxieties and needs, the worship service must still compete with other agencies and organizations for the priority of their attention. Once, worship attendance was the first resort for the needy. Today, it has become the *last* resort for the needy, who have already tried psychotherapy, social services, 12-step programs, self-help books, and other aids.

Each lifestyle segment tends to be attracted to specific kinds of mission-targeted worship services. Their choices are guided by the nature of the blessing from worship, not simply the style of worship. Any given lifestyle segment may value a wide variety of worship characteristics, but usually at least *two or three worship expectations dominate.* In other words, there are two (or perhaps three) personal or spiritual needs that *compel* the people in any given lifestyle segment to take an interest in church worship. Seekers come to worship because they are broken, sad, lost, lonely, anxious, victimized, or trapped. They are specifically looking for God to heal, comfort, guide, befriend, encourage, vindicate, or liberate the seeker.

Style may be a factor in their choice of worship, but today this is only a secondary concern. Worship that accomplishes these blessings may be done in any number of styles (different kinds of technologies, music, instrumentations, liturgies, and so on). The most important thing is that the worship service blesses people in any given lifestyle segment in a particular way.

Christendom churches have difficulty understanding worship as a *mission event.* They prefer to understand worship as an opportunity to glorify God. Post-Christendom churches, however, understand that the best way to glorify God is to bless people in God's name. God gives the grace, but the experience of grace can be focused and shaped by worship designers.

There are seven basic kinds of worship in the post-Christendom world. "Good worship" is defined no longer by the internal priorities of the church institution for liturgical or theological consistency, but by the external priorities of different publics seeking God's grace. Good worship is whatever works to bring people into the real presence of Christ, where they can experience God's grace in ways that are relevant to their needs.

Good Worship...	Brings people near to Christ as...	Through experiences of grace...	In a relevant way...
Inspirational	The Promise Keeper	Hopeful Attitudes	Motivational Preaching Powerful Rhythm
Coaching	The Spiritual Guide	Mentoring Relationships	Memorable Lyrics
Healing	The Healer	Healthy Lifestyle	Ritual Actions Ambient Music
Caregiving	The Comforter	Personal Support	Pastoral Presence Awesome Silence
Transformational	The New Being	Fresh Starts	Lay Witness and Story-telling Pop Music with New Meaning
Educational	The Perfect Human	Truth about Life	Expository Preaching Thoughtful Hymns
Mission-Connectional	The Vindicator	Acceptance and Justice	Advocacy and Internet Cross-Cultural Music

Note that sharing a Christian message, and equipping worship leaders, will be important for all options of worship. The message, however, may be "shared" in various ways (expository preaching, story-telling, imaging, drama, and so on). The worship leader may be credible as a spiritual person in various ways (ordained, lay, professional, amateur witness, and so on). Each worship alternative may be designed and implemented in different ways, with different leaders, to create opportunities for people to experience particular grace.

The "traditional" worship of churches with fewer than two hundred people (that is, "Church Families") is a blend of education and caregiving. The "traditional" worship of churches with more than two hundred people (that is, "Program Churches") is a blend of education and inspiration. Yet the most popular worship services today are blends of transformational, inspirational, coaching, healing, and mission-connectional experiences.

The point of all worship is to bring people into the *real presence* of Jesus Christ. Eucharist may be celebrated in any option of worship because the sacrament has significance in all seven ways. The import of Eucharist is shaped in part by the specific expectations that participants bring to the mission-targeted worship service. The words, prayers, creeds, and the manner in which the sacrament is shared with participants, can be shaped to focus the special nuance of Eucharist for the participants. The choice of words, method of distribution, and surrounding symbols and songs focus the real presence of God in particular ways.

Other sacramental acts may be particularly relevant to certain options of worship. Baptism, for example, is often central to transformational and inspirational worship. Unction and healing prayer are often central to caregiving and healing worship. Foot washing and commissioning (or ordination) are often central to mission-connectional worship. Confirmation may be central to educational worship, and interpersonal celebrations of fidelity (for example, renewal of marriage vows and other covenants) are often a focus in coaching worship.

It is difficult for any church to "blend" more than two (and occasionally three) mission purposes in a single worship service. This is why churches focus worship for specific lifestyle segments represented in their mission field. They do not try to make one size fit all, or to blend one worship service to bless everyone at the same time. Once one worship service becomes effective, the next worship service will be designed to address the primary personal and spiritual needs of another group of lifestyle segments. The difference is not in time or place, nor even technology and style, but in mission purpose.

Churches start an alternative worship service (different from their "traditional" experience) to bless a public that is currently under represented or completely unrepresented in their current membership:

- They want membership to mirror the proportionate demographic diversity of their primary mission field.
- They have a powerful heartburst for a special public in a particular neighborhood.
- They hope to "make a difference" in the community by motivating personal growth and social change.

An alternative worship service is *not intended* to bless currently active members of the church. If participants in "traditional" worship want to start attending "alternative" worship, they simply redevelop the "traditional" service first.

Worship today is less a part of the Christian year and more a part of a weekly spiritual life. Worship is only one piece of a larger spiritual life. People come to worship out of a spiritual life and leave worship to continue a spiritual life. "Success" is often best measured by *what happens after the worship service*.

- *Inspirational worship* results in greater risk-taking, more articulate evangelism, more generous giving, and a generally more countercultural lifestyle.
- *Coaching worship* results in participation in midweek small groups, highly accountable spiritual disciplines, and high-trust relationships.
- *Healing worship* results in stories of physical, emotional, mental, or relational wholeness; balanced and healthy

lifestyles; and connections with therapeutic and medical practices.

- *Caregiving worship* results in feelings of reassurance, community acceptance, higher participation in fellowship events and large groups, and active visitation of church and community members in need.

- *Transformational worship* results in freedom from addictions, participation in 12-step programs, radical career changes, conversions, radical attitude shifts, or dramatically altered personal circumstances.

- *Educational worship* results in knowledge of doctrine and Scripture, participation in Sunday school and Bible study groups, and institutional leadership.

- *Mission-connectional worship* results in greater sacrifice of time and talents, increased volunteerism for local and global outreach, and higher commitment to social action and evangelism.

When worship was diversified merely by *time of day* or *style*, church leaders measured success by attendance, financial giving, and harmony. Today, worship is diversified by mission purposes, and the leaders measure success in other ways.

There are three basic reasons why worship services fail. They are boring (dull and de-energizing), irrelevant (disconnected from daily living and unexpected life crises), and pointless (leading nowhere beyond institutional responsibilities and heritage protection). Therefore, in order for a new worship service to succeed, there must be a strong motivation for people to return again and again.

Remember that each lifestyle segment may be interested in more than one option of worship and may gravitate toward two or perhaps three kinds of worship. Their interest in different kinds of worship will also evolve through life stages, or suddenly change due to new circumstances. Just as lifestyle segments are fluid, so also worship design is fluid in order to be energizing, relevant, and purposeful.

Designing worship to bless a peculiar public with a particular grace is a different way of thinking. It is also an ancient Christian way of thinking unique to the mission to the Gentiles. When St. Paul relocated worship away from the synagogue and into the private home of Titus Justus, controversy followed. There is similar controversy over worship design today. God confirms Paul's strategy of mission-targeted worship in a vision: "One night the Lord said to Paul in a vision, 'Do not be afraid, but speak and do not be silent; for I am with you, and no one will lay a hand on you to harm you, for there are many in this city who are my people'" (Acts 18:9-10). It is increasingly relevant in contemporary culture, where Christianity is no longer the dominant religion of culture.

Postmodern worship more closely resembles the worship of primitive Christianity in the Apostolic Age. It is extremely Christocentric and is intended as an experience of incarnation. Incarnation means that God's revelation is poured into human understanding or experience, and thus necessarily "overflows" the container of human reason. The design of worship is relatively simple: an awakening to a particular aspect of God's grace; a single, captivating insight into God's purpose of the worshiper's life; and a new hope that is taken away from worship as a precious gift to be cherished and used the rest of the week.

Inspirational Worship

Inspirational worship blesses people experiencing high anxiety by giving them renewed hope. It gives them high spirits and light hearts. They are motivated to give thanks, celebrate God's grace, and praise God's power. They expect worship to give them renewed strength and confidence for the coming week.

Anxiety about the future that drives people to worship is often a chronic condition of their lives. In the most profound sense, people are anxious about death and dying, or the fragility, impermanence, or transitory character of life. These life segments tend to be worried about both real and potential threats to their well-being (marriage and family tensions, unemployment, constant mobility, war, economic depression, environmental disaster, and so on). Everyone suffers from anxiety, but some lifestyle segments are more likely to seek out inspirational worship. These include people who aspire to be upwardly mobile as well as people who feel that they are losing social status, economic strength, or power over their lives. They are sometimes transient in their pursuit of jobs, careers, and suitable surroundings; or they are commuting long distances to connect their source of employment with affordable housing.

These lifestyle segments often include extended families, families with older children, and struggling singles. They are often straining to be "successful," but success may be measured in many ways (financial wealth, popularity and influence, personal fulfillment, social justice, and so on). They may be frustrated idealists or struggling to get by. They tend to gather in larger groups (in church or in public) so that the sheer size and volume of a gathering helps them feel part of a larger movement. Similarly, they often tend to surround themselves with multimedia and use all their senses to *feel* better.

The sheer number of lifestyle segments that gravitate toward this kind of worship as a primary or secondary choice indicates the significance of the *anxiety* and *hopelessness* that has pervaded North American culture in recent decades. Many churches (denominational and independent) have grown quite large because of their particular mission focus on inspirational worship.

The design of worship may be simple or complex. Worship can be classically liturgical, with powerful choirs and organ music, or it can be highly contemporary, with contemporary bands and pop Christian music. The magnitude and power of performance is suggestive of concerts and other "entertainment" venues, but the focus is always hope for tomorrow rather than escape from today. The chancel often resembles a stage, and the seating resembles a theater. Worship tends to be performance driven, and leaders are on a quest for quality. High-quality music tends to be more rhythmic than lyrical, and the beat is more important than the words. Visual images are important and may be static pictures or movies. Video screens prompt the order of worship and are always displaying different pictures. Indeed, the environment of worship tends to be multisensory and encourages worshipers to multitask.

The message is motivational rather than didactic. Metaphors and stories are usually grounded in one brief Scripture passage, and a memorable truth is both the theme of the service and the big idea participants take away with them. People are not expected to take notes. There are few announcements. There are few moments of silence, and no distractions to greet other worshipers during the service. The entire focus is on the motivational point that is developed and celebrated by song, image, drama, and word. Spontaneous expressions of enthusiasm are common (applause, laughter, or shouts of "Amen!").

The sacraments are celebrated with considerable drama and special effects (processions, unique lighting, crafted images, background music, and so on). If Eucharist is observed, the liturgy is usually sung (and sung well), with special music and dramatic liturgical demonstrations. The congregation usually lines up to receive the sacrament standing, while music plays in the background, so that the pace of worship keeps moving.

The motivational speaker may be ordained but often does not emerge from traditional seminary training. Lay pastors, clergy with prior careers in other sectors, and leaders with strong cross-cultural influences are more common. The leadership team, however, is very professional and well trained. They may be artists or technicians who are intentionally exercising their skills for Christ. They may accept smaller salaries or moonlight from parallel professional careers. Worship is well rehearsed, but it can also invite improvisation and spontaneity. Despite the quest for quality, personal sincerity is vital. It is not unusual for musicians or technicians to give a personal witness of hope.

The outcome of inspirational worship is hope or renewed confidence in life. This is usually manifest through increased charitable giving and increased volunteerism for a variety of causes and nonprofit organizations. People often exit worship with smiles and comment that they are better able to take on the challenges of the coming week.

Coaching Worship

Coaching worship blesses people with practical help to live a Christian lifestyle at home, work, and play. It is especially appreciated by seekers who are lost, confused, or looking for quality relationships and moral guidance. It generally encourages positive thinking, greater self-confidence, and effective lifestyles. It focuses on everyday behavior and personal decision making, rather than on intellectual theories and abstract ideals.

Coaching worship is especially popular among lifestyle segments that seek advice and dialogue to improve all areas of life (for example, family life, business practice, personal health, and even retirement and recreation). These lifestyle segments include relatively stable groups of people with positive future prospects (white-collar suburbanites, entrepreneurial singles and couples, and students). These also include lifestyle segments that are struggling with concrete problems about safety and security, and people who are entering or exiting key phases of life (birth, adolescence, marriage, middle age, retirement, and so on).

This option of worship attracts a very wide cross section of the North American public (second only to "inspirational worship" in public esteem). It is especially helpful for lifestyle segments that are upwardly mobile or adjusting to a new country and culture. Coaching worship is a common alternative for newly planted or large churches. The topic for the day is often advertised on a changeable, illuminated marquee outside the building. Attendance is often driven by participation in small affinity groups during the week, and small-group participants often sit together in the sanctuary.

People tend to arrive early so that they can share significant conversations about life over refreshments and connect with friends. This worship is often supported by multiple choices in hospitality that encourage people to linger, and trained volunteers often engage people in conversation related to the topic of the day. When they enter the worship center, the music has already started, so that the conversations outside and inside blend seamlessly.

Coaching worship is designed around a practical topic or theme related to living a Christian lifestyle. Sermon titles often begin "How to..." People are encouraged to bring refreshments into the worship center. The order of worship is usually quite informal. Songs are distinctively Christian, but with a popular sound. Bands and ensembles are preferable to choirs. Worship relies on technologies familiar in daily life. This often includes computer-generated images and film clips that elaborate on the theme of the day. Live drama and personal stories are common.

The sacraments are celebrated in simple and informal ways. Eucharist tends to be shorter and intimate. If there is a liturgy, it uses common language and shorter sentences, and assumes people do not have a sophisticated educational background in liberal arts. If people are sitting in table groups or clusters, the sacrament may be distributed to each table. Depending on the values and beliefs of the church, the elements may be ordinary bread and juice rather than wafers and wine.

Dialogue is an important part of worship. The sermon is very practical and may last thirty minutes or more (interrupted by relevant video clips or dramas). There is often an opportunity for discussion, and questions can be spoken or texted to the leader. Speakers may not be ordained, and their credibility lies in their experience and expertise related to the topic of the day. There is little ceremony, and the offering may be collected as people depart the building. Hospitality and worship space are often merged, and conversation before and after worship is encouraged. The environment often includes small tables and movable chairs. It is very "family friendly," providing play space for children, rocking chairs for young mothers, bottle warmers for infants, and so on.

Coaching worship motivates people to participate in small groups during the week or in short-term mission teams. Small-group leaders are often spotlighted during the worship service, and opportunities for personal spiritual growth advertised. Worship always refers to the next step to mature as a disciple and grounds practical concerns in a broader practice of spiritual life. It also draws people into additional steps for self-discovery through personal service. Short-term mission projects, particularly aimed to address local issues, are often highlighted in worship.

The outcome of coaching worship is holistic personal growth and a commitment to faithful living seven days a week. Church leaders often track how many worship participants show up later in the week in some form of affinity or curriculum group. People often exit worship carrying resources related to the topic and comment on how helpful the message was to address a concrete issue in their daily lives.

Healing Worship

Healing worship blesses people with renewed health, wholeness, and vitality. Healing may be physical, emotional, mental, relational, or spiritual. It may be sudden and even unexpected, or it may be linked to therapeutic processes and ongoing counseling or medical care. Either way, healing is considered miraculous. God does something to restore or regenerate life that cannot be explained simply by psychological or medical analysis. There is a deeper meaning and significance to the experience of healing that is linked to God's power.

Healing worship is related to "transformational" and "caregiving" worship, but today these other forms of worship are so popular and distinct that it is helpful for church planners to separate them. As we shall see, "transformational" worship is linked specifically to recovery from addiction and conversion because both experiences are so radical that one feels "born again" through the intervention of a Higher Power. "Caregiving" worship accepts marginalized people and reassures those with chronic conditions or constant life struggles. "Healing" worship has a distinct focus on acute crises, seemingly irreconcilable relationships, and seemingly incurable problems.

This emphasis has made healing worship one of the fastest-growing worship options in North America. Ironically, the great promise of higher education and scientific research has generated a gap of frustration because people feel their brokenness even more keenly. The experience of healing that might once have been part of any worship service is now sought with greater urgency in a specialized worship service.

The lifestyle segments that prioritize healing worship often have difficult or dangerous lifestyles. They may include "grassroots" people who are just getting by, hardworking rural and urban core people, military families and veterans, and lifestyles at high risk for health issues caused by poor diets, poverty, occupational hazards, or environmental factors. These people tend to prefer small congregations that maximize intimacy or 12-step groups that combine spirituality and rehabilitation. They often connect with other health care and social services.

However, lifestyle segments seeking healing worship may also include people with relatively stable, predictable, and healthy lives who suddenly feel marginalized as "exceptions to the norm" because of some unexpected crisis. Lifestyle segments associated with the middle class are particularly beleaguered today. These include well-educated people stuck in low-income occupations and high-income people with only limited specialized training. Lifestyle segments that generally believe life is fair and "people usually get what they deserve" may be especially confused or despairing and seek out healing worship.

The first group of people may have strong ties to Christian traditions, and particularly with churches that readily celebrate miraculous events in history or daily life. The second group of people often does not have strong ties to Christian traditions or has drifted away from Christian traditions that readily celebrate reasonable faith to explore alternative spiritualities.

Healing worship may be very informal or extremely ritualized. If there is a sermon, it is often by a lay witness to healing events in his or her own life. The tone is generally quiet and meditative, but the senses are stimulated by soft background music or chanting and static visual images (paintings, murals, stained glass, photographs, and so on). Incense may be used. Touch is important, and people are usually encouraged to sit more closely together and greet one another with sincerity and enthusiasm. Lighting is often dim, and candles may be used for meditative focus or illumination. Liturgy often relies on simple responses or may be projected on-screen for greater ease in reading.

If Eucharist is celebrated, the liturgy is usually simple and in common language, although it may be offered in translation or signing for the deaf. The sacrament is very personal and is often served to individuals as they come forward and kneel. Unction, baptismal remembrance, blessings by "laying on of hands," foot washing, and other ceremonies may also be used. Personal healing prayer with a priest or mentor is usually available.

The leaders of healing prayer are often ordained priests, specially designated laity, or men and women with reputations as spiritually disciplined people. They often wear clothing or symbols that emphasize their spiritual credibility.

The outcome of healing worship is ongoing involvement in therapeutic processes, intentional reconciliation with estranged friends and loved ones, and greater contentment with one's life situation. The continuation of healing worship depends on the number of people who actually do experience healing, or who experience greater serenity in life. People often exit worship with signs of emotional involvement and express thanks for personal improvements to their health or outlook on life.

Caregiving Worship

Caregiving worship is one of two kinds of worship that are often called "traditional" (the other is "educational" worship). This is because many churches use the metaphor of "family" to describe themselves. Family members are expected to care for one another, uncritically include one another, and assimilate "outsiders" to become "insiders." Caregiving is the primary way churches create, maintain, and treasure the experiences of belonging and harmony.

Caregiving worship emphasizes mutual support in times of trouble, family crisis, or life-cycle transitions. There is a strong emphasis on comfort, compassion, and inclusion. New members are expected to adapt themselves to the customs of their new church family, but they are received kindly and without judgment. Conflict is wrong and strongly avoided. People are expected to honor each other and readily forgive one another.

The lifestyle segments that prefer caregiving worship also tend to favor educational worship. These lifestyle segments are usually well aware of Christian traditions and often experience the church as an oasis in the midst of trouble, or a rock that brings stability to their lives. Heartfelt experience of the immediacy and approachability of Christ is more important than knowledge of doctrine or clarity about ideological principles. These lifestyle segments are often burdened by loneliness and long to be accepted in a supportive community. They are deeply troubled by any kind of instability and cautious about change. They are extraordinarily generous to each other and to outsiders in need, but generally not great risk-takers.

Age is a major factor for attendance in caregiving worship. Empty nesters and seniors tend to gravitate toward caregiving worship. So also do people in small towns or aging urban neighborhoods. People in contexts experiencing dramatic urbanization and families in multi-generational households gravitate toward this kind of worship. These are people in stages of life when the number of relationships and opportunities lost is now greater than the number of relationships and opportunities gained.

Despite the overall aging of society, the number of lifestyle segments yearning for caregiving worship may actually be declining. This is because the same lifestyle groups value other types of fellowship groups (service clubs, sports associations, hobby and craft groups, and so on) that can offer the same caregiving without the financial expense for personnel and property maintenance. Their desire to avoid conflict may also deter them from attending caregiving worship because factional fighting, personality conflicts, or denominational controversies erode the harmony they seek. In short, the church may be less effective in caregiving than other, nonreligious organizations.

Caregiving worship may be highly structured or very informal, but the tone is usually meditative. Announcements may take a great deal of time. Updates about the life struggles of individual members are shared, and people go out of their way to renew friendships. Greetings, appreciations, and passing the peace are often extravagant. Memorials are recognized; gestures of affection between generations are emphasized; pastoral prayers are extended. Music is more lyrical, but an old or satisfying tune is more important than the words. Worship includes moments of awesome silence, and the environment is often warmly but colorfully illuminated.

If Eucharist is celebrated, it follows both denominational and local traditions. People may come forward or receive the sacrament in pews. Representatives of the church are commissioned to take communion to people restricted to home, hospital, or other institutions. It is celebrated most as "the tie that binds" us to one another and God. Baptisms primarily signify inclusion in the family of God. Youth confirmations and membership vows are highlighted during the year and often on holidays.

The message is pastoral. The common lectionary is often used, but only one of the prescribed lessons is the focus of attention. Sermons tend to be shorter and more anecdotal. Video technology is used primarily to enlarge the words for liturgy or hymns, share announcements, or display static images for meditation. The environment displays many traditional symbols. The most effective seating patterns are rows and semicircles, and sometimes with flexible seating. Musical presentations by small amateur choirs or ensembles appeal to more traditional aesthetic tastes. The sincerity of performers is more important than the quality of performance.

The leaders of caregiving worship are usually seminary graduates and ordained. They often have specialized training in clinical pastoral counseling. People expect them to be excellent visitors among members, and well connected with hospitals, nursing homes, day cares, elementary schools, and high schools. One common outcome of caregiving worship is that participants not only feel comforted and encouraged, but they are also motivated to visit in homes and institutions. People exit caregiving worship to linger outside talking with friends and often comment about the love and harmony of the fellowship.

Transformational Worship

Transformational worship blesses people who feel trapped by addiction or circumstance with freedom and a fresh start. It is an opportunity to "turn around" one's life, or to become a "new creature" by the grace of God. Church members may perceive this kind of worship as an opportunity for repentance and the reversal of bad habits. Seekers may perceive this kind of worship as an opportunity to be rescued from a dire fate. Some churches call this option a "recovery" service, because it focuses on breaking self-destructive habits of substance abuse. Other churches link this worship with "revival" meetings in their faith traditions, because it focuses on conversion and breaking free from sin.

The transformational worship alternative is one of the fastest-growing options today. One reason is that addiction is one of the greatest health issues in North America, and poverty is one of the greatest social issues worldwide. Of course, experiences of entrapment are shared by many publics and occasionally by individuals in any lifestyle segment. Another reason is that mass migrations (mobility and diversity) have opened people to new religious perspectives and encouraged assimilation into new cultures.

Lifestyle segments especially interested in this worship alternative include first- and second-generation immigrants, struggling urban families, rural and small-town people in regions of dramatic population decline, and urban and big-city people in regions of dramatic population growth. These lifestyle segments tend to include people transitioning to unfamiliar affluence, transitioning to uncomfortable poverty, or struggling with very difficult circumstances. They may include people who are detached from family, relationships, or home and people with low self-esteem and a sense of powerlessness.

These are often people for whom other kinds of worship have become empty or unhelpful. They are hoping to connect with a profound experience of the Holy lying behind or beyond more traditional forms of worship. They want to feel the touch of God directly, rather than through the proxy of institutional leaders and programs. They also may find their current careers, living arrangements, and relationships to be pointless, unhealthy, or unfulfilling. They are especially interested in personal and powerful experiences with the Holy that can break cycles of self-destruction or despair.

Transformational worship can be quite structured, but most commonly, services are informal and very interactive. The environment may contain symbols of faith, but it is often very plain and simple. Participants are likely to move about, so that space is open and chairs are movable. Music can be of any style or instrumentation, but the flow of music ranges from meditative to exaltation. Rhythm is more important than lyric. The centerpiece of worship is the time of prayer, during which people wait for God to act and then express themselves as they feel spiritually inspired. There is no time limit, and indeed, time seems to stand still. There may be a guided process for individuals to surrender to God, or worship may be more chaotic. Regardless, there is a strong sense of mysterious power and divine love.

The message is often brief and personal. The leader may be a lay witness, rather than an ordained professional. The order of service is so flexible that it is rarely printed, and spontaneity is encouraged. Unexpected events are expected. No one is entirely in control of what happens. The experience of worship itself underlines surrender to God and trust that God will bless whatever happens.

The sacraments of Eucharist or baptism may well be a part of worship and require a priest or spiritual leader. The liturgy for the sacrament is usually brief and in common language, but the celebration will be very dramatic and joyful. Aside from musicians and readers, there are leaders trained to assist people who are emotionally overcome, who can counsel with participants immediately after the worship service.

Worship leaders are more like "mediums" than "authorities." They help participants interact with the Holy, but they may not be able to describe what happens and why. They are cautious about imposing their personal interpretation of events and encourage participants to decide for themselves what events mean through subsequent prayer.

The outcome of worship is that some people experience a change in their lives that they describe as miraculous; and other people are motivated to pursue a deeper devotional life in the hope of experiencing the immanence of God. People exit to participate in 12-step groups and often make major changes about personal behavior, career goals, and social action. They often boast that they are a "new person" or "born again."

Educational Worship

Educational worship is the second kind of worship that is frequently called "traditional." In part, this is because Protestant churches (in particular) emphasized lay training in biblical interpretation, theological reflection, and proper worship. Ordained leaders were therefore deployed to instruct laity through preaching and teaching, and lay leaders focused on maturing the membership to understand the sacraments and exercise various ministries of education and personal support. In the modern era, educational worship has also been traditionally associated with liberal arts education and social assimilation. The prophetic witness associated with educational witness focused on ethical discernment, moral example, and political advocacy.

This worship is intended to help people understand the nature of God, the condition and destiny of the world, the call of Christ, the significance of the church and sacraments, the meaning of Scripture, the message of hope, and moral choice. This worship tends to assume a basic awareness of Christian practice, and it motivates worshipers to pursue further study, daily spiritual habits, and Christian service.

The love of learning and the desire for community are usually two sides of the same longing for lifestyle segments that gravitate to educational worship. This is because the intuition of "being lost" is connected with the feeling of "being alone." The perfection of Christ, therefore, is both renewed clarity about eternal truths *and also* renewed unity with like-minded believers. Educational worship also addresses the spiritual longing to belong in a community of common faith and ecumenical cooperation.

The lifestyle segments that most value educational worship tend to be well aware of Christian tradition, but rocked by questions arising from experiences of evil, rational critiques of religion, and secular threats to spiritual life. Many lifestyle segments have experience with postsecondary education and the liberal arts, or are particularly concerned about right belief and correct behavior. Other lifestyle segments may have little or basic education and be relatively poor, but they value learning and expect Sunday morning to be the one educational moment in their week that provides doctrinal and moral perspective. Not surprisingly, educational worship often flourishes in mission fields that include a college or university, or in mission fields in which there is a marked absence of entertainment and educational opportunities.

Note that many of these lifestyle segments have been the backbone of many institutional churches and denominations. However, these lifestyle segments are either declining or evolving in directions that value worship less. The decline of appreciation for educational worship parallels the decline of liberal arts education in favor of specialized training, the diversification of educational methodologies away from the spoken and printed word to sound and image, and the blending of "education" and "entertainment" in contemporary society.

Worship is structured in a manner that can be replicated among churches of any particular denomination. Standardization of worship sanctuaries, liturgies, preaching cycles, children's stories, and hymnals allows participants to "feel right at home" no matter what corner of the country they might be relocating to or visiting. The Christian year and common lectionary are important, although not always rigidly followed. There is a set pattern to approach God for confession and assurance, hear/read and understand Scriptures, respond with offerings of money and prayers of thanksgiving, and commit to financial support and personal service.

In churches with strong sacramental traditions, liturgies are often lengthy and rely more on spoken and written words than high drama. There are many strong allusions to historical events and biblical themes that should be recognized by knowledgeable participants. Access to the table requires membership, or at least a mature understanding of the meaning of repentance and the nature of grace. The authority of the celebrant depends more on the ability to explain faith and model high integrity. He or she is usually ordained, seminary trained, and certified by the denomination.

The message in educational worship is shared as expository preaching. Sermons are at least twenty minutes, sometimes longer. They are delivered and received as advanced training for mature Christians. People are expected to remember several points and may take notes. The accompanying "children's message" is often a shorter version for beginners. The lecture format means that people sit in rows to listen carefully. Dialogue is reserved for later Sunday school or midweek Bible study. Music may be in many styles and instrumentations, but songs or hymns are usually more lyrical. The words matter. They elaborate the theme or Scripture of the sermon.

The outcome of worship is that people participate in study groups, volunteer for committees, serve on mission teams, and give generously to the church as the agent of mission. A common outcome of educational worship is that people depart expressing appreciation for the insights of the sermon, the beauty of the music, or the moral challenge of the Gospel. People are more thoughtful, better informed, and increasingly bold to behave in countercultural ways that follow moral principles.

Mission-Connectional Worship

Mission-connectional worship is one of the least common forms of worship in North America, but it is more common around the world.

Immigration and cross-cultural experience is causing this kind of worship to grow in Australia, Canada, and parts of Western Europe, and it is becoming a clear alternative for emerging church movements in the United States and England. It is also driven by emerging X and Y ("buster" and "echo") generations, and by the growth in faith-based nonprofit organizations that involve volunteers in hands-on missions around the world.

The lifestyle segments that gravitate toward mission-connectional worship tend to be young, multicultural, and mobile. They build relationships of trust easily and are comfortable with both face-to-face and long-distance relationships. They tend to be comfortable with technology and do not feel any loss of intimacy when they use it. These lifestyle segments prefer learning methodologies that *begin* with mission and *precipitate* reflection. They have a high tolerance for risk and are willing to reshape their personal lifestyles in a good cause.

Mission-connectional worship is all about mission, nothing more and nothing less. It has little to do with honoring membership privileges or sustaining heritage organizations. Mission is the focus of the prayers. Mission teams are regularly dedicated and commissioned in worship. Mission partners are routinely included in worship, either in person or via real-time Internet links. Mission teams regularly sit together in worship. Conversations before and after worship are about practical service projects of the church.

The message of worship focuses entirely on key outreach ministries supported by the giving and volunteerism of the church or potential outreach concerns that should be the focus of attention in the future. The speaker may not be ordained or seminary trained and is more likely a nonprofit leader with experience and expertise in a specific mission project. It is important to understand that evangelism and social action are two sides of the same coin in this worship service. Strong Christology and celebration of the relevance of Christian faith are central to both the motivation and work of social action. Prayer is considered vital for the success of mission and sustaining mission volunteers.

If Eucharist is celebrated, it may be in multiple languages. It may be developed as part of an "agape feast" that deliberately provides cross-cultural or symbolic food choices. The sacrament reinforces counter-cultural behavioral norms that reject secularism and celebrate Christian identity. The celebrant may or may not be ordained, and his or her credibility depends not only on spiritual discipline but also on practical missionary experience.

The environment of worship is usually very utilitarian or multi-purpose, but up-to-date communication technology is crucial. There is a wireless connection to the Internet, and large video screens provide constant images of mission and connect worshipers to multiple broadcasts of local and world events. There is a "newsroom" quality to the worship center. Worship regularly uses audio and video links to connect worshipers with mission partners or volunteer teams at mission sites. Participants show their respect for worship by texting friends during worship.

The worship service can include music of any genre, but leaders are intentional about selecting music from a variety of cultural sources. Liturgy may be in two or more languages, and the worship leader may well be fluent in at least one other language. Worship may advocate public policy related to issues of survival, quality of life, the development of human potential, interpersonal relationships, and holistic health. Worshipers are usually given multiple options for designated giving and promised that minimal money will be diverted to overhead costs of the organization. People are expected to give volunteer time and energy, along with financial contributions and daily prayer.

The outcome of worship is that people are motivated for public service and equipped to share their faith. People never share faith without public service, and they never do public service without sharing faith. The values and beliefs of the church are very explicit on websites, but also in the design of worship and the symbols inside the worship environment. It is expected that these values and beliefs will be explicit in the lifestyles of worship participants. Small groups and mission teams will be held accountable for the values and beliefs celebrated in worship. Every worshiper becomes a "missionary," and every social service volunteer is committed to regular worship in person or online.

9. Education Alternatives

People learn in different ways. In the past, we described these differences generationally and culturally. Younger people used different processes and resources than older people did. For example, younger people relied on active dialogue, drama, video, and music; older people relied on passive concentration or oral or print communication. Some cultures preferred storytelling and learned from the elders; other cultures preferred conversation and learned from their peers.

These distinctions have now become so complicated that generational and cultural distinctions no longer apply. The pressures of work and the opportunities of leisure have multiplied the technologies and methods for learning among all generations. Global networks and mass migrations have blurred cultural boundaries. The fastest-growing group of Internet users is seniors; younger people are rediscovering print, albeit with hyperlinks that connect to blogs and websites, video clips and music. Oral cultures are accessing keyboards and texting their friends; print cultures are downloading music while they surf the Web.

The world facing the church today can no longer be classified simply as "literate" or "illiterate." Elsewhere I have described the new millennium as an omni-symbolic society of postliterate tribes.[1] Symbols replace or interface with abstract concepts and words, and meaning is elaborated through small groups and networks rather than books and classrooms. Of course, education is evolving differently, at different speeds, among different lifestyle segments.

It is possible to describe the preferences of lifestyle segments. Once again, these are *tendencies* only, and there are infinite variations from neighborhood to neighborhood. Yet these tendencies are useful for the strategic planning of school boards, businesses, nonprofits, and churches. Today, each lifestyle segment tends to learn through distinct methods and technologies, and prioritizes certain areas of inquiry. Their choices are guided by their level of education, media preferences, technology awareness, cultural backgrounds, and peer relationships.

The educational preferences most relevant for church planning can be grouped into three categories: form, content, and relationship. The form of education may be curricular or experiential. The content of education may be biblical or topical. The relationship of education may be generational or peer group.

For example, the traditional church model from the early twentieth century is a Sunday school that is segmented into age-based classes that read a printed curriculum from a denominational publisher based on Bible study. That model grew great Sunday schools for children and adults prior to 1940 and is still used in various forms by many established churches.

However, established churches in the late twentieth century began reshaping Sunday school into cross-generational peer groups that rotated students among different experiences (crafts, music, drama, storytelling, and so on) that were all based on a single topic or big idea. That model has also been implemented in various ways for different lifestyle segments.

Some lifestyle segments are apt to have very strong preferences for form, content, and relationship. They may even use their preference as a kind of test for the overall credibility of a congregation. Other lifestyle segments may be comfortable with more than one option for form, content, or group.

Form

The form in which Christian education is delivered matters a great deal for different lifestyle segments. Their different opinions reflect the shift away from print to image, film, song, dialogue, and multisensory symbols as a primary way of learning about anything. This is not just a shift in technology. It is a shift away from words, sentences, and paragraphs as a primary method to communicate truth. Printed words may be important only to supplement the power of images, film clips, and songs—or even interior decorations, pop art, and advertising. Crafts, drama, dance, and other interactive learning experiences may help postmodern generations learn better than would reading the printed word or listening to oral lectures.

Curricular

Christian education is oriented around printed books and study guides. While these may contain static images, the text is the primary means to communicate truth. Children, youth, and adults learn through reading the printed word, or through listening to prepared lectures. Learning is a matter of intellectual engagement. The ability of students to read at a level considered appropriate to their age is crucial. Students advance in Christian education as they expand their vocabulary and master grammar. Christian maturity is measured by acquired knowledge.

The educational environment tends to be more passive. Learning takes place in a classroom. The chairs encourage good posture and are arranged around tables that hold printed materials. Multiple electrical outlets may encourage the use of laptop computers, but these are principally used to download documents or take notes. Aside from educational props (whiteboards, newsprint, bookshelves, and so on), the space is intentionally plain so that there are no visual distractions.

The lifestyle segments that prefer curricular forms of education tend to be older (that is, over forty-five). They also tend to have postsecondary educations, or value higher education for their children. Many have basic experience with a core liberal arts curriculum in public or private schools and universities. On the other hand, some lifestyle segments are less educated but have a strong core value for more analytical education and factual learning. They may reside in rural or remote environments, and Sunday morning is the prime time for continuing education. They may also live in urban environments on very low incomes, without access to emerging technologies.

These lifestyle segments (urban or rural, wealthy or poor, with greater or lesser formal education) tend to associate "truth" with "knowledge" and expect education to provide practical insights that can be readily applied to daily living. Curricula often reflect their assumption that for every question, there can be reasonable answers, and that these answers can best be expressed in words. Study books, workbooks, and magazines may be designed with teaching, followed by discussion questions or "fill-in-the-blank" responses. They tend to focus on what is universally true, rather than what may be contextually relevant.

Experiential

Christian education is oriented around sensory stimulation, dialogue, and activities. While these may include written and spoken words, these are only a secondary means to focus or interpret experience. Children, youth, and adults learn through sights, sounds, smells, tastes, and touch. Learning is a matter of physical and emotional engagement. The ability of students to cooperate, exercise imagination, and explore ideas (regardless of age) is crucial. Students advance in Christian education as they learn new skills and express themselves with greater sophistication. Christian maturity is measured by responsible behavior and attitudes.

The lifestyle segments that prefer experiential forms of education tend to be younger (that is, under forty-five). They may not have post-secondary education. If they do, it may be in visual or performing arts, applied sciences, business, and specialized training. They value career advancement and social mobility. Some lifestyle segments are of non-Western European descent and value less structured learning environments.

These lifestyle segments assume that "truth" is larger than "knowledge." They are given to lateral thinking and metaphorical imagining. Some of these lifestyle segments are suburbanites or live in exurban environments with an ethnic mix. Others may surround university environments and include people who are starting out in new careers, living on their own for the first time, or aspiring to be assimilated into a new culture. Other lifestyle segments that prefer experiential learning methodologies include people who rely on cross-generational or individual mentoring rather than formal classroom education.

The educational environment tends to be more active. Learning takes place in, or among, various activity centers. Workbenches provide space for crafts; chairs are more comfortable and grouped in conversation areas; open space allows bodily movement. Technology primarily supports static images, video, and enhanced sound effects. Music tends to be pervasive. The space is intentionally decorated for mood and filled with symbols.

Content

The content of Christian education also matters a great deal for different lifestyle segments. Denominational or theological perspectives may be more influential to determine educational content among active veteran church members, rather than lifestyle. However, among marginal and inactive members, and certainly among the general public disconnected with Christian faith and practice, the expectations of a lifestyle segment will be much more influential. If a church has a priority to include marginal members and seekers in Christian education, then it will be important to capture their interest.

The two basic choices for Christian education content reflect the shift of North American culture from Christendom to post-Christendom realities. In the past, churches could assume a broad cultural consensus about moral behavior, belief in God, and acceptable civility in private and public life. We could even assume some basic awareness of the Bible in the Old and New Testaments. That normative cultural consciousness is diminishing everywhere. The shift is faster and more dramatic among some lifestyle segments, but everyone is affected.

Biblical

The content of Christian education focuses on the Old and New Testaments (and selected ancient Christian literature considered to be of unique value). Bible stories, salvation history, Jewish and Christian teaching and poetry, prophecy, and apocalyptic expectation are vital. The actual verses may be memorized, but the events and ideas are remembered and cherished. The goal of learning is biblical literacy and fluency.

The lifestyle segments that prefer strong biblical content for Christian education tend to be those that historically have been closely associated with institutional church membership. They tend to be anxious about postmodern confusion over spiritual or moral absolutes and want their children to be well anchored in Christian doctrine and tradition. Adults want to go deeper into Judeo-Christian history and the development of Christian thought. They want to establish their spiritual identity amid the diversity of religions.

Note that these lifestyle segments may prefer to explore the content of Scripture using curricular or experiential methods. However they do it, they tend to assume that understanding the Bible is critical to religious practice, theological reflection, and public service. They usually have a strong appreciation for the established church that may extend to appreciation for denominational perspective and seminary education for clergy. They tend to assume that the content of faith needs to be communicated and guided by spiritually mature or professionally trained leaders.

The content of Christian education is tied to certain categories of worship (especially educational, caregiving, and inspirational). Sunday school education and adult devotional literature may be integrated with a worship design strategy that uses a lectionary and follows the festivals of the Christian year. The biblical content will be interpreted historically and doctrinally.

Topical

The content of Christian education focuses on contemporary issues, ethical principles, public policies, controversial debates, and comparative religions. Books, periodicals, films, and other resources become the focus of study. These may be compared to the Bible, the sacred works of other religions, or the diversity of learned opinion. The goal of learning is ethical integrity, cross-cultural sensitivity, and enlightened behavior.

This content of Christian education is also tied to categories of worship (especially coaching, mission-connection, and transformation). Sunday school education and adult study may be connected to the practical topics of preaching or specific themes for worship. These are integrated with current events, the calendar of public holidays and special occasions, and particular issues of local or global concern.

The lifestyle segments that prefer strong topical content for Christian education tend to be those that are more critical of institutional religions and less active in organized churches. They tend to be anxious about modern stereotypes and assumptions and want their children to have critical tools to discern truth for themselves. Adults want to apply Christian values and beliefs to daily living and resolve the ambiguities of real life. They want to establish their personal integrity amid the diversity of cultures.

Again, these lifestyle segments may explore the content of religion using curricular or experiential methods. However they do it, they tend to assume that understanding the Bible is helpful, but not critical, to religious practice, theological reflection, and public service. They appreciate experienced and expert advice but look for it more widely beyond the church. Global issues, ethical dilemmas, and crises of faith in general tend to be more urgent for them than denominational perspectives or ecumenical dialogue.

Relationship

What people learn is significantly influenced by the company they keep. This insight is particularly significant for churches because spiritual maturity is not as dependent on the brain capacity or physical growth of students. An individual's most influential peer group was once defined by people of the same approximate age. This is still true in some contexts. Increasingly, however, one's most influential peer group is determined by other factors: shared life experience, common interests, special gifts or disabilities, quality of home life, language skills, relative affluence, and so on.

There are two basic strategies for grouping people together in a learning context. The more modern approach classifies people by age; the increasingly postmodern approach classifies people by shared enthusiasms and urgent needs (regardless of age). The postmodern approach is often linked to premodern educational practices. In the ancient world, education was more relational. Professionals with specific areas of expertise did not communicate specialized information to suit the assumed intellectual capacity of a student. Instead, mentors with broad experience and particular passions gathered students of various ages in a small group for individually customized tutoring. While the modern professional graduates students into another class with a new professional, the ancient mentor maintained a relationship with a small group of students over time.

Three factors are reshaping the expectations of lifestyle segments in regard to how students are grouped together for the most effective learning: the unique nature of the spiritual maturation process, the diversity of backgrounds that disposes students to learn, and the decline of the Sunday school. This last has perhaps been the most influential for churches. Many churches simply do not have sufficient students or teachers to fill the roster of a traditional generational education system. Curriculum developers are taking this into account. Small churches simply gather "younger" and "older" children into two groups.

The same shift is occurring in adult Sunday schools. Some lifestyle segments prefer to group adults by age: twentysomethings, middle-aged, seniors, and so on. Other lifestyle segments group adults according to phase of life: Young Adults, Homebuilders, Parenthood, Empty Nesters, Retirees, and so on. The shift toward grouping people together by shared enthusiasms or urgent needs continues this trend.

Generational

Some lifestyle segments prefer to mirror public school practices and organize classes into generational groups. Age is the primary factor. Sunday schools are organized K-12, followed by a confirmation class. Youth groups are divided between junior high and high school. After that, groups tend to be organized around phase of life rather than age: university students, singles, married without children, married with young children, and so on. The assumption is that people of similar age will naturally gravitate toward one another because they share the same life issues.

Adult education also separated people into age groups. The generations that demographers commonly call "Silents," "Builders," and "Boomers" tend to gather together. Long-established churches may have Sunday school classes named in remembrance of key church members who defined the generation. The "Young Adult Class" may actually have been formed in the 1960s, and the membership includes early wave "boomers" who are fifty-five to sixty-five.

The majority of lifestyle segments tends to prefer grouping people together generationally to promote learning. Their adaptation to educational methods tends to follow trends in public education in general. They also tend to follow trends in Christian schools (Roman Catholic, Lutheran, Baptist, and so on) that are generally more conservative and traditional in educational methodology. Some of these lifestyle segments are the beneficiaries of modern educational methods. They have occupations that are more professional, or in executive or middle management. They may also be more affluent and successful. Other lifestyle segments aspire to the success attributed to modern educational methods. They may be new immigrants or more blue-collar, but they are committed to traditional age-based learning as a means toward a better life.

Peer Group

A more postmodern approach is emerging that groups people by affinity rather than age. This affinity may be around some shared enthusiasm or interest, or a particular lifestyle orientation, or some urgent need or disability. In a sense, this takes clubs or "friendship circles" that were once extracurricular in traditional public education and makes these groupings primary for a cross-generational educational experience. People of different ages (sometimes teenagers and seniors) gather in more interactive spaces, using more interactive resources. Grouping by peers usually implies a more experiential learning process, although the content may be biblical or topical.

The decline of Sunday school participation, and the special interests of a limited number of teachers, has driven many churches to this alternative. Children may not gather in age groups, but in classes that include a wide range of ages with a common interest in some service project, topic of study, or particular technology. One group might read stories, another group might watch movies, and yet another group might learn about mission needs and perform service projects. Instead of a generic youth group embracing all teens, the church might launch several smaller youth groups focused on sports, Internet, music, or other topics of interest.

Adult education can be even more radical. Classes may not only focus on particular short- or long-term interests but also include a wider age range of participants. Youth and seniors may participate together in distinct activities or specialized discussions. This approach emphasizes the spontaneous mentoring that can happen alongside or underneath whatever formal curriculum or topic shapes the group. The *real* goal of Christian education is to transfer core values and convictions from one generation to another.

The lifestyle segments that prefer peer grouping for Christian education tend to appreciate individual uniqueness rather than generic developmental patterns. They tend to be very sensitive to gifted children, creative adults, and anyone with special needs. They may well prefer alternative educational models to traditional public education. Some lifestyle segments include people who are professional entrepreneurs, artists, educators, and social service workers, as well as those who are likely to change career paths several times. Other lifestyle segments include people who have limited formal education or have been unsuccessful fitting into generic educational systems.

It is important to note that while lifestyle segments may have clear preferences around the previous alternatives for Christian education (for example, biblical or topical, curricular or experiential), a few segments may be less concerned about grouping. As long as their preference is addressed in the other categories, they are content to gather in either generational or peer group ways. If the church is large, some lifestyle segments prefer to have options. Some children, youth, and adults thrive in one kind of grouping rather than another, and even change over time. Parents may seek to place one child in generational learning and another in peer group learning.

10. Small-Group Alternatives

One of the great revolutions in the church today is that Sunday school is no longer the cornerstone of Christian education for many churches. The expectations of a growing number of lifestyle segments are changing, including those that are traditionally the backbone of institutional church membership.

This has been driven in part by the mobility and economic demands of recent decades. Households with children are busier than ever, participating in amateur sports and pursuing special interests seven days a week. Dual careers are common, and individuals may hold more than one job. There are more nonprofit organizations competing for volunteers than ever before. This all means that people need more flexibility to choose the time and place for personal and spiritual growth.

This change is also being driven by the evolving learning methodologies described previously. More and more, people are relying on guided conversation with peer groups as the preferred method for personal and spiritual growth. Usually this is face-to-face, but small groups can also include participants at a long distance through a host of new social media. Even if groups use a curriculum to focus conversation, they prefer intimate dialogue to passive listening, and they prefer informal environments, outside of a classroom, where food and fellowship can be enhanced.

Small groups are not simply groups that are small. They are

structured groups with a designated or rotated leader, united around a common affinity (task, enthusiasm, need, project, or other focus) that is a high priority in their lives right now. The affinity is the reason why busy people prioritize time to get together. Personal growth is more important than simple fellowship. God is central. Relationships and faith deepen. Most groups are time limited, or at least have intentional mentoring moments when individuals have a deliberate choice whether to continue in a group or move on to another group that takes them deeper and farther.

There may be an overarching strategy to multiply, intermingle, and expand small groups, but each small group behaves as an independent unit. They have freedom to create a covenant for the time and location of gathering and determine the degree of confidentiality, timeline of commitment, and conditions of membership. Small groups are designed for peer accountability and mutual support. Each participant helps the others maintain spiritual disciplines and is a primary caregiver in times of need. Small groups do not necessarily focus on doctrine, but the core values and bedrock beliefs of the church define the boundaries for small-group dialogue.

This parallels the multiplication of many different kinds of 12-step programs today. These groups provide spiritual discipline, mutual mentoring, and peer accountability to overcome addictions, change lifestyle habits, and generally improve the quality of life. The overall strategy has appealed to all lifestyle segments in North America today. The basic elements include strong fellowship and deepening intimacy, shared activities or concerns, learning key principles of faith or receiving coaching for healthy and effective living, and intercessory prayer.

The variables of Christian education defined previously still apply to lifestyle segment preferences. Small groups may be curricular or experiential, biblical or topical, generational or peer group. Two new variables can be traced among lifestyle segments. Some prefer small groups that have designated leaders, and others prefer groups in which leadership is rotated from meeting to meeting. Some prefer to structure groups around a curriculum (study book, series of exercises, and so on), and some prefer to structure groups around a shared affinity (topic of interest, urgent need, and so on).

In the latter half of the twentieth century, specific church traditions dictated the kinds of small groups offered. Evangelical and Catholic churches often preferred structured curricula, while mainstream Protestant and Pentecostal churches often preferred more experiential processes. Evangelical churches often preferred biblical content. Catholic churches often preferred lifestyle topics like marriage enrichment and Christian parenting. Pentecostal churches often preferred spiritual practices like prayer and healing, and mainstream Protestant churches often preferred a wide range of topics adapting Christian values to daily living.

Today, lifestyle segment expectations are more likely to dictate small-group activities rather than the agendas of church traditions. The affinities that draw the attention of the public often depend on their trust of the local church. The easiest small groups to start usually have affinities related to hobbies, crafts, sports, and music. Other groups might focus on specific short-term local or global mission projects. Greater trust is required for churches to provide peer mentoring for career and vocational discernment. The highest trust is required for churches to provide small therapeutic groups for addiction intervention, rehabilitation, recovery, and relationships.

The small-group experience is very fluid and diverse. Participants may move in and out of different kinds of small groups for different stages in their personal and spiritual growth. Lifestyle segments may prefer to *start* with one kind of small group, but subsequently *travel* through other kinds of groups. Each transition is guided by the mentoring of a pastor, staff leader, or small-group leader:[1]

- *Discovery Groups* are all about exploring oneself, one's relationships, and one's experience of God. These can be built around any affinity, but the goal of the group is to "discover" deeper meaning in life. Any lifestyle segment may be attracted to these opportunities, but especially those lifestyle segments that have discretionary time that they might invest in continuing education, hobbies, and other personal interests. Some lifestyle segments that include hardworking laborers, dual-career couples, or young families may not be sufficiently motivated to spend precious time on these "extras" in daily life. Such groups are often the entry point into small-group experience for the "Boomer" generation. Discovery Groups are often associated with worship options for coaching and education, and with church leaders who are enablers and disciplers.

- *Destiny Groups* help people discern their calling that will bring personal fulfillment, or their vocation that will shape their career choices, so that they can be a faithful part of God's plan. This kind of group appeals especially to lifestyle segments that are in transition between cultures, careers, life stages, and economies, as well as those wrestling with circumstances that hold them back from expressing their full potential. Such groups are often the entry point into small-group experience for the "Buster" generation. Destiny Groups are often associated with worship options for inspiration and transformation, and with church leaders who are visionaries and mentors.

- *Mission Groups* help people form partnerships to fulfill their gifts and callings by doing high-quality, effective ministries that bless the local community and wider world. These are not just task groups, but spiritual partnerships that match external outreach with internal spiritual discipline. They have the same relational and spiritual accountability as any true small group. This kind of group appeals especially to younger lifestyle segments that are unattached, mobile risk-takers, or to older lifestyle segments that are retired, empty nesters, and modestly affluent. Such groups are often the entry point into the small-group experience for the "Echo" generation. Mission Groups are often associated with worship options for healing and mission connection, and with church leaders who are CEOs and pilgrims.

Of course, these distinctions are only *tendencies*. Especially in the category of "small groups," there is no substitute for strategic listening in each local context.

Leadership

One of the important differences between true small groups and groups that are simply small is that true small groups emphasize strong leadership. The leader guides the group through whatever process they have established as their routine, facilitates communication by encouraging the shy to speak out and the vocal to listen carefully, welcomes new members, interprets and focuses accountability to group principles, and generally creates an environment for personal growth.

Leadership in a midweek small group is perhaps more important than leadership in Sunday school. The leader must work harder to overcome distractions, manage time, and balance the activities of prayer, action, learning, and sharing. The traditional isolation, time restraints, and behavioral assumptions of Sunday morning are not present midweek. The place of meeting is usually not in the church building, and the leader must plan ahead more intentionally to provide whatever resources are necessary for the meeting.

Small-group ministry usually has higher expectations for leadership than the average Sunday school—or at least they are more rigorously applied. Small-group leaders are generally expected to be credible spiritual leaders of the church, and their lifestyle models the core values and bedrock beliefs of the congregation. They have a high commitment to personal and spiritual growth, the maturity to manage different personalities in a group, the openness to listen to different perspectives without judgment, and the courage to cope with the emotions and conflicts of deepening intimacy.

Rotated Leaders

Some lifestyle segments prefer to participate in small groups where leadership is *rotated*. The group decides from week to week who will facilitate group process the next time. This is particularly common when group participants all share similar levels of spiritual maturity or topical expertise, or when the discussion of a group meeting relies on the expertise of a print or video resource. The church board may recognize a group, and each group might receive regular prayers in worship, but there is no particular leader who is accountable for the success or failure of a group.

Basic training and regular coaching for small groups is not a high priority. Lifestyle segments often welcome a broad orientation to small-group life and may use a manual that each leader follows when it is his or her turn to guide a meeting. These lifestyle segments often rely on the pastor or professional staff to intervene in any small-group crisis, or occasionally to participate in a small group to ensure its alignment with the mission and identity of the church. The pastor or staff may occasionally coach group leaders to facilitate conversations (especially to encourage shy people, manage vocal people, and resolve personality conflicts), but such coaching is usually initiated by the occasional group leader.

Rotated leaders tend to emphasize their responsibilities as hosts and facilitators. They create a healthy environment for conversation and confidentiality, provide refreshments, manage time, and welcome newcomers. If there is a curriculum (print, video, or Internet), they enable access to the resource.

Lifestyle segments prefer rotated leaders for different reasons. Some prefer to rotate leadership because they do not have strong values for training. They assume most church members can have the gifts to host and facilitate a small group. Other lifestyle segments rotate leadership because participants all have strong opinions and want to ensure that every perspective has an opportunity to influence discussion. Still other lifestyle segments rotate leadership because their primary investment in small groups is to develop or maintain friendships, encourage personal support in life struggles, or pray for one another. Some lifestyle segments assume a broad consensus about key values and beliefs in both church and community and rely on peer pressure to hold one another accountable for spiritual disciplines.

Designated Leaders

Some lifestyle segments prefer to participate in small groups where there is a *designated* leader. This leader is officially appointed by the pastor or priest, authorized by the church board, and occasionally commissioned in worship. Designated leaders usually receive formal training, although the rigor of that training may vary from church to church. Training may simply be a day apart, or it may require multiple sessions and regular upgrade coaching through the year. Training ensures that the leader lives up to the expectations defined earlier, and it often provides advanced preparation in conflict resolution, shaping spiritual habits, and faith formation.

The designated leader guides the group from start to finish. The leader sets the covenant for meeting time, timeline, location, and confidentiality. The leader may choose a curriculum, arbitrate who can be a member of the group, and manage unexpected crises. Most importantly, the designated leader keeps the group focused on the purpose of the group, aligned with the mission of the church, within the boundaries of values and convictions defined by the church. This protects the unity of the church and guards against unwanted factions and frictions.

Lifestyle segments that prefer designated leaders have different motivations. Some are very sensitive to status and authority and want the group leader to have the endorsement of the church. Others value the importance of training and insist that any leader should be especially equipped to lead a team. Still others struggle with low self-esteem and do not expect that any group participant will have the expertise or confidence to lead a group. These lifestyle segments generally value small groups for educational content, spiritual integrity, and practical help to overcome problems and improve quality of life. They may look to many other informal clubs and associations to build friendships.

Remember that some lifestyle segments may be quite ambivalent about small-group leadership. They will accept designated leaders and take their turn in rotational leadership. The most ambivalent lifestyle segments seem to be relatively affluent suburbanites with stable careers. They may have also moved less frequently and maintain residence in the same community or neighborhood over longer periods. If they "shop" for a "good church," they may be more concerned about the choices for small-group topics and the way small groups are structured.

Structure

The basic principles of small-group process (prayer, action, learning, sharing) are common to all lifestyle segment expectations for small groups. Most lifestyle segments will readily embrace the habit of creating covenants that establish goals and convenient practices customized for group participants. However, there are distinct tendencies to choose between groups that are based on a curriculum versus groups that are based on affinity.

In the previous discussion of educational preferences, I contrasted choices in content between "curricular" and "topical." This emphasized the preference of some lifestyle segments for groups that used some standardized print, video, or audio resource for group study and the preference of others for groups that pursue a topic of common interest that might use any number of resources or rely simply on the personal perspectives of participants.

Here, the preference of lifestyle segments is based on different ways to define the focus of the group. Some lifestyle segments prefer the focus to be a particular resource that is the object of study. Discussion is organized around that study guide and does not stray far from the study guide. This is particularly useful for lifestyle segments that prefer groups with rotated leaders. Other lifestyle segments prefer the focus to be a particular affinity. Discussion may refer to many resources but always involves some shared enthusiasm. Discussion is organized around shared identity or common concern. This is particularly common for lifestyle segments that prefer designated leaders.

The choice between curriculum-based and affinity-based groups is not really determined by age. It may be influenced by cultural heritage. Western Europeans familiar with the public or private educational systems and educational philosophies of the Enlightenment and Industrial Revolution may tend to prefer curriculum-based groups (just as they may prefer curriculum-based methods for Christian education). Publics with different heritages (Eastern European, African, Asian, East Asian, Caribbean, Creole, South American, and Aboriginal) may tend to prefer affinity-based small groups. Some lifestyle segments may eschew any structure of "small group" and prefer one-to-one mentoring relationships or extended family personal growth environments.

Curriculum Groups

A "curriculum" is a specific study guide. It may be print or multi-media. The study guide *defines* the group. Lifestyle segments that prefer this kind of small group often name the group after the guide. These include various kinds of Bible study groups, groups that use denominational study books to explore Scripture and doctrine, and groups that study specific resources about Christian financial management, church growth, marriage enrichment, and other topics. The structure of the group is set by the prescribed exercises, discussion questions, or stories in the resource.

Fewer and fewer lifestyle segments have a general tendency to prefer Curriculum Groups. The lifestyle segments that do are often groups that have been traditional participants in established churches, and who are more likely to value Christian education resources authorized by denominations and released through denominational publishing houses. They are also lifestyle segments that prefer highly structured learning experiences. These segments tend to build relationships around intentional dialogue, rather than follow dialogue as it evolves from deepening relationships.

Note that only some lifestyle segments that prefer curricula as the methodology for Christian education also prefer curriculum-based small groups. This is because Christian education is often associated with Sunday school. The same people who prefer curricular methods for children's education (kindergarten through fifth or eighth grade) may not actually prefer curriculum-based small groups that are mid-week and focus on teens and adults. Youth groups, for example, may be organized by affinity rather than curriculum. Adult groups may be organized by topics rather than curriculum.

The lifestyle segments that do extend their preference for curriculum from Sunday school for all ages to midweek small groups tend to be strongly committed to established Protestant and Catholic traditions. They are more concerned with maintaining uniformity for faith and practice and use small groups as a means to establish closer ties with a particular tradition. Small groups are a means to assimilate newcomers into church membership and to bind members more closely together into a common identity that contrasts with that of the general public. The curriculum is often provided by a denominational office or a trusted agent compatible with a particular tradition.

The sophistication of the curriculum used by small groups will vary according to the affluence and educational level of participants. Some resources may be of considerable theological depth, while others may be very practical, exploring liturgical practices, ethical issues, or Christian seasons of the year.

It is important to distinguish between a "class" and a "curriculum-based small group." A "class" is a modern grouping of individuals who gather in a classroom environment to learn a particular subject. Their interaction with each other is largely coincidental, because their primary focus is the teacher or resource for the class. When the class is over, each individual goes his or her own way and applies the information independently.

A "curriculum-based small group" is a postmodern grouping of covenanted participants who gather in an informal conversation environment. While they focus on a particular subject, their interaction with each other is very intentional and the primary way they learn. Each individual intentionally helps others learn, and the leader not only teaches or presents the curriculum, but deliberately guides participants to develop their spiritual lives and build trusting relationships. When the group is over, participants remain in friendship and mutual support of one another.

Affinity Groups

An "affinity" is much more than a topic. It may be a shared cultural identity, language, or tradition; or a shared hobby, activity, or interest; or a shared problem or need. The most common affinity groups focus on crafts, hobbies, music, and other interests. Affinities might also include shared mission activities or social service priorities. Personal support or therapeutic groups for addiction recovery, rehabilitation, and health are all types of affinity groups. Finally, groups that combine people who all share specific life challenges are affinity groups: singles, single parents, unemployed, physically disabled, retirees, and so on.

More and more lifestyle segments prefer affinity groups. These people tend to embrace a more relational and fluid style of personal growth. The primary goal is to deepen relationships and then allow discussion to evolve out of the increasing honesty and trust of the group. These lifestyle segments feel too constrained by any specific resource and are often wary of the hidden biases of denominationally approved study guides. They often appreciate cross-disciplinary, cross-cultural, and interreligious dialogue.

Note that lifestyle segments that prefer experiential methods for Christian education (that is, Sunday school) usually prefer affinity-based small groups. These small groups may or may not use audio, video, and Internet technology to enhance conversations. The goal is simply to make the small group as dialogical and interactive as possible. This might involve a visiting "expert" to make presentations, but dialogue will always be a major strategy of the group.

Remember that the choice to study a curriculum (book, video, exercise, and so on) may also fit into the overall preference for affinity groups. In these cases, the participants are pragmatically committed to a study process as the best way to address some shared enthusiasm, but the study of a curriculum is not their natural tendency. Once that small group ends, they are likely to return to an affinity-based group.

Affinity groups might also be described as peer mentoring groups. Participants are "peers" in any sense of shared experience, and the goal of the group is to help one another go deeper into a shared enthusiasm, and further in using a shared enthusiasm to bless people beyond the group. Therefore, an affinity group might also become a mission group. This is not a task group or committee, because they continue the small-group disciplines of prayer, learning, and intimate sharing even as they are engaged in a particular activity.

11. Outreach Alternatives

Church planners want to discern potential for outreach among each lifestyle segment. Alternatively, they want to discover what kinds of outreach are most likely to motivate the generosity of their own volunteers. Generalizations in this area of ministry are more difficult, because the motivation for outreach can be very personal. It is vitally important that any generalization based on lifestyle segment expectations be tested *in context* through listening strategies like prayer walks, focus groups, listening triads, and interviews with local social service, health care, and educational professionals. Church planners should bear in mind two influential factors.

First, there are four distinct ways in which any lifestyle segment might engage outreach. Although each method of outreach can *affect* the mission field in positive ways, some methods *accelerate* church growth more than others do.[1] Church growth *accelerates* faster in the following order (from least powerful to most powerful):

- Property loan or rental (for example, permitting outside groups to use church property for activities)

- Board leadership (for example, appointing a church member to serve as a director for a nonprofit agency)

- Charitable contribution (for example, raising money for a good cause or forwarding money to an agency beyond the congregation)

171

- Volunteer support (for example, committing church members to volunteer "hands-on" in mission work)

The first method results in the least church growth, while the last method results in the most church growth. This is because volunteers who are "hands-on" in mission grow as leaders, and their interaction with seekers invites more people into church life. Therefore, whatever category of outreach is most relevant to a lifestyle segment, it is usually more productive to follow this strategic planning principle: *only support mission with property or money if you send church volunteers as well.*

Demographic studies can reveal the charitable giving priorities of the major lifestyle segments in any given mission field. These include contributions to the following:

- Religious organizations
- Educational institutions
- Social service programs
- Public radio
- Public television
- Private foundations
- Health care
- Environmental causes
- Political organizations

This research helps leaders identify the priorities for a specific region or lifestyle segment, and can also set a benchmark for generosity that can be compared favorably or unfavorably with the current generosity of church members.

Once again, each lifestyle segment has distinct priorities when they volunteer their resources. Some lifestyle segments prefer a church stewardship and financial management strategy that encourages designated giving (rather than unified budgets) so that they can focus charitable donations. These preferences are explained later in this book in the section for lifestyle expectations for church financial management. Although it would be difficult to generalize for a lifestyle segment, specific individuals and households might focus charitable donations in one category of outreach and devote their volunteer energy to another category of outreach.

A second factor to bear in mind is that each lifestyle segment might have different preferences for outreach they *receive from others* and outreach that they are predisposed to *give to others.* It is probably easier to generalize the former than the latter. Preferences for outreach *received* will be determined by contextual needs and aspirations within each lifestyle segment, whereas preferences for outreach *given* will be shaped by many things (including the priorities of a denomination and the heartbursts inspired by the Holy Spirit).

There are seven basic categories of outreach. Expectations for outreach *received* and outreach *given* may be the same for many lifestyle segments. However, church planners may want to make two distinct lists. The options include *survival, recovery, health, quality of life, human potential, interpersonal relationships, and human destiny.* These are shaped by the life context and the spiritualities that are common for each lifestyle segment.

Survival

When church people think of outreach, their first thought is almost always ministries of survival. This kind of outreach focuses on basic needs for food, shelter, and clothing; subsistence income; and basic health care. Outreach often addresses acute, short-term needs. Emergency relief, especially for natural disasters, and occasionally from mob violence and war, often evokes passionate self-sacrifice from many lifestyle segments.

Longer-term care often involves "depot" ministries. These are ministries that collect, store, and distribute food, clothing, old furniture, and basic household utensils. Many churches dedicate unused space in the church building or rent distribution facilities convenient to those in need. Similarly, churches may transform unused space into dormitories or shelters for the homeless, or serve basic nourishing food to the poor.

Much of survival outreach can be done with just basic training for volunteers. Aside from hands-on service, churches do mission through redevelopment of space and in-kind donations and often rely on financial subsidies from the community or denomination. More complex survival ministries, like medical clinics and job placement centers for temporary labor, may require trained and paid personnel, and volunteers are more likely to serve on nonprofit boards.

Survival ministries may be favored by lifestyle segments that are either very poor (offering hands-on service) or very affluent (offering professional expertise). Very poor lifestyle segments may include newly arrived immigrants, individuals and couples just starting independent living and new careers, the flotsam and jetsam of disadvantaged people often described as "urban grit," struggling agricultural and mining communities, fixed-income seniors, and anyone who is just "getting by." Very affluent lifestyle segments may include white-collar suburbanites, philanthropically minded upper classes, entrepreneurial professionals, and small-town solid citizens.

These lifestyle segments are all groups to which nonprofit agencies look for volunteers. The people in these lifestyle segments are often volunteering for more than one charitable organization during the year or are often clients of more than one charitable organization a year.

Recovery

Addiction is one of the top health issues in North America today, and certainly it pervades all lifestyle segments. Nevertheless, certain segments will elevate this outreach ministry as a higher priority than others. Any addiction intervention program may be the focus. Programs often address dependencies on alcohol, illegal or prescription drugs, tobacco, gambling, and pornography, but almost any obsessive behavior can be the focus.

The program strategy may involve peer accountability or professional therapy. Twelve-step programs, personal counseling, healing worship services, holistic remedies, and spiritual disciplines may all be involved. Small groups, clinics, and halfway houses may be some of the tactics. Churches often work in collaboration with other nonprofit organizations and networks.

Lifestyle groups that may be particularly interested in receiving this outreach also include groups that are very affluent or very poor, but especially those that are subject to peer pressure or prone to broken relationships, or who live in geographical or cultural isolation. Age may not be a decisive factor, because the abuse of prescription drugs and over-the-counter pharmaceuticals is growing among older generations. Teenagers and aging boomers can all have addictions to gambling and pornography. Lifestyle segments that tend to be rootless; fringe to the surrounding normative publics, especially materialistic or consumer oriented; status conscious; or separated from family support are all more vulnerable to self-destructive behavior patterns that they chronically deny.

The desire to *contribute* to recovery ministries depends more on personal and family experience than on belonging to any particular lifestyle segment. However, the same lifestyle segments that are most vulnerable to addiction may also provide the most active and generous volunteers to address addiction issues. The continuity of identity between volunteers and clients is probably more important in this particular outreach option than in any other. Credibility depends on a profound empathy with those in need.

Health

The health care crisis may be more severe in the United States than in Canada and Australia, but worry about health is universal as the overall population ages. This outreach area may focus on mental or physical fitness, disease prevention, wellness, healing and rehabilitation, and therapy. Programs are often related to counseling centers, healing therapies, diet and exercise disciplines, and holistic spiritualities.

Churches often focus on professional staff development (parish nurses, visiting pastors, and Christian counselors). They may also partner with health care institutions to provide support groups for people who are fighting disease, caregivers in homes or institutions, and extra activities for people with disabilities. Day care for seniors is a growing ministry for households caring for aging parents. These are often tied to tactics for healthy hospitality, caregiving and healing strategies for mission-targeted worship, and midweek small groups.

Lifestyle segments seeking this kind of outreach are often in more-established communities (older suburbs, small towns, and rural communities) where there is a higher expectation for families to take care of their own, but family systems are breaking down to do it. Churches often function as extended families to provide informal, semiprofessional, or professional support. Institutional visitation, parish nurse ministries, wellness clinics, counseling centers, and other forms of outreach abound.

Some urban lifestyle segments are losing direct access to health services because they lack insurance or face long waiting lists. Poorer and older lifestyle segments may not be able to afford additional health services in an increasingly two-tiered system. This creates opportunities for lifestyle segments oriented around professional specialties to provide free clinics, therapeutic ministries, mental health resources, and counseling services. More affluent lifestyle segments see opportunities to fund faith-based health care nonprofits.

Quality of Life

There are a number of lifestyle segments for whom the previous outreach concerns are not high priorities. These lifestyle segments may already have the basic necessities of life, are less pressured by obsessive behavior and addictions, and are more middle-aged and generally healthy. They tend to be more stable than mobile. Many own homes or have realistic expectations to own homes. They value the common good and seek good relationships in their neighborhoods. Their concerns have to do with social well-being. Their priorities are to improve the quality of personal, family, and community life.

Some of these lifestyle segments include younger and older families. They are particularly concerned about quality education and interested in programs for tutoring, higher education, specialized training, good schools, sound curricula, and extracurricular activities. They may look for Christian education alternatives to public schools, or for churches that are highly active in the wider school system. They appreciate programs that protect children from bullying and provide safe, cross-cultural opportunities for family interaction.

Quality-of-life programs are often related to crime prevention, safety, and environmental protection. People are concerned about eliminating gangs, prostitution, drug dealing, and poverty. They seek leadership for conflict intervention and mediation and join advocacy campaigns against prejudice and for peace. Quality-of-life concerns may be local, regional, or global. The issues vary among lifestyle segments, but the priority is to provide environments for personal safety, healthy family life, efficient systems of justice, and mutual respect.

Opportunities to improve quality of life are often unfortunately neglected in small towns and established communities. Churches may feel obliged to feed the homeless, for example, but the few people motivated to do it must travel some distance to accomplish the mission. The disparity of context undermines empathy. Meanwhile, important issues in their own local communities may be ignored. Growing churches tend to meet local needs first, and then expand in ever-widening circles of outreach.

Interpersonal Relationships

The top priority for many people today is safe, healthy, stable intimacy. This is particularly true for college-town communities, younger singles and families, and people starting out in new phases of life. It is also true for people in military service, people living in rural or remote regions, and seniors who live separately from their children or who are widows and widowers in an aging population.

This kind of outreach focuses on marriage enrichment (and divorce recovery), healthy expressions of sexuality, sexual orientation, and safe intimate friendships. Programs often include marriage counseling and enrichment, divorce counseling, parenting counseling and training, cross-generational small groups, and any number of different fellowship and recreational ministries.

As North American culture diversifies, sensitive support and advocacy for nontraditional relationships are also significant forms of outreach. This often makes this kind of outreach more controversial within churches or in communities. It tests the *real* core values of a church and challenges the myths of "acceptance" and "friendliness" that many churches boast.

The Internet has opened a whole new world of social networks with both opportunities and dangers. This form of outreach often involves both face-to-face and digital communication. Intimacy across distances, cultures, languages, and customs is empowering and enhances multicultural relationships. Younger generations in particular consider cross-cultural sensitivity as a sign of personal and spiritual maturity.

Therefore, the lifestyle segments most interested in this kind of outreach are often more mobile than stable. A large proportion may be single (never married, divorced, or widowed) or live in relationships that are often under stress (remote environments, military personnel, or tense multicultural contexts). Some lifestyle segments are struggling to balance careers and relationships (for example, dual-career households, working families with unsupervised children, or mature households with teens). The more lifestyle segments fragment and multiply, creating more and more microcultures, the more this area of outreach becomes urgent.

Human Potential

The financial instability of the global economy, migrations of people, and employment problems for younger adults have steadily raised the importance of discovering personal potential as a high priority for outreach. Programs tend to focus on personal and vocational fulfillment, higher education, specialized training, and career counseling. The core convictions of many churches regarding spiritual gifts and individual calling connects with the aspirations of many people who feel they have yet to tap their real potential as human beings.

The inequities of the workplace and the prejudices of modern culture have pushed human potential outreach from education to advocacy. Many lifestyle segments seek help overcoming discrimination (race, gender, age, language, physical and mental disability, and so on), or overcoming poverty (paying the cost of higher education and professional training). Church programs may include foundations and scholarship funds, legal aid, corporate workshops, and vision discernment retreats.

The same lifestyle segments that are preoccupied with interpersonal relationships are often similarly concerned about human potential. This is the other side of balancing relationships and careers. These lifestyle segments are often younger or middle aged, as issues of vocation, retraining, and rethinking personal priorities become urgent. Some lifestyle segments include a high proportion of people who are "in between": between homes, between marriages, between careers, between phases of life. Any life transition elicits concerns to discern human potential.

Churches may partner with community colleges, retreat centers, and campgrounds and may create interactive websites, blogs, and coaching networks. The lifestyle segments with the highest priority for developing human potential are often very mobile, and their lower incomes do not seem to match their educational accomplishments. People in these lifestyle segments may change career paths several times, but they do not necessarily equate career success with personal fulfillment. Many are looking for opportunities to volunteer in meaningful social services, and those who can afford it are willing to travel abroad and sacrifice leisure for service. They are particularly interested in nonprofits that give them opportunities for leadership.

Human Destiny

Confidence in "salvation" can take many forms among different lifestyle segments. It can include a sense of ultimate forgiveness and acceptance, personal alignment with God's purpose in history, or surrender of lifestyle to divine will. In the context of demographic sensitivity, a primary concern for personal or community destiny emerges from complex patterns of personal and social circumstance.

The lifestyle segments that tend to be most interested in human destiny are often very conscious of social status, second- and third-generation immigrants who are anxious about preserving their roots as they adapt cautiously to new cultural expectations, mature generations in stable communities who are anxious to honor valued traditions in the face of dramatic cultural change, or well-educated and successful professionals who are reevaluating their lives and looking for hope.

This outreach priority is growing because it is no longer limited to "old-fashioned" strategies for conversion. Even lifestyle segments that are highly educated and relatively comfortable with scientific theories of the origin of humankind are increasingly asking questions about life after death, cosmic purpose, generational continuity, and the goal of history.

Outreach may have a classical focus on repentance, conversion, and baptism. However, other programs encourage whole-life stewardship and making lifestyle adjustments to align with God's purpose for creation. Some programs include classic revivals, personal witness, neighborhood canvassing, Bible distributions, and prayer chains. However, other contemporary strategies include combinations of preaching and small-group discussion, interreligious dialogue, creative celebrations of the sacraments, and other spiritual disciplines. Many of the lifestyle segments for whom human destiny is a priority also welcome high accountability for church membership and spiritual practices.

12. Facility and Technology Alternatives

Lifestyle segment preferences for programs in hospitality, worship, Christian education, small groups, and outreach clearly imply preferences for facilities and technologies:

- Hospitality preferences for "multiple" and "healthy choices" may imply preferences for kitchen upgrades, food service technologies (for example, coffee preparation), and environmental concerns for fresh air, natural light, and seating. The same lifestyle segments that prefer "the basics" and "takeout" often prefer hospitality rooms to be church basements or fellowship halls, with stackable chairs, a few metal tables, and large steel urns to brew coffee.

- Worship preferences presume adjustments for performance or participation. These imply choices for seating, stage and chancel space, acoustics and sight lines, and audio, video, and environmental control technologies. For example, preferences for inspirational worship may lead to preferences for rows of comfortable theater seating and image projection, and preferences for transformational worship may lead to preferences for movable chairs and multiple microphones. Many established churches are clearly designed for educational worship and therefore use intentional rows of fixed pews, raised lecterns, and amplified audio systems.

- Christian education preferences also imply expectations for facility and technology. For example, lifestyle segments that prefer generational and curricular education also tend to prefer well-lit, plain, traditional classrooms, with tables and chairs sized for age. Meanwhile, lifestyle segments that prefer peer group and experiential education may prefer rooms with variable lighting, color and images, and craft tables or computer centers.

- Small-group preferences reflect particular sensitivity to environments that facilitate intimacy, communication, and meditation. Curriculum-based groups gravitate toward more traditional classrooms. They may prefer to meet at the church building rather than private homes. Affinity-based groups gravitate toward social environments. They prefer to be surrounded by the equipment necessary to pursue their shared interest and meet in neutral, more public spaces. Twelve-step groups strive to protect confidentiality and may require rooms that are private, soundproof, and flexibly decorated.

- Outreach preferences directly guide how facilities and technologies are used. The success of a mission depends on the usefulness of the tools. For example, "survival" ministries require multipurpose facilities and lots of storage, or high mobility and instant communication. "Interpersonal" ministries may require warm environments and Internet technology. Traditional outreach ministries about "human destiny" often utilized natural environments (campgrounds and outdoor chapels) or deliberately used transitional physical settings (tents and drive-in theaters) to encourage spiritual transformations (conversions and lifestyle changes).

Church planners should not underestimate the symbolic power of facilities and technologies to communicate acceptance to distinct lifestyle segments. After all, the first glimpse of any public of a church is often its architecture and communication "hardware." People automatically make assumptions about the programs and process "software" that these facilities and technologies promote.

Normally, form follows function. In other words, the facilities and technologies are designed to deliver certain kinds of programs that are relevant to obtain specific measurable results. In order to reach any given lifestyle segment, leaders design the appropriate programs and then design the facilities and upgrade the technologies to deliver the programs successfully. The "form" (facility and technology) is just a container in which the programs are delivered.

However, each lifestyle segment is naturally self-centered. The natural habit of any given lifestyle segment is to consider their preferred "containers" to be the best. All others are flawed because they are irrelevant or ineffective *for us*. This leads to friction among lifestyle segments. Lifestyle segments may regard the same thing as too fancy or too plain, too quiet or too noisy, too awesome or too unfriendly.

Churches often exaggerate this self-centeredness further by false assumptions about sacred space and sacred techniques. What makes any space, object, or technique "sacred" is that it becomes a vehicle through which God touches our lives directly, but there is no general rule about what that space might look like or how that technique might operate. At one time, many things now considered by some lifestyle segments as "sacred" were considered scandalous: pews, organs, coffeemakers, indoor plumbing, central heating, and air conditioning, to name a few.

The common mistake of many church planners is to assume a particular kind of facility or technology to be sacred, and then expect the diverse and changing lifestyle segments of the community to accept it. Not only does this undermine the success of any given program, but it also encourages each lifestyle segment to perceive the church as irrelevant and judgmental. Because most churches claim to be "friendly," the inability of churches to let form follow function makes them vulnerable to charges of hypocrisy. The more adaptable a church becomes to shape space and technique around lifestyle segment preferences, the more its reputation for friendliness and relevance grows. Consider the following examples:

- A small town is overcome by exurban expansion. The people in the historic, resident lifestyle segment who happen to be church members all live in small bungalows, labor in blue-collar agricultural jobs, and eat out in local diners. The people moving in are affluent commuters living in estate homes who regularly eat out in ethnic restaurants and savor specialty refreshments. In order to welcome these new lifestyle segments, the church needs to renovate the food court, multiply choices, and buy cappuccino makers. Yet the resident members are appalled at the "waste of money."

- An urban core church with a tall steeple, gothic architecture, and historic sanctuary (with oak pews, stained glass, and celebrated pipe organ) wants to reach lifestyle segments in the neighborhoods surrounding the building. They decide to offer a transformational worship service connected with 12-step "recovery groups." Yet they are insensitive to the lifestyle expectations for interactive space, participation, contemporary instruments, and serving stations in the worship center. They insist the only place to really "worship" is in their sanctuary, and they wonder why the new worship service attracts so few people.

- A suburban church wants to grow its Sunday school. Most members are over fifty and empty nesters, but leaders are aware that young families are moving into growing subdivisions of town houses, apartments, and starter homes. The church needs to shift to a new educational strategy of cross-generational activities and experiential learning centers. They try to raise money to upgrade classrooms for video and computer technologies, drama, and crafts space, but traditional givers need to be persuaded that this is essential and not just trendy.

- A rural church feels called to become a community center and home to much-needed social services. However,
  the county has just bypassed the church property when
  expanding the highway, and the church building is isolated more than a hundred yards away down a dirt road,
  hidden in the woods, beside the cemetery. They need to
  relocate and rebuild, but they must convince the matri-
  archs and patriarchs that this break with tradition is a
  faithful mission decision.

In each case, churches are faced with the daunting challenge to
develop relevant facilities and technologies that will bless new lifestyle
segments and emerging generations. The church is literally a "comfort
zone," and only extreme sensitivity to changing expectations and God's
mission will encourage people to take the risk.

Facility

Although there *can* be great variety in regard to church architecture, it is remarkable *how little* variety there really is! The basic tendencies between "ecclesiastical" and "utilitarian" are often revealed in
the midst of church planting. Even while new Christian communities
gather in homes or rented facilities, people may decorate in certain
ways to create traditional "churchy" space. New churches often reach
a consolidation phase in which they buy property and either build or
renovate buildings. Some lifestyle segments will prefer Roman, Gothic,
or Byzantine architectural designs that deliberately remind worshipers
of ancient roots. Other lifestyle segments will go out of their way to
avoid these designs in favor of utilitarian facilities that emphasize the
relevance of the church to culture.

Affluence may be a factor in this decision. More affluent lifestyle
segments may celebrate the extra cost of ecclesiastical designs as a sign
of their appreciation of God's grace through material generosity. Poorer
lifestyle segments may deliberately reject ecclesiastical architecture as
too showy and praise God through demonstrations of austerity.

A more significant factor may be the tension between permanence and mobility. Some lifestyle segments (rich or poor) are habitually "on the move." Ecclesiastical architecture conveys a sense of permanence and suggests that the builders will remain in one place for generations. Many lifestyle segments, however, are more nomadic. They may only be confident of their residence for a few months or years and want to be able to sell the property quickly and reinvest in another church building somewhere else. Ecclesiastical architectures are notoriously hard to sell, and that reality may or may not be exactly what a group of people wants to recognize and advertise.

As North American culture diversifies, several social factors encourage a trend toward more utilitarian churches. Churches (and denominations) have fewer financial resources; individuals and families are more transient. It is also true, however, that multicultural populations tend to encourage religious organizations to "blend in" rather than "stand out." And in a secular society, overt religious behavior is more likely to undermine credibility and invite criticism. Is it possible that the more ecclesiastical the building looks, the less seeker-sensitive the congregation is? This may not be true at all in the hearts of the believers, but it may accurately describe the perceptions of emerging lifestyle segments.

Ecclesiastical

Ecclesiastical architecture makes a building "look like a church." It cannot be mistaken by observers as anything else. It replicates, or at least approximates, structures traditionally associated with churches: arches and apses, steeples and towers, and doors and windows with curves and points. The glass is colored or opaque and may be stained and leaded. Even in a new building, when contemporary by-laws require easy access, the church deliberately includes flights of stairs (and pays for extra ramps and elevators) to communicate the spirituality of "ascending" to the holy place.

The church designates a sanctuary, which is deliberately set aside for limited (sacred) use. Seating may be pews or chairs, but deliberately arranged in rows so participants face forward. The chancel or stage is raised and includes specialized furniture (pulpits, altars, fonts, and so on) that have special designated uses. The rest of the building may be more flexible, but the floor plan usually makes the sanctuary the hub for movement, and the design and color scheme of corridors, offices, and classrooms harmonizes with the central worship space.

Many old, urban church buildings have undergone several renovations and additions. Investigating the changing architecture of the facility over time is like an archeological history of changing lifestyle segments. The common transition from highly ornate, ecclesiastical construction to very plain, utilitarian construction often reveals the neighborhood changes around the church as new lifestyle segments have replaced the original ones.

Utilitarian

Utilitarian architecture makes the church "look like normal." It fits in with the rest of the buildings in the neighborhood or community. If it weren't for a sign or an exterior symbol, the church building could easily be mistaken for a movie theater, retail store, medical building, warehouse, or gymnasium. This may be cheaper than ecclesiastical architecture, but there is a theological point being made. These lifestyle segments do not emphasize the "otherness" of sacred space, but rather claim all kinds of space to be potentially sacred.

The interior of the facility is just as utilitarian as the exterior. The word "sanctuary" may not even be used to describe the worship center, because it is multipurpose space. The same room that is used for worship may be used for mission activities, fellowship gatherings, community meetings, and even child care centers. All the other rooms of the building may be deliberately multipurpose as well, with the exception of the pastor's office and the nursery.

Many suburban, small-town, and rural church buildings have also experienced several renovations and additions, especially if the congregation started as a church plant and grew. This time, the changing architecture of the building may reflect the evolution of a lifestyle segment through different phases of life. The building may have begun as a very utilitarian facility, but the later addition of a distinct "sanctuary" may have a decidedly "ecclesiastical" look. Once it was a community center; now members claim a specific tradition. Once stackable chairs were sufficient, and now pews are essential. The people in the lifestyle segment, and the church, have matured.

Symbols

Church leaders should never underestimate the power of a facility as a symbol of meaning. Architecture always *signifies* something. The church facility makes an unspoken, visual statement about the identity and purpose of a church. Church people have chosen to rent, build, or reside in a specific structure, rather than other structures, for a reason. That reason usually has nothing to do with financial resources, and everything to do with the core values and faith convictions held by the church people.

As lifestyle segments evolve, and church buildings age, the disconnections between the symbol system embedded in the facility and the shifting values and beliefs of church members can cause serious conflict. Church leaders are often surprised by the anger and conflict that seemingly simple improvements can precipitate:

- The removal of a pew to install handicapped access
- The replacement of a stained-glass window to provide fresh air or improve light
- The use of an electronic organ to replace pipes

Church leaders may be equally surprised by the anger and conflict over changes that seemed to add meaning when none was perceived:

- The introduction of padded cathedral chairs to replace stackable metal chairs
- The replacement of a music stand with a lectern for preaching
- The demolition of an intentionally "temporary" meeting room to build a permanent sanctuary

The facility itself has significance. It may not be consciously remembered until it is gone, or intentionally articulated until it is threatened. The more the facility becomes sacred in itself, rather than pointing toward something intangible and eternal, the more the symbol becomes an idol.

Most people associate symbols with visual signs, pictures, sculptures, images, and devotional objects that reveal the standards of accountability and faith convictions of the community. Lifestyle segments tend to have one of two basic preferences: "Christendom" and "Contemporary." The choice depends less on affluence and mobility, and more on age and attitude. The "Stations of the Cross," for example, can be depicted in styles deliberately reminiscent of the Middle Ages or Renaissance, or in styles that deliberately highlight multicultural realities and scenes of current life.

Christendom

Exterior and interior signs and architectural details use historic symbols associated with Christianity. These include commonly recognizable crosses, famous scenes from Bible stories, and architectural styles associated with Christian historical epochs (Gothic points, Norman arches, and so on). There are also symbols that have doctrinal significance, but which require interpretation by expert or experienced church leaders (symbols for the Trinity, Four Gospels, the Hand or Eye of God, and so on). Stained-glass windows often depict images of the saints or other historic Christian figures. These symbols were used to supplement preaching and teaching in the past, but today they simply convey a sense of continuity with salvation history and unity with the church.

In the sanctuary, Christendom symbols more effectively support worship services that have mission purposes for caregiving, inspiration, and education. These are often considered more "traditional" forms of worship, and the symbolic and architectural environment mirrors this appreciation of the struggle and victory of the church over the years. The space is quite different from other public space and is uniquely sacred. Participants know that they are a part of history.

Contemporary

Exterior and interior signs and architectural details use symbols that have broader spiritual significance. These are more immediately recognizable by young or new Christians, or by seekers for whom the history of the church is less relevant to personal spiritual growth. Symbols may include images from nature (flowers, greenery, seeds, sunrise), images related to life-cycle changes (water, wedding rings, musical notes and notations), or images that connect to popular perceptions of religion (open Bible, tablet of Ten Commandments, praying hands). Stained glass may depict victories in social justice, environmental recovery, or important figures in recent social transformation. These symbols may not be mentioned in preaching and teaching, but they convey the core values and bedrock faith convictions that shape the particular identity of a specific congregation.

In the sanctuary, contemporary symbols more effectively support worship services that have mission purposes for healing, coaching, personal transformation, and mission connection. These are often considered "non-traditional" and "seeker sensitive." The architecture deliberately mirrors the structures of other public spaces. It is more important that the unique symbols make the space "safe" rather than particularly "sacred." This means participants know what to expect from worship and how they will be treated by leaders of the church.

Technology

Church people often assume that "technology" refers to electronic devices. In fact, the term refers to any useful tool. Electronic devices like microphones and amplifiers, computers, LCD screens, projectors, digital instruments, electric guitars, cappuccino makers, dishwashers, and central vacuum cleaners are all technologies. Central heating ducts, air conditioning units, indoor plumbing, sealed window casements, and emergency lights are also technologies. Chairs, carpets, elevators, and even pulpits, lecterns, and pipe organs are also technologies.

Each lifestyle segment tends to consider certain technologies more useful than others. What they consider "useful" in hospitals, schools, and private homes may be different from what they consider "useful" in church. Businesses that manufacture or sell technologies (appliances, utilities, kitchen wares, musical instruments, furniture, floor coverings, and so on) market their wares in different ways to different lifestyle segments. Some lifestyle segments consider surround sound, LCD video screens, and flexible seating *useful*, and some segments consider these things *useless*. Some consider dishwashers and air-conditioning essential, and some consider these unnecessary extravagances. Certain technologies might not only be unimportant, but downright harmful to the church in the view of a lifestyle segment. Perhaps they contradict core values for simplicity, or they undermine the effectiveness of ministries.

Of course, there is great variation even within a lifestyle segment. Older generations tend to be more comfortable with older technologies, and younger generations tend to be more comfortable with newer technologies. Young or old, people also tend to be early, middle, and late adopters of emerging technologies. Some define their identity of openness, creativity, and risk by demonstrating their willingness to invest in emerging technologies, and others define their identity of carefulness, caution, and judiciousness by demonstrating their hesitation to invest in emerging technologies.

Church people who prefer ecclesiastical facilities and Christendom symbols also tend to be "late adopters" (careful and cautious about technology). Prior to 2000, these preferences were the most common among church members. This meant that churches were often ten to twenty years *behind* community businesses, schools, government services, and military branches in technology use. This shifted dramatically in the 1990s as computer and Internet capabilities became necessities for daily living. In the emerging millennium, churches are becoming much more aggressive to catch up with technology and are generally behind the rest of the community by only five to ten years.

Some church people may entrench certain technologies as "sacred" practices. This, too, reflects the general skepticism of some lifestyle segments about technologies that are perceived as radically changing their way of life. For example, the churches that insist that sanctuary seating *must* rely on unpadded, wooden pews, arranged in rows, as the *only* true means of worship may include lifestyle segments that *also* rely on unpadded plastic chairs and metal desks arranged in rows as the *only* effective way to educate schoolchildren. Meanwhile, the churches that upgrade to padded, movable chairs arranged in circles and conversation areas for worship may be motivated to do so because they include lifestyle segments that pressure the school to develop experiential learning centers. Church people who prefer utilitarian facilities and contemporary Christian symbols are more likely to be early adopters of new technologies. For them, the *purpose* may be sacred, but the *technologies* used to achieve the purpose are not.

There are two basic preferences regarding technology: modern and postmodern. Modern technologies include tools and tactics that emerged with the Age of Enlightenment in the eighteenth century and developed through the Industrial Revolution of the nineteenth and early twentieth centuries. The continuity of tools and tactics in agriculture, manufacturing, mining, transportation, communication, education, and early scientific investigation perfected over this time period became standard for most Christian churches. It is important to understand that when people in various lifestyle segments refer to "old" or "traditional" methods, they do *not* really mean ancient or premodern technologies that served the church for hundreds of years. They refer to tools and tactics that have become commonplace in the last centuries until the middle of the twentieth century.

Exactly when the postmodern world began to emerge is a matter of debate. Perhaps it began in the 1940s with the emergence of computer technology, or the 1960s with the emergence of the Internet. Certainly, a revolution in miniaturization and communication was transforming culture by 1981 with the introduction of the PC ("personal computer") and by 1990 with the expansion of the Internet. The very methods through which people sought abundant life dramatically changed. Technologies were being used to interconnect rational, emotional, relational, and spiritual aspects of life. As the world became a global village, so also the compartmentalization of inner life between body, mind, and spirit blended into a whole. The different perceptions of technology reveal distinct attitudes or unspoken philosophies about life.

Modern

Technology is used primarily to enhance print and oral communication. Emphasis is placed on audio and acoustical improvements. Indoors, this includes new and improved microphones and speaker systems; aids for the hard of hearing; and fabrics, tapestries, or acoustical tiles to reduce echo effects. Sanctuaries may be remodeled to elevate pulpits and lecterns, or make room for signing for the deaf. Outdoors, this means changeable and illuminated signage, security systems, ramps, and walkways. These lifestyle segments prefer lengthy printed bulletins and newsletters. Bulletin inserts supplement or duplicate oral announcements in the worship service.

Reliance on hard copy encourages progressive modern people to improve their recycling efforts for paper and printer ink. A computer may be used for word processing, printing, and filing, but many other software programs may be ignored. Storage space is important, as these lifestyle segments often keep old hymnbooks, Bibles, and Sunday school curricula for future use.

Aside from upgrades in print and oral communication, these lifestyle segments lag behind the rest of the community in other technologies. They often rely on large steel urns to brew caffeinated and decaffeinated coffees but consider more elaborate equipment to brew espresso coffee or herbal tea as unnecessary. Seating in the sanctuary and education buildings is very traditional, and office and meeting space is furnished to the standards and tastes of 1965 (around the peak of church membership in North America). Furnishings often include recycled items from the home renovations of members, so that the décor of the church reflects the décor of private homes ten years previously.

The priority to upgrade print and oral communication reflects the rationalism of the modern era. Truth is expressed in and through words more than anything else. This is reflected in musical choices. The lyrics are more important than the rhythms, and the musical instruments must be quiet enough to let people concentrate on the words that are the real message. Lifestyle segments that prefer modern technologies tend to assume that truth and meaning are essentially reasonable, relative, and controllable. These lifestyle segments often include people ages fifty-five to eighty (first-wave "boomer," "silent," and "builder" generations) and also second-generation immigrants who distance themselves from old cultural forms and seek to improve their lives through education and hard work.

Postmodern

Technology is primarily used to create environments; intensify sensory experience of sound, sight, touch, taste, and smell; and communicate on several conscious and unconscious levels, with very different kinds of people, all at once. Emphasis is particularly placed on visual communication, dramatic participation, and immediate interaction. Indoors, this includes computerized imaging with still pictures and videos, colorful and highly accessorized rooms, and wireless Internet networks. Sanctuaries may be remodeled to provide excellent sight lines and elevated stage space for drama, dance, and experimental music ensembles. Outdoors, this means digital signs and ultrabright video screens, ambient music for courtyards, and encrypted Internet and other electronic security measures.

Focus on audio and video, seamless social networks, and ongoing Internet connections encourages renovation of traditional space to upgrade electrical supply and link personal media devices. The liturgy and messages can be supplemented by images and surround sound, and even intercessory prayers can be interfaced with Internet news feeds. Participants in worship and continuing education events can browse websites and multitask. The worship service may be simulcast to other sites, or repeated in podcasts. Mobile members can participate in church activities in real time from anywhere in the world.

These lifestyle segments match or lead technology innovations in the community beyond media technology. They prefer the latest kitchen technologies designed for mobile lifestyles. Their priority is less space for food preparation, and more options for reheating and fast freezing. Seating in worship centers and education space is often very flexible to encourage freedom of movement, dialogue, and artistic expression. Furnishings are usually utilitarian, but high quality, and are comparable to the décor of the homes of church leaders.

The priority to integrate all five senses for personal growth reflects the omniliterate and beyond-rational attitudes of the postmodern era. Truth cannot be contained in words alone, and certainly not in one-sided verbal presentations. Conversation and meditation are two sides of the same coin. Dialogue, unity with nature, appreciation of the arts, and intensely personal meditation are all vehicles for truth. This is reflected in musical choices. Rhythms are just as important as lyrics, and the combination of sound and image (for example, music video) or sound and activity (for example, music and exercise) adds meaning to daily life. Lifestyle segments that prefer postmodern technologies tend to assume that truth and meaning are experienced, dynamic, and ultimately uncontrollable. These lifestyle segments often include younger people (with postmodern preferences intensifying with each young generation under age fifty-five). They also tend to include lifestyle segments with non-Western European origins.

13. Stewardship and Financial Management Alternatives

The church manages risk with one eye on organizational stability and mission effectiveness and the other eye on expectations for personal sacrifice by members and financial generosity. In each category, there are two tensions that lifestyle segments balance in different ways, just as they balance their own personal and household finances in different ways:

- *Organizational stability* for a church is generally encouraged by unified budgets, just as family stability is generally encouraged by a common pool of money shared by all members of a household. Mission effectiveness for a church is generally encouraged by designated giving, just as personal growth is encouraged by separate pools of money controlled by each member of a household.

- *Financial generosity* for a church, and for a household, is generally encouraged by informed philanthropy. Individuals gather detailed information about charities and decide what percentage of their personal disposable income they are willing to give to specific public services. On the other hand, personal sacrifice for a church, and for a household, is generally encouraged by lifestyle coaching.

Individuals shape their lifestyles around certain attitudes and habits, and daily money management reflects their core values and convictions.

The way lifestyle segments balance these aspects of risk management in their personal and household lives is usually reflected in their expectations for the church.

Lifestyle segment preferences for leadership often reveal preferences for different kinds of fund-raising and financial management habits. Individual participants in any given lifestyle segment may have individual income preferences and investment strategies, but they generally expect the church to manage money in certain ways:

- Leaders who are characteristically Caregivers and Enablers tend to be more cautious about risk and more traditional in money management. They prefer unified budgets so they can subsidize programs by consensus and avoid fractious competition. They prefer informed philanthropy so they can help church members make financial decisions that can be justified in institutional settings and partner with other charitable organizations or denominational agencies. Their members often describe themselves as a "church family," and this identity assumes financial management habits that are practiced in their own households.

- Leaders who are characteristically CEOs and Visionaries tend to be selectively cautious or adventurous in money management and want the budget to align perfectly with the vision and strategic outcomes defined annually by the organization. Therefore, they tend to prefer unified budgets to protect organizational stability, but lifestyle coaching (and not just informed philanthropy) to train members to model generous lifestyles. Their members often describe themselves as a "body of Christ," and this identity implies a common resource of energy, but individual specializations and unique personalities.

- Leaders who are characteristically Disciplers, Mentors, and Pilgrims tend to be risk-takers. They want personal financial management to be accountable to extreme standards of Christian practice. They want individual Christians to align their whole lives with a clear personal mission. Therefore, they tend to prioritize designated giving and lifestyle coaching at the risk of organizational stability. Their members often describe themselves as a "mission movement" or "pilgrim band," and this identity encourages trust for individuals to have greater control of how they give and spend money.

Leaders determine the congregation's approach to finances, and the cultural conditioning of the lifestyle segment to which the leader belongs will determine that leader's attitude. Caregivers and Enablers tend to finance program development first and assume that personal growth will emerge from program participation. Disciplers, Mentors, and Pilgrims tend to finance leadership development first and assume that programs will emerge as people grow. CEOs and Visionaries tend to blend program and leadership development, pragmatically doing whatever it takes to achieve organizational outcomes.

This pattern explains the comparative success (or lack of success) of various kinds of stewardship resources produced by denominations, Christian publishers, and individual congregations. As the diversity of lifestyle segments grows, it becomes increasingly difficult to mass distribute an effective stewardship resource. I already described the strategic mistake of labeling any particular facility or technology "sacred" in the previous section. That same mistake is often repeated by churches in regard to financial management. Churches are prone to label some fund-raising and financial management strategies as good or bad (biblical, traditional, or authorized, as opposed to corporate, entrepreneurial, or competitive). In fact, different fund-raising and management strategies are simply effective in one lifestyle segment and ineffective in another.

Most denominational stewardship resources are designed to support pastors who are Caregivers and Enablers serving "family churches." This is how most seminaries train pastors, and this is how most churches are shaped. However, these churches tend to be shrinking as lifestyle segment diversity increases, and the stewardship resources are less and less effective. They all tend to emphasize organizational stability and financial generosity and encourage unified budgets and informed philanthropy. Many of these stewardship resources originally included tactics for every-member visitation, but these tactics usually disappear in favor of newsletters, announcements, and fund-raising projects. This is because personal, lively *conversation* around financial priorities is not really necessary if the ultimate goals are organizational stability and financial generosity.

Church resources designed by megachurches, multisite churches, and individual congregations tend to support pastors who are Disciplers, Mentors, and Pilgrims. They may or may not be traditionally trained in seminaries. These churches are often growing because they are more sensitive to the diversity of lifestyle segments emerging around them. Their stewardship resources emphasize mission effectiveness and personal sacrifice and encourage designated giving and lifestyle coaching. These stewardship resources almost always include tactics for household visitation or small-group discussion. This is because personal, lively *interaction* around financial priorities with a credible spiritual leader or elder is *necessary* if the ultimate goals are mission effectiveness and personal sacrifice.

Both the business and the nonprofit sectors have largely awakened to the connection among leadership, lifestyle segments, and financial management preferences. Retailers for homes, cars, appliances, and other high-cost items have multiplied options for financing. Even credit card companies realize that it is in their self-interest to provide more options to balance their business stability with sensitivity to client aspirations. Charitable organizations have also been responsive to the changing, diversifying preferences of lifestyle segments, and charitable giving and volunteerism has been consistently growing. Only the institutional church lags behind. Churches still tend to assume that the stability of the ecclesiastical institution and the limited goal of personal financial generosity are all that matter to the public. In fact, many publics have other priorities.

There are two basic categories or tensions for stewardship and financial management, and each one involves the balance of two distinct tendencies.

The Tension between Stability and Effectiveness

This tension may best be understood as risk management. Financial consultants help individuals develop their investment portfolios based on their unique personalities and ambitions. Clients who seek high financial returns in shorter periods of time invest in stocks that are more vulnerable to economic and social changes. Clients who are more cautious about upsetting their stable lifestyles invest in stocks that may have lower yields but are less vulnerable to change. Most clients in a time of economic turmoil balance their investment portfolios to manage risk.

The same is true for churches. Church leaders develop a financial plan that reflects the expectations and anxieties of the lifestyle segments surrounding the church. Churches that want to maximize effectiveness are very open to change and eager to have a large impact on the mission field. They take great risks in order to achieve significant change. Churches that want to ensure institutional stability are less open to internal change and more conservative in outreach. They take few risks in order to maintain institutional stability. Some lifestyle segments balance the financial management plan to maximize mission; other lifestyle segments balance the financial management plan to maximize stability.

Unified Budgets

Some lifestyle segments prefer unified budgets. This budget may be a "line" budget, in which every income and expense occupies a distinct line in the ledger, or it may be a "narrative" budget, in which income streams and expenses are grouped to describe distinct ministries. The point, however, is the same. They assume that people will contribute money to a single organizational budget, and a central administrative board will disburse funds for personnel, program, property, and other institutional overhead.

There may be a few options. Income from bequests and trusts may be designated for specific uses (property repairs, organ funds, memorials, and so on). Options for giving may be expanded to include debt retirement, capital improvements, denominational funds, or memorials in addition to the general fund for operations. Still, these lifestyle segments prefer to give money to the institution itself, rather than designate their giving to any particular ministry or mission of the church. They trust a central administrative board to set priorities and disburse funds.

The result is that creative ideas and innovative missions are almost always considered "second-mile giving," and the top priority (or "first-mile giving") is always the perpetuation of ongoing programs, salaries, and maintenance. Churches preserve stability first and evaluate risk with extreme caution. The central administrative board is usually made up of members with longer tenure and a high priority to honor the programmatic comfort zones and historical consciousness of the members.

Unified budgets are often encouraged by denominations. This ensures that a portion of congregational giving is reliably forwarded to fund denominational salaries, publishing, and global mission projects. It avoids competitiveness in fund-raising and reduces the potential for conflict. It also allows denominations to engage in extraordinary ministries and support unpopular causes because the central administration determines how funds will be disbursed from the general income stream.

The lifestyle segments that prefer unified budgets, and therefore balance the financial management plan in favor of institutional stability, tend to be those publics that have historically been church members. They also tend to be older, married, and in fairly traditional family units. They tend to be homeowners rather than renters, and they tend to have average residency over five years in any one location. They may also be the adult children of veteran churchgoers, who follow parental expectations for social networking and assimilation.

Designated Giving

Some lifestyle segments prefer to give to distinct capital pools. They want to designate their giving. The capital pools are not just narrative descriptions of different ministries, but distinct giving destinations. These lifestyle segments want to maintain control of their giving so that money that is given for a particular purpose *must actually be spent* for that purpose and nothing else. There may still be a central administrative board, and even a single bank account, but the accounting must be so transparent that givers can be confident that their contributions go to the program, mission, or project that is their personal priority.

There are many giving options. In addition to a general fund to pay property maintenance and necessary institutional fees, every ongoing program or creative project competes for attention. These lifestyle segments prefer to customize their own charitable giving portfolio. Innovative programs are more readily funded, and ongoing programs must demonstrate their effectiveness in higher mission impact in order to continue to receive funding. Ministries and missions become the "first-mile giving," and whatever is left over is given to institutional maintenance as "second-mile giving."

This pattern of designated giving extends to personnel funding. Lifestyle segments that prefer designated giving are less likely to value tenured leadership. Paid staff leaders are evaluated on mission results rather than certifications or denominational allegiance. Lifestyle segments that prefer unified budgets tend to value pastors who are Caregivers or Enablers, while lifestyle segments that prefer designated giving tend to value pastors who are CEOs, Visionaries, Mentors, and Pilgrims.

Designated giving is often discouraged by denominations. Mission might yield more results, and ministries may be forced to be more effective. However, the denomination is less able to fund extraordinary projects or unpopular causes. Competitiveness in fund-raising increases the risk of conflict. It is more difficult to train and place clergy. Historical sites may not be well preserved, and classic programs may be underfunded.

The lifestyle segments that prefer designated giving, and therefore balance the financial plan in favor of mission effectiveness, tend to be those publics that have historically tended to be fringe to church membership. Increasingly, they are also publics traditionally associated with church membership that have become alienated from denominations through disagreements about public policy or scandals regarding funded personnel. These lifestyle segments tend to be younger, single, or in nontraditional relationships, and nontraditional households. They tend to be renters rather than homeowners and live very mobile lifestyles.

The Tension between Sacrifice and Generosity

This tension may best be understood as measuring the cost of discipleship. "Generosity" is usually associated with *financial* giving in particular and is a response to informed philanthropy. "Sacrifice" is more broadly associated with seven distinct "cost centers":[1]

- The cost of changing tradition
- The cost of changing attitude
- The cost of changing leadership
- The cost of changing organization
- The cost of changing property
- The cost of upgrading technology
- The cost of financial investment

The "cost of discipleship" more broadly represents the degree of personal sacrifice, and the readiness to endure personal stress, that will be expected of church members.

Life coaches help people align their lifestyles to express their compassion and pursue important goals. In a free-market economic culture, and in countries of great affluence, discipleship is measured by financial generosity. On the other hand, life coaches also help people shape their lifestyles so that they can prioritize time and energy. People will reduce waste, simplify living, and concentrate resources to achieve what is most important to them.

The same is true for churches. "Stewardship" has always been a more complex ecclesiastical term than many pastors or denominations suspect. Some lifestyle segments think of "stewardship" simply in terms of financial generosity and concentrate their efforts on fund-raising. Other lifestyle segments think of "stewardship" more broadly in terms of lifestyle changes and concentrate their efforts on expanding compassion and prioritizing good causes.

Charitable giving to nonprofit organizations, foundations, health care institutions, and educational centers has been growing exponentially in North America every year (with a brief plateau in 2001), despite economic recessions. However, benevolent giving to churches in particular has been on a plateau since around 1965. One reason for this is that charities in social sectors other than the church have understood how lifestyle segments strive to balance the cost of discipleship in different ways. They can customize year-round strategies for lifestyle coaching in addition to specific programs for fund-raising.

Informed Philanthropy

Some lifestyle segments think of stewardship primarily as financial generosity. They are motivated to give money through informed philanthropy. This means that they prefer to gather all possible information about how any ministry or mission project will raise, invest, and disburse money to achieve its benevolent goals. They want to know the ethical and theological assumptions of money managers, the networks or partnerships with which they work, and the measurable outcomes they strive to achieve.

These lifestyle segments are particularly keen to avoid unreasonable institutional overhead costs, and churches have been particularly vulnerable to this criticism in recent decades. People fear that churches will divert money to shore up unnecessary staffing models and organizational structures from traditional institutional practices, or abuse the trust of investors and use funds for unadvertised purposes. These lifestyle segments are increasingly likely to compare church overhead costs with those of other parachurch or charitable organizations and give money to these other organizations rather than the church.

Information can come in any form: sermons or lectures, printed books and pamphlets, video clips, and Internet websites. If an every-member visitation is part of the fund-raising strategy, then visitors must be personally excited about the ministries and mission projects of the church and quite knowledgeable about financial management and mission results. Visitors are often officers and committee members.

The response to information can also come in any form: cash, checks, and pledges. These lifestyle segments are less likely to preauthorize debits from their account on an ongoing basis, preferring to update their information and make separate, informed decisions. If the lifestyle segment prefers unified budgets, this means that the church may do several fund-raising projects each year. If the lifestyle segment prefers designated giving, this means there will be constant and competing fund-raising programs through the year.

The lifestyle segments that prefer informed philanthropy are often traditional participants in established churches. They tend to be older and more affluent, with occupational backgrounds from middle management in business, government, and education, and likely to manage a larger investment portfolio for retirement. They also tend to be of Anglo-European descent, living in culturally homogeneous households, in fairly traditional marriages or relationships. In addition to church donations, they often make donations to public radio, health and education institutions, and established charitable nonprofits. Financial commitments are made independently by each household, usually with complete confidentiality. They expect to receive a tax receipt, and therefore they are most urgent to gather philanthropic information in the fall of each year.

Lifestyle Coaching

Some lifestyle segments think of stewardship primarily as a lifestyle choice. They make financial commitments only in a wider context of lifestyle adjustments. Indeed, they rarely give money to ministries or mission projects in which they do not have a personal, vested interest. They often actively volunteer in the ministries or missions to which they donate money, or they personally participate in learning events, public policy debates, or activities sponsored by the organization that receives their money. Their financial giving choices mirror their lifestyle preferences and express their personal passions and priorities.

These lifestyle segments are particularly eager to avoid any hint of hypocrisy, and churches have been particularly vulnerable to this criticism in recent decades. They will not give to a church mission for the poor or homeless, for example, if they know that the pastor, board members, or denominational leaders drive expensive cars or live extravagant lifestyles. These lifestyle segments will compare the lifestyle integrity of church leaders to that of nonprofit or social service leaders and give money to the charity with the best leadership model.

Lifestyle coaching has many dimensions. Personal counseling, programs, curricula, and training events all help people align their daily living (including daily living expenses) to specific core values and mission purposes. People are coached to simplify their lifestyles, divest themselves of unnecessary things, invest their time and energy in essential goals, eliminate debt to credit card companies and banks, and embrace tithing. They may even go so far as to embrace "reverse tithing" (an attitude with which people dedicate everything to God and expect to receive a small portion back to survive). If an every-member visitation is part of the lifestyle coaching strategy, then visitors must be passionate about the vision of the church and models of spiritual life. Visitors are often staff, small-group leaders, and board members.

The response to lifestyle coaching is simpler, more purposeful living. People tend deliberately to choose smaller homes, more efficient transportation, more environmentally friendly consumer habits, and less self-centered and more volunteer-oriented vacations. They often support mission-driven debt by a church because they have achieved debt freedom as a household. If the lifestyle segments prefer unified budgets, then they will have very high expectations for the moral character and spiritual credibility of staff and boards. If the lifestyle segments prefer designated giving, then they will expect congregational or denominational volunteers to be active in the ministries or missions that are funded and directly interact with church members to update progress and results.

The lifestyle segments that prefer lifestyle coaching are often relatively new or renewed Christians, or active participants in new church developments. They tend to be younger and less affluent, with occupational backgrounds from senior management, small business ownership, or blue-collar labor; they are more likely to have occupational backgrounds in manufacturing and transportation, service industries, clerical work, and health care; they often rely on basic pension plans and government help for retirement. They also tend to be from east European, south European, Hispanic, East Indian, Caribbean, Pacific Rim, or aboriginal heritages or live in heterogeneous households and multicultural relationships. In addition to church participation, they tend to volunteer their time for other local community social services. Financial commitments are often made in conversation with a peer group. They may not expect a tax receipt, but they give considerable thought to spending their tax refund.

14. Communication Alternatives

Each lifestyle segment tends to rely on distinct kinds of media to share information and network with colleagues. Because there is a variety of media, these preferences tend to be combinations of media preferences. There will be continuity between their preferences in communication and their preferences in the other ministry application areas:

- Communication includes how people make new acquaintances and connect with friends and family. Compare these preferences with the hospitality alternatives preferred by each lifestyle segment. For example, people who prefer "the basics" often also prefer verbal announcements, face-to-face gatherings, and simple, black-and-white printed newsletters. People who prefer "multiple choices" or "healthy choices" often also prefer hospitality environments with color, natural light, and background music. People who prefer "takeout" often also prefer television, Internet, and multiple sources of communication simultaneously.

- Communication includes how people experience God and what spiritual yearnings dominate their personal needs. Compare these preferences with the worship alternatives preferred by each lifestyle segment. For example, people who prefer inspirational worship often prefer to communicate through more sophisticated audio and video systems, while people who prefer caregiving and healing worship often prefer intimate gatherings. People who prefer coaching worship often prefer television, radio, and Internet rather than print, while people who prefer educational worship often prefer print. Transformational worship may be ultrasophisticated or extremely simple, while people who prefer mission-connectional worship often value the Internet and multimedia.

- Communication includes how people teach, train, and share knowledge and which media are most effective to help them learn anything. Compare these preferences with the educational and small-group alternatives preferred by each lifestyle segment. For example, people who prefer a curriculum to study often embrace print and television, but people who prefer dialogue and activities often prefer face-to-face gatherings or social networks.

- Communication includes how lifestyle segments advertise and which media captures the consumer's attention. Compare these preferences to the outreach alternatives preferred by each lifestyle segment. For example, people who connect with survival ministries often prefer print and radio; those who connect with quality of life issues often prefer telephone and television. People who connect with health care concerns often prefer personal gatherings, and those who connect with interpersonal relationship needs often gravitate toward social media on the Internet.

The most obvious comparisons to make are with "modern" and "postmodern" preferences of technology. Communication alternatives have many significant nuances, however, and there may be a "modern" and "postmodern" application for each media choice.

Methods of communication are important because of what they *reveal* or *symbolize* about the community and congregation. What a communication method actually does, and what a communication method actually signifies, can be quite distinct. Communication technology has symbolic meaning that shapes the identity of a local church that sometimes contrasts with that of the lifestyle segments of the community:

- For example, some lifestyle segments may acquire digital technology for video capability in the sanctuary but use it to project printed words on a screen only rather than images, video clips, or live video streams. Their preferred communication method is actually verbal announcements and print, but they want to establish an identity that is more postmodern (young and upbeat).

- Or for example, some lifestyle segments use printed bulletin inserts and verbal announcements in worship, but these are commonly discarded or ignored. Information is actually shared over the telephone or in family gatherings through the week. The verbal announcements and printed information simply project the self-image of friendliness to strangers, openness, and transparency of decision making.

In the age of information, the significance of any method of communication is that it reveals who holds power in the church. The information shared is actually less important than the subliminal message of who controls the flow of information. For example, the same individuals *always* make verbal announcements; a specific team *always* determines images projected; one committee *always* launches the "telephone tree"; the pastor or certain staff leaders *always* edit the radio broadcasts.

Announcements

People share information and acquire knowledge through formal, verbal announcements made in public gatherings. These might include town meetings, regular meetings of clubs, parent-teacher associations, annual meetings for social service organizations, and Sunday worship services. Announcements are often highly structured. They are given at a specific time in the meeting, from a specific podium, and with specific time restraints. They may be repeated in print form or forwarded via other media.

Small churches in large, diverse communities may rely on verbal announcements even if the wider community relies on other methods. These churches are usually very homogeneous and do not mirror the demographic diversity of the public. Verbal announcements may actually not be very effective, but they establish continuity with tradition, encourage a sense of group identity, and often reinforce the control of particular leaders.

Lifestyle segments that genuinely prefer announcements are often older, less technologically sophisticated, and less affluent. They enjoy routine, prefer to work in committees and task groups, and have a high regard for authoritative leaders who are certified, elected, or appointed.

Print

People share information and acquire knowledge through hard copy: books, newspapers, magazines, and periodicals. They communicate through written letters, mass mailings, and institutional newsletters. They respond to visual advertising using still images in magazines, packaging, and billboards that include explanatory words or slogans. They tend to think in a straight line, following a logical argument that is highlighted by bullet points and ends with no more than three insights, conclusions, or recommendations for action.

Because reading has been the principal method of sharing information and acquiring knowledge since the invention of the printing press and is closely associated with popular access to the Bible, this is the most common form of communication in churches, even if it is no longer the most common method among many lifestyle segments. Most sermons are produced *as if* they will be read, even if they are never actually published once preached. Churches that strive to be seeker sensitive often assume that reading will be the preferred method of communication by outsiders. The modern version of this prompts churches to create longer and more detailed printed bulletins. The postmodern version of this leads churches to project the printed words of songs and liturgies.

Lifestyle segments that prefer print are often over forty-five. Their phase of life is often college and career start, adult with older children, empty nester, enrichment years, or retired. They usually have some postsecondary education that emphasizes liberal arts. They are more likely to work in education, health care, government, executive management, and financial sectors. They are fluent in the primary language of the surrounding community.

Radio

People share information and acquire knowledge through AM or FM broadcasts, at home, or in vehicles, and often the radio is constantly in the background at home, work, and play. They share information through local audio broadcasts and respond to audio advertising that uses drama and sound effects. These lifestyle segments prefer a mix of music and talk radio. They may also participate in limited dialogue to express opinions on the air.

The modern version of this records sermons and worship services for later distribution as tapes or CDs. The postmodern expression is a preference for satellite radio. People prefer specialty stations for specific genres of music or specific topics of conversation. Talk radio may be recorded for later podcasts on specialized websites.

Churches that appeal to these lifestyle segments often imitate the radio experience in worship. Worship designers may combine or blend several genres of music and often provide brief verbal commentary to interpret lyrics or explain liturgical elements. There may be limited opportunities for spontaneous announcements or opinions from the congregation. Services or sermons are often taped, duplicated, and distributed for visitors, marginal members, or shut-ins.

A wide range of lifestyle segments can have a preference for radio. They may be extremely sedentary or extremely mobile. They often have occupations that are mechanical, repetitive, or even boring, but with the multiple options of satellite radio, people of any occupation can become a niche market for a radio station. Some lifestyle segments may prefer radio because they are very active outdoors or involved in sports. First- and second-generation immigrants may rely on radio as a way to stay connected with their culture of origin or to become assimilated into their country of adoption.

Television

People share information and acquire knowledge through television programs and commercials. The television is constantly in the background at home. They are adept at "channel surfing" and may actually be following multiple sources of entertainment and news at any given time. They share information through local cable networks and respond to visual advertising using images that attract attention and stir emotion. They use television shopping channels to purchase personal and household items and gifts. They rent movies and may record programs. They are increasingly prone to marathon viewings of recorded programs.

The postmodern expression is satellite television and pay-per-view. This allows people who prefer television to access specialty stations (much like satellite radio). They may transfer television programs, movies, and commercials to mobile devices. They use computer enhancements and three-dimensional imaging to create virtual realities.

Churches that appeal to these lifestyle segments make extensive use of video screens in worship, Christian education, and advertising. They use both still images and streaming video and never permit a blank video screen in worship. Christian education material will be primarily visual, with little or no print supplement beyond a list of discussion questions. Churches use television screens (monitors) indoors and outdoors to advertise upcoming events or highlight the vision of the church. Because television is often associated with "entertainment," churches that consistently use video may be criticized as shallow. However, because each church program is like a different television channel, a wider diversity of lifestyle segments can often connect with church activities in some way.

Many lifestyle segments have a preference for television today.

They tend to be over thirty, and their educational background may be specialized rather than liberal arts. There may be a correlation between preference for television and diminished writing and reading skills. They are more likely to turn on the TV or watch a movie than read a book, although they may read magazines with lots of pictures. They are more likely to watch television news as another form of entertainment. These lifestyle segments often are avid consumers, follow fashion trends, and imitate pop-culture role models.

Telephone

People share information and acquire knowledge through telephone conversations, intentional telephone chains, and automated phone calls. These may be simple reminders to do things, contribute to charitable causes, and pay bills, or these may be long discussions about people and events. They may be individual or conference calls. The postmodern expressions are cell phones, chat rooms, and Internet voice calling. These mobile strategies allow people to talk personally with almost anyone, anytime and anywhere.

Churches that appeal to these lifestyle segments make extensive use of "telephone trees" and "prayer chains" to share information about coming events and personal needs. They usually avoid answering machines because they are impersonal and prefer to pay staff or train laity for 24/7 availability. They often share conference calls or include absent committee members through high-quality speakerphones or computers with desktop microphones and external speakers. The pastor may not be expected to be in the office, but is always reachable with a phone call.

Many lifestyle segments have a preference for telephones, although the clear trend is for cordless, mobile communication. People expect to leave messages on voicemail but are frustrated by complex automated systems that deprive them of the opportunity to talk to a "real person." Their need for relationship requires personal conversation. Internet conversations that allow both sight and sound in conversing with other human beings are preferred. This need is so universal that people who prefer telephone communication consider access to be a basic human right and bitterly resent profiteering from corporations and eavesdropping by governments or media conglomerates.

Lifestyle segments that prefer telephone communication often ignore other features on a cell phone. ("Smart phone" users better identified with Internet communications than telephone communications). They leave their mobile phones on and are frequently interrupted by phone calls, but do not spend much time downloading apps, playing games, or surfing the Web. They are open to telemarketing, although they often complain about it. These people tend to be upwardly mobile economically and professionally, but not yet in senior management or tenured positions.

Internet

People share information and acquire knowledge by surfing the Web, browsing websites, and participating in blogs. They are adept at using search engines with key words or phrases. They regularly contribute to online social networks and exchange e-mail and text messages frequently. They carry on simultaneous conversations and may be texting distant friends at the same time that they are talking face-to-face. Their mobile devices are constantly emitting different sounds to indicate messages received. People in this lifestyle segment respond well to pop-up advertising.

Churches that appeal to these lifestyle segments make the entire church building a wireless "hot spot." The worship center often has multiple video screens, one or more of which are always linked to a news service or mission website. Participants may feel free to link to websites mentioned during the service and text questions and comments to the worship leaders during the service. They readily connect with worship from other sites. They often prefer to sit comfortably with friends in a social setting outside the church building and access preachers, prayers, and songs remotely. They readily access church websites and look for interactive and online study groups.

These lifestyle segments are enthusiastic about using social media. They treat Internet conversations with the same intimacy as face-to-face conversations and may be surprisingly unguarded about sharing personal information and candid opinions. They are more likely to text than talk and are more tolerant of inevitable misunderstandings.

The number of lifestyle segments that include a preference for the Internet is growing rapidly. Those who *primarily* rely on the Internet for communication are usually under forty-five, with very mobile lifestyles, living in areas of greater population density. They may be early adopters for new hardware and software and use cell phones primarily for surfing, texting, socializing, and gaming (more than e-mail or phone calls). These people find that focusing on a single medium at a time is boring. They are not distracted by multiple inputs of image, sound, and data.

Gatherings

People share information and acquire knowledge by "hanging out" among peers of similar age, phase of life, or interests. Gatherings are not *meetings* in which there are formal agendas and announcements. These are informal, face-to-face gatherings without an agenda or timeline where recreation, relationship, and reflection are more important than learning, training, or decision making. Gathering spots may include coffee houses, pubs, health food stores, sports arenas, entertainment centers, food courts, or music venues. People readily respond to informal bulletin board advertising, free promotions, and spontaneous opportunities for short-term service.

Churches that appeal to these lifestyle segments create gathering spots within the church building, or off-site within walking distance of neighborhoods or apartment complexes where these lifestyle segments live. Staff leaders are usually extraverted personalities with a gift for conversation. Lay leaders are often trained in hospitality as greeters and refreshment servers or in ministries as fitness instructors or coaches. A specific religious atmosphere can provide a sense of safety, but aggressive evangelism, dogmatism, intolerance, or judgmental attitudes will drive this lifestyle segment away.

Some lifestyle segments that prefer gatherings as a primary means of communication tend to be under thirty-five, single or in nontraditional relationships, and without children. They tend to be ambitious but just starting out in careers. They tend to be renters and are often burdened with high debt. They may gravitate toward university centers but may not be students. They often enjoy cross-cultural environments and like to be surrounded by television or Internet media. They are generally poor financial contributors to charitable causes but are willing hands to do short-term beneficial services.

Other lifestyle segments that prefer gatherings as a primary means of communication may be over sixty-five, single, familiar with tradi-·tional gender-based relationships, and distant from family. They tend to be ambivalent about their former careers and anxious about the future. They are anxious about cross-cultural environments and do not appreciate the distractions of other media. They gravitate toward service clubs and special interest groups and are selective in philanthropic giving. Many are eager volunteers, provided there is a strong socializing element in service.

Multimedia Networks

People communicate in all of the above ways. They often do this simultaneously, using enhanced digital and wireless technology. For example, they may enjoy "gatherings" but text friends who are just across the room. They may talk by cell phone or voice software, interact using several social media, and upload and download photographs at the same time. They may listen to announcements but surf the Web to follow their curiosity sparked by a key word in the meeting. These people seamlessly carry on conversations to and from their destinations, and across various media, and with different partners, without missing a beat. They often do this deliberately in busy environments, with the accompaniment of music or streaming video.

Churches that appeal to these lifestyle segments train staff and volunteers to communicate on the fly, in shorter bursts of information, punctuated with question marks and provocative sayings that elicit a response and continue ongoing dialogue. Repetition and visibility are key strategies. They keep the name of a spiritual leader, or the name of a church, fresh in the minds of people for reference in times of trouble, and they run alongside these mobile lifestyle segments for Christian companionship. Churches use multimedia networks to spread news quickly of emerging mission opportunities, advocacy opportunities, and special events.

Although many lifestyle segments are including mobile phones, Internet, and peer group gatherings among their communication preferences, fewer go to the extreme of highly integrated networks. These tend to be young, single or in experimental relationships, and open to crossing cultural boundaries. They may be working at multiple part-time jobs in entertainment, food preparation, retail, manufacturing, transportation, and financial sectors. They usually have some post-secondary education but are more likely lateral thinkers rather than strategic planners.

15. Synthesis: Two Contrasting Examples

Church leaders are compelled to study demographic information because it is so remarkably *useful*. One can gather all the research in pure demographics, psychographics, lifestyle segments, and heartbursts into a practical aid to strategic planning. In a moment, I will share two very different examples, but first I want to highlight important insights about the assumptions we make and the conclusions we draw.

First, the power of demographic research does not lie in *analysis*, but in *synthesis*. It is not enough simply to "take apart" a microculture to study how it is constituted and its motivations, behavior, and thought processes. That may satisfy the curiosity of a research scientist, but it does not advance God's purpose to bless the world. We must "put it all together" in a fresh and profound way. We must take analysis further to uncover the significance of this information for the human quest for meaning and the divine urgency for blessing each microculture in unique ways.

In other words, demographic *analysis* alone only reinforces a profound subject-object dualism between church and world. The microculture is like a blob on a microscope's slide, and the scientist stands objectively apart, eyeing the blob from a distance. But our job as Christian disciples is not to stand apart in rapt curiosity. It is to involve ourselves in the unfolding drama of divine grace. We are not satisfied with an "I" and "You" relationship. We are drawn into an "I" and "Thou" relationship. Synthesis means that we put all the pieces of demographic research together, and that we put it together in a special way. We put it together in a way that reveals the peculiar human condition of a microculture, and the special grace of God toward that microculture, and that illumines the specific ways the church can participate in that event of incarnation.

Second, although *analysis* may be a science, *synthesis* is an art. This actually makes the work of church leaders more difficult. If it were only a matter of analysis, we might one day feed all the complexities of demographic categories and lifestyle attitudes into a vast computer in the cloud, press "enter," sit back and watch the computer generate a detailed tactical map, press "print," distribute it to ministry area leaders, and anticipate the certainty of institutional growth and social change. Instead, we have to pray about it. We have to think it through, test the results, think some more, pray some more, and listen some more. We have to explore. We have to "prayer walk" the neighborhoods and play with the search engines. We have to experiment, learning from both successes and failures. And we have to do all of this over and over again, because, if we blink, the mission field is different. If lifestyle segments morph, fade, and emerge faster and faster in the postmodern world, then church leaders must work and pray harder in the post-Christendom world.

The following two examples will also illustrate how the art of synthesis occurs. These two examples were shaped by several sources:

- The lifestyle group and segment studies of *Experian*[1] provide detailed information about who these microcultures are, where and how they live, how they view the world and survive, and even their digital behavior. *Experian* is one of a number of companies that gather millions of data bytes, analyze them with sophisticated algorithms, and provide information to corporations, retailers, municipal developers, school boards, local and regional governments, hospitals, and social service agencies. I have done these syntheses using other providers as well.

- These studies also rely on psychographic research from *MissionInsite*, which provides pure demographic information and a variety of topographic, street, and satellite views of communities and neighborhoods. This unique search engine allows church planners to explore specified mission fields they create for themselves and track opportunities for mission as communities evolve. The examples below are just two of more than seventy lifestyle segments for which I have described ministry applications.[2]

- Both studies are enhanced by my experience as a pastor and consultant in growing churches and church plants and networking with church leaders "on the ground" who are using the listening techniques I described earlier in this book. They are also the ones who pray constantly for the microcultures around them and who spiritually agonize about finding ways to bring extraordinary blessings to specific kinds of publics. It is this background that particularly informs the "heartburst" insights regarding ministry applications to specific microcultures.

All three sources help create the synthesis of ministry applications that guides strategic planning. If we compare *synthesis* to nature photography, we recognize immediately the importance of a tripod stand on which to place the camera lens. A quality image requires a solid foundation. One leg is the objective research that analyzes every scrap of information. The second leg is the subjective experience that immerses itself in the attitudes and moods of the mission field. The third leg is the spiritual discipline that prayerfully links human need and divine grace. Consider the "click" of the camera as the beat of your heart.

Here are two examples that illustrate how synthesis can be so useful for church leaders.[3] The first example outlines the ministry applications for a lifestyle segment that *Experian* calls *Unspoiled Splendor*. This segment is part of a group titled "Thriving Boomers" and represents a group of older, empty-nest, baby boomer couples living in small-town and rural communities often found in Midwestern and Western states. They tend to be friendly toward the church and are often of particular interest to pastors renewing established churches. The second segment *Experian* calls *Fast Track Couples*, who are part of a different group titled "Promising Families." *Fast Track Couples* are active, upper-middle-class suburban couples, under thirty-five, with or without children, living upwardly mobile lifestyles. They are often found on the fringe of midsize cities in the West, Midwest, and South. They are often quite alienated from the church and are of interest to church planters.

I have deliberately chosen these two segments because churches often lump together middle-class couples and families as if one set of ministry strategies can be easily blended to attract and bless both groups. Nothing could be farther from the truth. Many under-thirty-five *Fast Track Couples* might easily be the grandchildren of the aging boomers comprising *Unspoiled Splendor*. They may be couples, and they may value family life, but after that, there is little common ground. Their expectations for hospitality, worship, education, small groups, and outreach—to say nothing of their ideas on property, financial management, and communication—are so different that no amount of blending or compromise will satisfy both at the same time.

Unspoiled Splendor[4]

Imagine taking a drive out of the city, beyond the suburbs, skirting small towns, and driving down paved country lanes (but not dirt or gravel roads). In the West or Midwest, you see certain kinds of homes repeatedly. These homes are relatively recent estate homes built on formerly agricultural land. The house itself may not be over two thousand square feet, but it will be set on a large lot that is well landscaped.

The winding driveway also leads to a new, well-maintained barn or large shed at the back. Inside, you will see a high-end, extended cab, made-in-USA pickup truck, plus at least one additional vehicle that may be a hybrid, and catch glimpses of small tractors with various mowing, towing, snow-blowing attachments. The barn may well have a second floor dedicated as a woodworking shop.

These boomer couples have deliberately chosen to remain in, or relocate to, quite rural or even remote regions. However, these are not aging "hippies" seeking "flower power." They are socially conservative, hardworking, mainstream households that prefer to blend in rather than stand out. They tend to be spiritual *and* religious, living lifestyles that are sensitive to God and creation and connecting with established churches. Many are in agricultural careers, and more work in mid-level professional or retail jobs.

Despite their retiring ways, these people tend to have a global perspective. They often hold moderate to conservative social views and are surprisingly unconcerned about the environment. They can still be motivated to join a protest march, but on the whole they prefer to live a balanced life that maximizes personal fulfillment. Religion can, and should be, reasonable, and the church should help them expand their horizons.

These people dig deep roots in the community. They care about their neighbors, volunteer in community social services, and take leadership in municipalities. They will provide board and committee leadership for a local congregation and step up to mentor the next generation. They gravitate toward socially conservative established churches, Catholic or Protestant, and are not particularly ambitious to think outside the box or challenge traditional authorities. However, they will have strong opinions about what makes a just society and a faithful church, so they will sign denominational petitions and criticize the worship service.

Leadership: Enabler or Caregiver, Discipler[5]

Most people will prefer to connect with a small to medium-sized church that is networked with similar churches into a wider "parish"; some may be willing to drive farther to a central location in order to participate in a larger, resource-size church. On the whole, however, they value small population centers and join churches in part to keep those communities vital.

The pastor of the church is classically trained in seminary and usually ordained by a denomination. Even if the church is independent, the pastor is well connected with a network of clergy who share a common tradition. The pastor's focus is less on preaching and more on discipling. He or she may be young or old, but prioritizes time to mature members in Christian faith and equip them for service. The pastor does not need to be a great preacher but should be doctrinally sound and spiritually disciplined. He or she is a great small-group leader, builds mentoring relationships, and helps individuals through the life cycles and the ups and downs of Christian living.

In a small church, the pastor combines enabling with caregiving. He or she visits homes and residential communities and provides counseling and personal support. In a larger, regional church, the pastor combines enabling with discipling. He or she identifies, equips, sends, and evaluates volunteer teams to do caregiving ministries and outreach services.

Key Leadership Insight:

If Eucharist is part of the church tradition, the pastor takes a priestly role quite seriously, and Eucharist often functions as a healing or mystical focus of Sunday worship and personal visitations.

Hospitality: The Basics, Multiple Choices

People in this lifestyle segment are apt to come to church early and linger afterwards. Sunday morning is an opportunity to connect with friends and neighbors once a week. Committee and board meetings may take place before or after worship on Sunday, rather than midweek. Greeters do not need to be trained but are chosen for their outgoing natures and tolerant attitudes. Ushers are unnecessary.

More attention should be given to training refreshment servers. They should be able to address participants by first name and confident enough in their faith to engage in significant conversations about God, life, relationships, service projects, and so on. Refreshments are "basic," but "basic" means something different in this rural, agricultural context. "Basic" refreshments may include fresh grains, fruits, vegetables, and milk products alongside regular and decaf coffee. Sugary delights are welcome, but they are usually homemade.

Key Hospitality Insight:

People are apt to gather in their friendship circles and miss a newcomer. Train and deploy a team of "minglers" who deliberately welcome visitors and introduce them to others.

Worship: Educational, Caregiving, or Inspirational

When people in this lifestyle segment say they prefer "traditional" worship, they are usually thinking of the *best* worship experiences in their *personal* history. Good worship is not necessarily what the seminary or denomination thinks best, but what has been most influential in their local experience.

Smaller churches are usually a blend of educational and caregiving worship. The educational part includes a strong (albeit brief) expository sermon that is loosely connected to the lectionary or Christian year and predictable orders of worship with standardized prayers. The caregiving part includes personal intercessory prayers, extensive personal greetings, shared concerns, meditative moments, and children's stories, and leaders adjust the pace of worship to the slowest participant. Specific small churches networked as a wider parish may have special healing services as well.

Larger churches are usually a blend of educational and inspirational worship. The same educational elements are included, but the pace of worship is much faster. There is more music and music participation, and music is more upbeat. There is a greater emphasis on praise and thanksgiving. Larger churches may offer two or three services for different generations but never try to blend the service aimed at this lifestyle segment too much.

Key Worship Insight:

The pastor may have to be mobile from church to church, so lay leadership training becomes more and more important. This lifestyle segment definitely appreciates lay worship leadership, but only if leaders are excellent communicators and authentic spiritual role models.

Education: Curricular, Biblical or Topical, Peer Group

The educational backgrounds for people in this segment include high school, with some basic college degrees and specialized training. They are more likely to rely on structured educational events using a book, workbook, or curriculum. The curriculum may be tied to the lectionary used in worship or the Christian year, but they will also observe major cultural holidays like Mother's Day, Halloween, and Thanksgiving.

The children's Sunday school may be relatively small, with brief seasonal attendance in the mid fall and winter and attendance falling off sharply after grade 5. People in this segment prefer young children to older children because the latter do not value their worship preference. The young children may also be grandchildren.

In smaller churches, Sunday school may be replaced by a strong nursery and preschool, plus a "Children's Church" that gathers children of all ages. However, if the size and resources of the church permit, they will likely opt for age-based classrooms. Content will usually emphasize Bible stories rather than Bible studies, and some curricula will emphasize contemporary topics.

Adult commitment to Sunday school is mixed. Those adults with strong and consistent backgrounds in traditional Protestant churches may continue the practice of Sunday morning classes. These are usually early in the morning, led by an older and highly respected member (or pastor), and people remain in the same class for a long time. Increasingly, however, adults tend to replace Sunday school with expanded hospitality on Sunday morning and transfer Christian education to midweek small-group experiences.

Key Education Insight:

Even though couples in this lifestyle segment no longer have children at home, they have strong opinions about Sunday school method and content. There may be stress when introducing new educational methods or content.

Small Group: Rotated Leaders, Curriculum

Small groups primarily focus on relationships and mutual support, and the actual content of discussion may be secondary. Groups tend to stay in touch over an extended period of time. They may not communicate through social media when they are traveling, but people in this segment will soon reconnect with their group once they return. Affinities include outdoor recreational activities and indoor crafts, and special interests for antiques, gardening, and home decorating. Groups often rely on a book or workbook to guide conversations, especially if there is a "Leader's Guide" to create a lesson plan and enhance participation. The book is often set aside for the sake of friendly conversations.

Leadership is rotated because no one likes to stand out, and everyone wants to share authority. Basic training may be difficult to develop, and the pastor or overseeing leader will need to rely on 24/7 coaching to help groups deepen group life and resolve personality conflicts. Rotating group leaders rely on a curriculum with relatively easily implementation in order to focus conversation.

Key Small-Group Insight:

Groups and group leaders are often hesitant to enforce too much accountability. They are more likely to tolerate bad behavior in a group, even if it plateaus spiritual growth, because relationships are longstanding, and they do not want to disrupt harmony.

Outreach:
(For Themselves) Quality of Life, Interpersonal Relationships
(For Others) Survival, Human Potential

People in this lifestyle segment can be very compassionate, particularly for local or regional outreach. Perhaps surprisingly, they are less concerned about environmental or health issues, but they respond generously to family or community emergencies, gather and distribute the necessities of daily living (food, clothes, used furniture, and so on), and create opportunities for education (particularly for disadvantaged youth and adults). They feel great urgency to protect children and support police checks for vulnerable sector workers. They are strong advocates to sustain rural and small-town communities and to support traditional community events (fairs, socials, exhibitions, and so on).

They tend to spread their money around and donate to several local charities (within and beyond the church), but they also prefer to follow their money and get involved. They volunteer for nonprofit boards and are active in community social services. They may not have a big, bold vision for the future, but they can be very earnest about a variety of causes that capture their hearts. They are willing to write petitions, participate in marches, and advocate on behalf of victims of crime, prejudice, or poverty. People in this segment commonly say *we just want to make a difference!*

Key Outreach Insight:

People in this segment tend to believe in "gentle evangelism." They want to change hearts, impart faith, and witness, but do it in non-confrontational and educational ways.

Property and Technology: Ecclesiastical, Christendom, Modern

Unspoiled Splendor have lived in their current home up to fifteen years or more and have developed strong ties with the rural and small-town community. They are often passionate about preserving heritage buildings (including churches) and cautious about renovations or technology upgrades that might dramatically change the exterior or interior appearance of facilities. The church building is "sacred" space, not necessarily because it is consecrated ground, but because it embodies the history of the community.

Symbols are traditional and clearly Christian. The standard of audio and video technology is often whatever was "good enough" for their parents. Electrical circuits may not support highly amplified equipment, but plumbing and appliances for kitchens and washrooms will be updated. They will readily provide ramps and widen doorways for handicapped accessibility, but fear that elevators might compromise the aesthetics of the building. If a tornado or fire destroys a church building, they are apt to replace it with an exact replica. Churches usually have a nineteenth-century ecclesiastical appearance (white paint, steeple and bell, small narthex, hardwood sanctuary, and so on).

Important Administrative Issues:

People in this segment tend to be quite opinionated about any proposed change to facility or technology and will often lobby to preserve the status quo.

Stewardship and Financial Management: Unified Budgets or Designated Giving, Informed Philanthropy

These older boomer couples are careful with their money and frugal about spending. They will hunt for bargains even when they can afford high quality. They build large nest eggs for retirement and avoid debt. These attitudes are projected on the church as if it were an extended family. They preserve investments against a "rainy day" and are hesitant about capital campaigns (unless they are necessary to restore historic buildings or will clearly bless disadvantaged persons).

They give to unified budgets and expect regular and detailed financial statements. They prefer traditional, every-member visits and pledge to only a few funds (general, memorial, and debt retirement). However, they are quite open to special fund-raising during the year for mission projects. They often prefer paper offering envelopes over preauthorized withdrawals from their accounts and may wait until the end of the fiscal year to make a large donation. They often raise questions about spending in board or annual meetings and like to examine financial statements line by line. They may lobby to be appointed to finance and property committees.

Important Administrative Issues:

If the financial crisis of a small church forces a hard decision between sale of property and reduced personnel, they will often opt to reduce staff costs rather than sell, merge, or mothball property.

Communication: Print, Telephone, Gatherings

People in this lifestyle segment may use a generic Internet host like AOL, but they use the Internet mainly as a source of information and method of commerce. A church website may not be a high priority, and it will be seen primarily as a means to advertise and provide basic information about church programs. They may see a church website as another form of static, printed brochure.

They may not use e-mail very much (although this is changing rapidly). They rarely send text messages. They prefer printed newsletters and a master calendar on a wall in the church building. Printed announcements are reinforced by verbal repetition in worship and meetings. They reach the public through posters in community centers, public service buildings, restaurants, and sports arenas, and through direct mail.

They often rely on telephone communication direct to the home and will always have an answering machine ready to take a message. Because they travel, they will carry cell phones, but these are often quite basic and set to vibrate. The cell phone may not have an answering service. If they carry a smart phone, they will not use many of the features and rarely download apps.

Important Communication Issues:

Although couples that belong to *Unspoiled Splendor* are interested in outreach, they do not readily follow Internet links to learn more or participate in blogs. Always provide printed information or DVD movies to educate and motivate them about mission, or include a verbal "Moment for Mission" during the worship service.

Remember that these insights are all generalizations or trends. They need to be tested in every context using local surveys, perspectives from other community agencies, focus groups of members *and* nonmembers, listening-prayer triads, and so on. There will undoubtedly be differences in both degree and kind. Yet it is remarkable how these insights stand up to scrutiny time after time among churches in which *Unspoiled Splendor* is a dominant lifestyle segment in the community:

- A visionary pastor who is an excellent administrator, is a great motivational speaker, and has a passion for contemporary worship is less likely to succeed in this church than is an enabling pastor who is an excellent visitor, is an expert counselor, and has a passion for denominational history.

- Successful youth pastors eventually disharmonize the church and leave after nine months to two years, even though the adult members yearn for a successful youth ministry.

- Even the smallest change in worship can be stressful, especially if it involves upgrades in technology or renovations to space, or if it involves changes in musical style. Meanwhile, most people who join the church do so through transfer of membership and comment that their new church family *feels just like home.*

- Most outreach is accomplished through cooperation with social service agencies, rather than initiated by the church itself, and people often feel inhibitions about sharing their faith.

- Members prefer to practice accountability through redundant levels of management, with the last recourse being some form of congregational consensus or "town hall" meeting, rather than rigorous adherence to core values and mission alignment. Ad hoc committees are more important than measurable outcomes.

- It is usually easier to raise money for property maintenance, renovation, or new buildings than to raise money for additional staff.

- Marketing budgets will emphasize newspaper ads and direct mailings, but not website development. The pastor is more likely to get phone calls on his or her day off than responses to a blog post.

These preferences, and the positive or negative impact on church health, are really not theological or even denominational. They reflect the behavior and attitude of the lifestyle segment itself.

Contrast this behavior and attitude with a second, very different lifestyle segment. *Fast Track Couples* represent the active, upper-middle-class, and highly mobile couples and families in which the adults are under thirty-five. Some of these adults, at least, are the grandchildren of *Unspoiled Splendor* boomers. Their parents (the children of *Unspoiled Boomers*) dropped out of church, highly skeptical of religion. They were the middle-age generation that went missing from the institutional church and, contrary to past expectation, never did return once they got married and had children themselves. *Fast Track Couples* may be indifferent to the church but are no longer hostile. If they did come to church, what kind of church would it be?

Fast Track Couples[6]

Imagine taking a drive beyond the downtown core of small Midwestern and Southern cities. Drive beyond the established suburbs, beyond the beltway and box stores. The four-lane commuter roads are reduced to two lanes, and for a few miles these roads are rutted and broken due to the transport of heavy equipment. Large, new subdivisions of homes and town houses suddenly appear where crops once grew. The lots are relatively small and the trees immature. Yards are minimally landscaped, and the decks are open to the hot sun, with a barbecue and lots of children's toys. There are three to five architectural styles, repeated over and over again. The driveways are short, but wide enough for an imported minivan and a gas-efficient used car for commuting.

The subdivision is often centered on a park, with a new school, a new day care, a new fire department, and perhaps some other public buildings that all have very utilitarian architectures. There may not be a church building. Weekdays, it is pretty quiet, as both adults work, but on weekends people are coming and going constantly as families head out to a zoo, park, or museum, and childless couples travel to sports and entertainment venues.

The mobility of this lifestyle segment is profound and makes it difficult for the church to either attract or bless them as they pass by. These people are mobile in so many ways: frequent moves, career shifts, late-night and weekend activities, and instant messaging. Their imported SUVs all have accessories that make them a second home, and their houses are more like a staging area than a residence.

People in this lifestyle segment often live in an ethical blur as well. There are few, if any, absolute principles in their lives, and they don't take much time to think about consistent moral behavior or spiritual habits. Their behavior is pragmatic and self-absorbed. They don't wrestle with issues beyond the front door and are not particularly involved in their local communities. This often means, however, that people in this lifestyle segment are starved for authentic, deep, and lasting relationships. A sense of emptiness or meaninglessness can suddenly overtake them, and they may turn to prescription and non-prescription drugs to medicate themselves. Unexpected tragedy can significantly disrupt their lives, and they often look for help in times of crisis.

They will participate in local parent-teacher organizations and might participate in the church if they are powerfully motivated. Their involvement in the church may be sporadic and driven by crisis. They may struggle with the absolutes of Christian faith and the expectations of Christian discipleship, but they are often very interested in spirituality in general. Many do not have a particularly strong church experience, and they do not readily understand worship traditions and the sacraments, or church decision-making habits and organizational leadership. Yet they are very curious, quick learners and respond well to basic training and coaching. Churches don't have much time, because these people may be moving within three years.

Some may be driven by relationships or day care needs toward new church developments. Everything about a church needs to be convenient. The building needs to be central, with easy parking and accessible entrances. Offices, nurseries, and worship centers need to be clearly marked. All resources should be instantly accessible through the Internet, including a podcast of the worship service that these people may well have missed because of busy weekend lives. Nothing should require too many turns, steps, pages, or clicks, nor should it require too much work, thought, or perspiration.

Leadership: Mentor, Discipler[7]

New church developments appeal to their relational lifestyles and keep faith relatively simple. They like to connect with a pastor who is a mature Christian, but capable of mentoring them "on the go." The pastor helps them build a solid foundation in basic beliefs, key biblical stories and concepts, and the essentials of Eucharist and baptism. He or she models accountability to core Christian values and embeds simple and effective spiritual habits.

The pastor does not need to be a great preacher or sophisticated worship designer. He or she must be a good communicator personally and digitally. The pastor regularly blogs on an interactive website, texts constantly, and participates in social media. Therapeutic counseling can be referred to other professionals. The pastor concentrates on the basics of Christian life and coaches how to live faithfully amid transient residences, careers, and even relationships. These pastors participate in ecumenical and cross-sector networks of like-minded clergy, so that they can hand off mobile relationships to another mentor.

Important Leadership Issues:

Leaders are rigorously aligned to the purpose of making and maturing disciples. Do not be sidetracked by property, fund-raising, programs, or advocacy. No tactic or property is sacred. Do whatever works.

Hospitality: Multiple Choices, Takeout

The word *mobility* has many nuances for this lifestyle segment of people under thirty-five. They live in a world of speed, flux, and blur. Couples without children are out late during the week and attending entertainment venues for sports or music over the weekend. The one-third of the couples with children is likely to use economical day care during the week and take family outings over the weekend. Their homes in new subdivisions are more like staging grounds for upcoming activities, and they are not very interested in housekeeping or yard maintenance. Fast convenience foods are normative.

Church hospitality understands this. Parking and access must be super easy. Greeters need to be effusively friendly and able to communicate three things in just a few seconds: sincere welcome, the message of the day, and the importance of an experience with Christ. The worship center provides tables and chairs, and people will come and go during worship for more coffee and dessert. No paper handouts. No seating instructions. Give everyone a password to the wireless Internet.

People may or may not show up, but if they do, it will be last minute. Provide lots of food, even if it means storing or giving away the leftovers. If you run out, people in this segment will make snap judgments about your stinginess and never come back. Put leftovers in take-away bags that they can carry off to sports events and family outings. Food can be basic, but splurge on excellent coffee and real cream. Provide multiple serving stations to cut down any waiting in lines.

Important Hospitality Issues:

Create a welcome center in a large vestibule that also provides refreshment serving stations and lots of room to mingle. Give away useful gifts to visitors (like flash drives imprinted with the church website or DVDs of contemporary Christian music).

Worship: Coaching, Inspirational

Worship is probably not the primary way people in this segment first connect with a church, and it may not be the primary way they sustain their relationship with the church. They are more likely to connect through a small group or through a day care center sponsored by the church. They may sustain their church connection through a relationship with the pastor, social media, and podcasts of the worship service.

Coaching worship based on practical themes of Christian living is the best method to sustain worship involvement. They may attend two or three worship services in a row to follow a relevant theme (although watching a podcast or participating in a blog may work just as well). Worship is informal and interactive. Be sure to include ample time for Q & A, and organize text messaging direct to the pastor during worship so that he or she can instantly respond to questions. Keep their attention by including video clips or live drama. Assume they are multitasking during worship. They mean no disrespect when they are tracking Internet links, posting comments on social media, and watching the news while the worship service is going on.

Music will be truly contemporary with the sounds currently playing on the radio. Do not expect them to sing. Most prefer to observe and appreciate either live music or music video. Keep the order of worship very simple. No need for bulletins that contain responsive readings. Limit Scripture to the essential texts of the Old or New Testaments. Make the celebration of Eucharist very personal, and help them connect with the real presence of Christ as a spiritual guide and constant companion.

Important Worship Issues:

Provide an *excellent* nursery and preschool. Make the worship service an adult experience without children's stories, and reduce the number of crying infants or hyperactive toddlers.

Education: Experiential, Topical or Biblical, Generational or Peer Group

Most adults are about thirty-five, and their children are grade 5 and usually younger. Some adults may have old-fashioned preferences for their young children and expect Bible stories and generational groupings. Most assume their children learn best through activities, sounds, and images. If they attend a large megachurch, they will expect a Bible-based program enhanced by lots of technology, crafts, and activities. They will expect the same in a small church plant, acknowledging that different ages may be grouped together.

It will be difficult to draw adults into Sunday school. They prefer Sunday school to be concurrent with worship, so that they spend less time at the church and more time on family outings. Alternatively, adults may linger in the refreshment center to watch TV, surf on wireless Internet, or converse. The few who participate in an intentional learning event usually focus on a topic of urgent interest (often related to parenting or relationships).

The Internet is a natural part of daily (even momentary) living, and print is a foreign medium that reminds them of boring classrooms, technical training, and corporate workshops that are all bad memories. Adults often need only the spark of a video to engage in lively discussion, or they will watch video of some expert on the theme for the day, or they will appreciate the Christian witness of a famous athlete or celebrity.

People in this lifestyle segment are not particularly open-minded, despite their progressive attitudes toward technology and change. They often make snap judgments about clergy, church people, programs, and policies. They may uncritically accept generalizations about age, race, culture, or nationality. They tend to expect that others should give them a break but are less likely to give a break to others. Churches often need to explain the basics of accountability and provide strong role models for compassion, generosity, and respect.

Important Education Issues:

Avoid mere chitchat. Make the most of your limited time with them by engaging in significant conversations. Talk openly and nonjudgmentally about important questions of faith or challenges in living. Constantly reinforce the core values and beliefs that are critical to the consensus of the faith community.

Small Group: Designated Leaders, Affinity

The mobility of people in this lifestyle segment often encourages shorter, shallower relationships. Their yearning for deeper relationships is a primary motivation to become involved in a midweek small group. Groups are usually short-term but may be very intense. Groups are very creative about where and when they meet. They always have a digital component, and participants will continue their conversations through e-mail, text message, and social media.

Topics will vary, but they tend to reflect the self-absorption of people in this lifestyle segment, who see themselves as the center of the universe. Therefore, affinities are not usually about global social or environmental issues or about local community issues. They usually focus on parenting, marriage enrichment, relationships, and sexuality; technologies, music, and video; or especially on amateur or professional sports, personal fitness, and career development.

Designated leaders are preferred. If people in this segment make time for a small group, they want to spend that time with an expert or mentor. This is someone who not only speaks knowledgably about the topic, but who demonstrates accountability and intentionally models Christian values.

Important Small-Group Issues:

Christian faith often comes through a mentoring moment when "the penny drops" and individuals or couples in this segment suddenly "get it." Once the habit of self-centeredness is broken, people in this segment can become strong Christian leaders and assertive witnesses.

Outreach:
(For Themselves) Human Potential, Interpersonal Relationships
(For Others) Human Potential, Relationships, and Recovery

People in this segment assume that the issues that are a high priority for them are the same for everybody. They can take an interest in any outreach event or program that helps them explore spiritual gifts, personality type, vocational goals, and career plans. They are also interested in the dynamics of interpersonal relationships. Singles often have trouble starting healthy relationships, and couples are often concerned about maintaining healthy intimacy. Their frenetic dual-career lifestyles raise many issues about parenting young children. Many parents are already investing in college funds and micromanaging the futures of their toddlers and grade-school children.

The secret "underside" of their lifestyle is that substance abuse is a constant temptation. The same lifestyle segment that loves thrill rides at the theme park may experiment with drugs, and their combined incomes may help sustain bad habits. They may have a priority to create recovery groups for others as a backwards way they can participate in such groups themselves.

Important Outreach Issues:

People in this segment are more open to the miraculous in the sense that authentic spirituality does not need to be rationally explained. Individuals may experience the transforming power of God through addiction recovery, renewed relationships, or unexpected and undeserved grace.

Property and Technology: Utilitarian, Contemporary, Postmodern

Fast Track Couples find ecclesiastical structures rather forbidding, and Christendom symbols are often incomprehensible. They may have visited traditional church facilities at a wedding or in their childhood, although that is increasingly rare. "Wired" or "fixed" environments that lack postmodern technologies seem anachronistic. Therefore, they prefer to connect with a church with a multipurpose design, wireless Internet, ample video screens, and cell phone freedom.

The hospitality and nursery space is especially important. The former should provide comfortable conversation areas and refreshment centers, and the latter should equal the best day care organizations in the region (fresh air, natural light, high security, updated equipment, and clean, undamaged toys).

Landscaping is relatively unimportant, but parking and accessibility are crucial. The architecture often resembles any other public or educational building, but symbols embedded in murals, floor mosaics, pictures, and sculptures represent scenes of nature, starbursts, colored lights, and other broadly spiritual motifs.

Important Administrative Issues:

These people are very status conscious. They may dress conservatively and avoid ceremony, but they like to be in a quality environment with excellent furnishings and updated technologies.

Stewardship and Financial Management: Designated Giving, Lifestyle Coaching

Couples in this segment combine dual incomes and acceptance of debt in order to afford whatever is new and popular. They are informed consumers and do not consider it indulgent to set aside money for fitness and recreation. They do understand, however, that spirituality is an important part of overall health, and they welcome coaching that can help them develop family budgets that balance essential and personal expenses with generosity toward the church and selected charities.

They prefer to meet a Christian financial advisor in a coffee shop, with two or three other couples, and develop a faithful financial plan, and they do not readily participate in traditional stewardship campaigns that include personal home visits and pledge cards. They are wary of financial waste through institutional overhead and often do not appreciate the necessity of personnel *and* property costs. They prefer to designate charitable giving to specific programs and may contribute to the operations of a church as what their grandparents might have called "second-mile giving."

Favorite priorities in giving often involve children's ministries, technology upgrades, and pastor support packages. It takes more persuasion for them to give to social services, denominational mission funds, and other program and support staff.

Important Administrative Issues:

If the church is in a financial crisis, they are more likely to prioritize money to sustain personnel even if they must sacrifice property.

However, they often expect the pastor to have an alternative source of income from grants or work in another sector.

Communication: Internet

The Internet in all facets is the clear communication preference. People access the Internet for communication, socializing, research, and financial transactions. They are frequent browsers. Anything in print must have many Internet links to which they can turn. Even worship videos are more authentic if they are accessed directly from websites, rather than from DVD or hard drive memory. These people will multitask during worship. They can listen, blog, text, explore related links, and watch an Internet news feed all at the same time.

The best way to reach them quickly, and with reminders, is through texting and social networks. Greeters should be equipped with smart phones, and texting a message to a visitor within thirty minutes of their departure from the facility is effective. Staff routinely text encouragement or inspirational thoughts to members and post to blogs. It is better to send text with links to a document in cyberspace than to attach a document to an e-mail. They may respond to cell phone calls but often allow voicemail services to accumulate messages before responding.

Important Communication Issues:

The nuances of a message are often lost in transmission. Be prepared for frequent misunderstandings and the occasional inappropriate comment that requires a measure of forgiveness and reconciliation.

Remember that the contrasts between *Unspoiled Splendor* and *Fast Track Couples* are not about what is right or wrong, but simply about what works or doesn't work. The grandchildren will never "mature" to embrace the ministry preferences of the grandparents, and the grandparents will never be "open" enough to embrace the ministry preferences of the grandchildren. This is why "blending" strategies rarely work, even between lifestyle segments that may otherwise like each other.

Imagine that small rural communities in the West, Midwest, and South are being overcome by the urban sprawl of small cities.

Nineteenth- and early twentieth-century church facilities that addressed the expectations of aging boomers of *Unspoiled Splendor* are now seeing the advancing subdivisions of *Fast Track Couples* just one or two side roads away. The aging boomer church members uncritically assume that these under-thirty-five couples might be attracted to their church, but they do not even begin to understand them. Ministry expectations are extremely different:

Expectation	Unspoiled Splendor	Fast Track Couples
Leadership	Enabler or Caregiver, Discipler	Mentor, Discipler
Hospitality	The Basics, Multiple Choices	Multiple Choices, Takeout
Worship	Educational, Caregiving, or Inspirational	Coaching, Inspirational
Education	Curricular, Biblical or Topical, Peer Group	Experiential, Topical or Biblical, Generational or Peer Group
Small Groups	Rotated Leaders, Curriculum	Designated Leaders, Affinity
Outreach	For Themselves: Quality of Life, Interpersonal Relationships For Others: Survival, Human Potential	For Themselves: Human Potential, Interpersonal Relationships For Others: Human Potential, Relationships, Recovery

Property, Symbol, and Technology	Ecclesiastical, Christendom, Modern	Utilitarian, Contemporary, Postmodern
Stewardship and Financial Management	Unified Budgets or Designated Giving, Informed Philanthropy	Designated Giving, Lifestyle Coaching
Communication	Print, Telephone, Gatherings	Internet Social Media

Strategic planners for a rural church that is overtaken by urban sprawl face some real challenges. There are a few intersections between ministry expectations. Although the under-thirty-five *Fast Track Couples* won't share the social conscience of boomers in *Unspoiled Splendor*, they do share a keen interest in developing human potential and personal relationships. The older boomers will sympathize with addiction recovery. Both groups share a conservative set of family values. They both consider Scripture to be authoritative and the basis of Christian education, although their interpretations may differ.

There are many more places where their expectations diverge. It will be hard to choose a pastor who will connect well with both groups. Yes, that pastor needs to be a "discipler," but time-management priorities for the pastor will be hugely different. The hospitality expectations of *Fast Track Couples* will appear needlessly extravagant and indulgent to *Unspoiled Splendor*. Both mission purpose and style of worship will be markedly different and impossible to blend. They will quarrel about any renovation to the kitchen (microwaves and freezers vs. ovens and cupboard space) and about any upgrades to the sanctuary (audio, video, and flexible seating vs. pulpits, memorial glass, and pews).

Unspoiled Splendor would love to have the additional kids in Sunday school and worship, but *Fast Track Couples* will hate how they want to organize the educational program and be embarrassed by the children's stories in worship. The long-standing fellowship groups with untrained leaders and poor accountability of the boomer segment will grate on the nerves of under-thirty-five couples who want deep intimacy, expert advice, and strong role models.

It will be hard to convince many *Fast Track Couples* to visit the church twice. Parking is poor. The ecclesiastical architecture is forbidding, and many of the Christendom symbols are obscure. The narthex is claustrophobic, and the technologies are not charming but anachronistic. Pews are just plain weird. The sound system that is good enough for the aging boomers is woefully inadequate to the under-thirty-five adults. The organ is unknown to pop radio, and there is neither space, nor electrical supply, nor inclination to make improvements to musical instrumentation in the Finance or Property Committees that are dominated by boomers. Nothing happens in the church without a meeting, and dual-career couples under thirty-five hate meetings. They don't really understand how much financial commitment is required to run a traditional church, they don't pledge to a unified budget, and they are skeptical that maintaining what (to them) is old, useless stuff is worthwhile anyway.

The fact is that the empty-nest boomers of *Unspoiled Splendor* have lived there fifteen years already, and an essential purpose of the church is to sustain small communities. They simply cannot recruit *Fast Track Couples* to support that unspoken vision. Those young couples will be gone within three years, and they need a church that will make a relationship with Christ personal, transformative, and portable.

Here are the paradoxical problems facing a church that wants to blend these two lifestyle segments:

Unspoiled Splendor	Fast Track Couples
A good pastor protects harmony, honors tradition, structures worship and exposits Scripture, loves little children, balances the budget, cares about the poor and disadvantaged, therapeutically counsels members, and is always available in the office.	A good pastor models accountability, thinks out of the box, encourages spontaneity, coaches Christian lifestyles, loves young parents, manages inevitable debt, cares about spiritual life, mentors leaders, and is always available online.

Unspoiled Splendor, cont.	Fast Track Couples, cont.
Great hospitality parks on the grass, greets effusively, moves people along into the sanctuary, provides basic coffee and just enough food, and encourages friendship circles to chat about whatever they like.	Great hospitality parks between solid lines, instantly communicates purpose, lets people linger before worship, offers espresso and more than enough food, and seeds significant conversations about God and life.
Great worship educates people about the meaning of Scripture, doctrine, and ethics; connects them with a liturgical tradition; highlights kids; gets everybody singing; prays for traveling mercies and needy members; and repeats important announcements.	Great worship coaches people to overcome real daily problems, connects them with Christ, highlights small groups, gets everybody "pumped" through images and rhythm, prays for a good reason not to give up, and embeds core values and essential beliefs.
Great children's education puts the kids in a classroom, gives them a Bible curriculum that illustrates moral principles, and shapes future church members. Great adult education is face-to-face and eyes to print, and it shapes lasting friendships.	Great children's education puts kids in a craft room, gives them a theme for the day that refers to the Bible and other things, and shapes a Christian lifestyle. Great adult education is heart to heart and eyes to image, and it shapes a career path.
Great small groups meet in short bursts, over a long period of time, to study the Bible or a book, while participants take turns leading. The primary result is love.	Great small groups meet in shorter bursts, for a short period of time, to share a common affinity, guided by a trained leader or expert. The primary result is growth.

Unspoiled Splendor, cont.	Fast Track Couples, cont.
Great outreach helps disadvantaged people survive or improves our own quality of life.	Great outreach helps people develop their human potential or deepens our interpersonal relationships.
A church should look like a church; the more ancient a symbol, the better; standard equipment should be accessible by the least technologically savvy church person.	A building is just a building; the more contemporary a symbol, the better; standard equipment should be useful to the most technologically savvy member or visitor.
Gather as much information as possible about institutional income and expenses, pledge to a unified budget, and be generous toward extra fundraising for mission projects.	Gather as much information as possible about mission, plan a diversified portfolio for designated giving to charities, and be generous toward the operational expenses of an organization that gets mission results.
Advertise through newspapers, posters, and brochures; communicate with members by telephone; and repeat verbal announcements as often as possible.	Advertise through websites, blogs, links, and pop-ups; communicate with members by Internet; and never interrupt worship with announcements.

If the established church is part of a denomination, then wise denominational planners will not even try to blend both lifestyle segments into one church. The risks of conflict are too great, and any attempt to satisfy both groups at once will probably result in disappointment for both. Instead of growing a church, they could lose a church entirely. There is a better strategy.

Plant a new church in borrowed space in the subdivision for the *Fast Track Couples*. Appoint a specially trained pastor with the gifts and skills uniquely valued by this lifestyle segment, who can financially support himself or herself with another job. Provide grants for technologies, lay training resources, and programs. Concentrate ministry on short-term, highly effective small group and informal coaching worship. Focus the mission on disciple making, anticipate a high rate of turnover in membership and leadership, and waste nothing on unnecessary overhead.

There are two choices for the established church of *Unspoiled Splendor*. One choice is to cluster the congregation in a wider parish. Centralize program staff to travel the circuit. Consolidate organization into one board and one budget, but encourage each congregation to develop its own style of worship and set its own mission priorities. A second choice is to sell this and other similar church buildings. Invest in a new and central property near a major intersection, and build an ecclesiastical structure with plenty of room to house memorials and artifacts. Pool resources to create a staff with specialists in worship design, children's ministries, small-group multiplication, and outreach coordination. Disperse outreach centers in each of the surrounding communities.

The great value of demographic research lies in just this kind of synthesis. Leaders can be deployed, ministries shaped, and properties adapted to bless specific lifestyle segments in unique ways. Many publics can be included in the Realm of God.

Appendix

Mission Impact: Ministry Applications

Place an "X" beside the expectations that best represent *current church membership* in the second column from the left.

Circle the expectations that best represent *the lifestyle segments you want to reach.*

Leadership			
Each lifestyle segment tends to gravitate toward certain kinds of leaders.		**Caregiver**	Merciful, compassionate, special training in pastoral care and counseling; strong visitor; on call 24/7. Usually ordained.
		Enabler	Approachable facilitator; special training in generational ministries; sensitive to lifestyle cycles; committed to tradition. Usually ordained.
		CEO	Organizer, fund-raiser, manages staff and volunteers; coordinates programs; excellent communicator. Ordained with administrative experience.

Leadership, cont.			
Any given lifestyle segment may value a wide variety of leadership traits, but usually at least *two leadership expectations dominate.*		**Visionary**	Strategic and long-term planner; strong motivator; cross-sector credibility; serious spiritual habits and discernment. Ordained or lay.
		Discipler	Strong spiritual habits; matures Christians, grows leaders, mobilizes teams; strong seeker sentivity, high accountability. Ordained or lay.
		Mentor	Penetrating intuition, extreme spiritual discipline; 1:1 focus on incarnational experience to break addictions and focus personal mission. Lay or neo-monastic.
		Pilgrim	Accountable spiritual life, cross-cultural journey; "priestly" persona, inter-faith insights; radical sacrifice and simplicity. Lay or neo-monastic.
Hospitality			
All ways the public is greeted, sheltered, nourished, connected and before, during, between, and after worship services.		**The Basics**	One size fits all. One layer of un-trained greeters; limited availability of generic foods; single serving station; no good-byes.
		Multiple	Different strokes for different folks. Layers of trained greeters, focus on newcomers. Ongoing food court. Immediate follow-up.
		Choices	Ongoing food court. Immediate follow-up.

Hospitality, cont.			
		Healthy Choices	Targeted hospitality. Layers of trained greeters; board or small-group leaders intentionally mingle; Health, allergy-conscious foods. Small group invitations.
		Takeout	Mobile hospitality. Designated roving greeters; take food into worship, and take food home from church. Digital, wireless communication; follow-up tweets and texts.
Worship			
Worship based on *compulsion,* not *shopping:* lonely, trapped, dying, lost, broken, discarded, and victimized.		**Educational Worship**	Bless people with information, interpretation, exposition, explanation, and advocacy. Link to tradition, take notes, and watch the clock. Words; aim at the head.
		Transformation Worship	Bless people with personal change and divine intervention. Rescue the trapped and addicted. Stories, drama, action, rhythm. Role models; aim at the gut.
Usually at least *two worship expectations dominate,* and it is difficult for any church to "blend" more than two purposes in one service.		**Inspirational Worship**	Bless people with high spirits and light hearts. Sing, applaud, shout, enjoy, and send people fearless and strong into the world. Images; aim at the heart.
		Coaching Worship	Bless people with practical help to live a Christian lifestyle at home, work, and play; informal, relational, and "how to." Video, drama, expertise. Aim at behavior.

Worship, cont.			
		Healing	Bless people with physical, mental, relational, spiritual healing. Prayer, rites, awesome silence. Chants, background music, sensory experience. Aim at the body.
		Caregiving	Bless people with belonging. Pass the peace, children's stories, classic hymns, pastoral prayers, traditions. Gentle reminders, positive vibes. Aim at continuity.
		Mission-Connection	Bless people with opportunities to covenant for mission, celebrate mission results. Cross-cultural, international, simultaneous witness and social service. High-tech.
		Worship	Tech.
Education			
Each lifestyle segment tends to learn through distinct methods and technologies, and prioritizes certain areas of inquiry. At least *three preferences dominate* related to orientation, content, and structure.		**Curricular**	Children, youth, and adult education are oriented around printed books or study guides. Passive, intellectual, classroom. Maturity measured by acquired knowledge.
		Experiential	Children, youth, and adult education are oriented around activities. More music, images, movement, interaction. Maturity measured by behavior patterns, attitudes.
		Biblical	Content focuses on the Old and New Testaments (and ancient Christian literature); interpreted historically, culturally, and doctrinally. Maturity means biblical literacy.

Education, cont.			
		Topical	Content on contemporary issues, ethical principles, or comparative religions. Faith applied to daily events. Maturity means ethical integrity and enlightened behavior.
		Generational	Gathers people by age, and parallel the grades of the public school system. Each age or grade to have private space and age-appropriate resources.
		Peer Group	Gather people by affinity or special interest, parallels the friendship circles that are "extra-curricular" to the public school. Common enthusiasm, multi-purpose space.
Small Groups			
Each lifestyle segment tends to bond differently, and organize their groups in distinctive ways. *Two preferences dominate* for organization and focus.		**Rotated Leaders**	Participants take turns leading the group. Leaders are primarily fellowship hosts and conversation facilitators. Limited training.
		Designated Leaders	Single leader guides the group from start to finish. Leaders are chosen for spiritual maturity, and guide spiritual growth. Significant training.
		Curriculum	Focus on a book, workbook, or structured program; chosen by the group or leader. The outcome of group participation is greater knowledge or self-awareness.
		Affinity	Focus on shared interest, enthusiasm, or activity. Personal growth occurs in the midst of the affinity, and the outcome is healthy behavior or mission.

Outreach			
Each lifestyle segment finds certain kinds of outreach more relevant than others.		**Survival**	Focus on basic needs for food, shelter, clothing, employment, and basic health care. Often related to food banks, shelters, recycling, job placement, and medical clinics.
		Recovery	Focus on addiction intervention, 12-step support, and counseling. Often address addictions (alcohol, drugs, tobacco, gambling, and pornography, etc.)
There may be differences in the outreach they wish to *receive*, and what they choose to *volunteer to do*.		**Health**	Focus on mental and physical fitness, disease prevention, healing and rehabilitation, and therapy, Often related to counseling, healing therapies, diet/exercise disciplines.
		Quality of life	Focus on social well-being. Often related to crime prevention, safety, immigration, environment; and conflict intervention, advocacy against violence and peace.
		Human Potential	Focus on personal/vocational fulfillment, education, and human rights. Often includes schools, training, career counseling, and intervention against discrimination.
		Interpersonal Relationships	Focus on family life, marriage, sexuality, and healthy friendships. Often includes marriage counseling and enrichment, divorce counseling, parenting counseling and training, and advocacy for nontraditional relationships.
		Human Destiny	Focus on repentance, conversion, stewardship, and alignment with God's purposes. Often includes revivals, witnessing, canvassing, Bible distribution, prayer chains.

Facility, Symbols, and Technology		
Lifestyle segments have individual likes and dislikes: the appearance of the facility; regarding visual symbols that express vision and values; technologies or tools to enhance meaning and communication.	*Facility*	
	Ecclesiastical	The facility must "look like a church": structures traditionally associated with churches: arches and apses, steeples, colored glass windows; linear seating, etc.
	Utilitarian	The facility must be "user-friendly": strictures resemble and function like public buildings, entertainment centers, or schools; versatile and flexible.
	Symbols	
	Christendom	Signs and architecture use historic symbols associated with Christianity. Symbols supplement classic preaching and teaching.
	Contemporary	Signs and architecture favor symbols and images of broader spiritual significance, which are immediately recognizable by non-Christians.
	Technology	

Facility, Symbols, and Technology, cont.			
		Modern	Technology primarily enhances print and oral communication. Audio and acoustical improvements; options for reading or listening; sight lines accessibility for seniors.
		Postmodern	Technology primarily enhances multisensory interaction. Surround-sound, image, and video improvements; Internet and social media; and multitasking.
Stewardship and Financial Management			
Lifestyle segments have individual income preferences and investment strategies. People manage risk with one eye on organizational stability and mission effectiveness; and the other eye on expectations for personal sacrifice by members and financial generosity.		*Stability and Effectiveness*	
		Unified Budgets	Contribute money to a single general fund, and trust central administrators to disburse funds for personnel, program, and institutional overhead. Stability first.
		Designated Giving	Contribute money to personal preferences, and administrators disburse money according to the giver's priorities. Effectiveness first.
		Sacrifice and Generosity	

Stewardship and Financial Management, cont.			
		Informed Philanthropy	Stewardship primarily a financial commitment. They prefer to make informed, independent, confidential commitments for a tax benefit.
		Lifestyle Coaching	Stewardship primarily a lifestyle. They prefer to receive individual counseling; follow models of generosity; expect life benefits in return for obedience.
Communication Alternatives			
Each lifestyle segment tends to rely on distinct kinds of media to receive and transmit information. Individual households may have a unique balance of communication preferences based on different age groups in the household; but they tend to rely on one or two combinations of the following alternatives.		**Newsprint**	Receive knowledge through newspapers, magazines, periodicals; share information through newsletters, mailings; respond to visual advertising.
		Radio	Receive knowledge through AM or FM broadcasts, at home or in vehicles, and often the radio is constantly in the background at home, work, and play.
		Television	Receive knowledge through television programs and commercials, and often the television is constantly on. Images attract attention and stir emotion.
		Telephone	Share information and ideas through oral communication on corded or wireless telephone. Personal conversation, telemarketing, always talking.

Communication Alternatives, cont.			
		Internet	Receive knowledge by surfing the Web, browsing websites, blogs, social networks, and respond well to pop-up advertising. E-mail and text.
		Gathering	Share information by "hanging out" with others in their affinity group at unique gathering spots; board advertising, free stuff and free promotions.
		Multi-Sources	Communicate in all of the above ways; often simultaneously, using enhanced digital and wireless technology; text across the room or en route.

Notes

1. The Mission Attitude

1. An exercise to discern the "mission mix" of a congregation can be found in my strategic planning guide *Accelerate Your Church* (www.MissionInsite.com).

2. The connection between demographic research and strategic planning methods is elaborated further in my book *Accelerate Your Church*, available as a PDF workbook from www.MissionInsite.com.

2. A Brief History of Applied Demographics

1. Several of my books addressed this changing environment of ethnicity, including *Kicking Habits* and *Moving Off the Map*. The former was translated into Spanish and Korean.

2. Several of my books were used to analyze best practices, reprioritize budgets, change programs, and manage stress during this phase of church redevelopment, including *Coaching Change* and *Growing Spiritual Redwoods* (written with my friend Bill Easum).

3. My book *Why Should I Believe You? Rediscovering Clergy Credibility* (Nashville: Abingdon Press, 2006) explores the issue of relevance and accountability in greater detail.

4. My book *Mission Mover* emerged from digital dialogue with an emerging generation of Christian leaders called to mission, but reluctant to go to seminary. The book identifies the new learning content and methodology. Other books, such as *GPS: Global Positioning for the Soul* and *Christian Mentoring: Helping Each Other Find Meaning and Purpose*, are also intended to equip a new kind of leader.

3. Progressive Lenses of Research

1. Mark Mather and Diana Lavery, "In U.S., Proportion Married at Lowest Recorded Levels," Population Reference Bureau, accessed April 6, 2013, http://www.prb.org/Articles/2010/usmarriagedecline.aspx.

2. Robert Longley, "U.S. Birth Rate Hits All-Time Low," About.com, accessed April 6, 2013, http://usgovinfo.about.com/cs/censusstatistic/a/aabirth rate.htm.

3. See http://www.med.uottawa.ca/sim/data/Birth_Rates.e.htm and http://www.vitalsignscanada.ca/en/research-53-health-incidence-of-low-birth-weight.

4. See my book *Why Should I Believe You?* (Nashville: Abingdon Press, 2006).

5. See my book *Spirited Leadership: Empowering People to Do What Matters* (Atlanta: Chalice Press, 2006), 19.

6. See more description in my books *Talisman* (Atlanta: Chalice Press, 2006) and *GPS: Global Positioning for the Soul* (BandyBooks, 2011), which can both be found on Amazon.com.

7. I first wrote of this tactic in my book *Moving Off the Map* (Nashville: Abingdon Press, 1998), 190–91.

4. Demographic Research and Planning

1. I describe strategic planning for churches in a six-week annual planning process in my book *Accelerate Your Church: Out of the Box and Beyond* (2010, downloaded from www.MissionInsite.com).

2. Bandy, *Accelerate Your Church.*

3. I use these categories in the church assessment guide *95 Questions to Shape the Future of Your Church* (Nashville: Abingdon Press, 2009).

4. Tom Bandy, *Moving Off the Map* (Nashville: Abingdon Press, 1998), 237–78.

5. A phrase I first heard from my friend Bill Easum as we wrote about the emerging "cultural wilderness" of the postmodern world in *Growing Spiritual Redwoods* (Nashville: Abingdon Press, 1997).

6. I recognize that there is a "National Shrine to St. Rita of Cascia" (www.saintritashrine.org) in Philadelphia, and a Society of St. Rita devoted to her message of peace and forgiveness, and other specific examples of innovative Christian communities. My illustration is only a hypothetical, but realistic description of what could be.

7. See also *Moving Off the Map*, 275–77.

8. This latter organization is based on boundaries rather than tasks and is sometimes described as "policy governance." See my book *Spirited Leadership: Empowering People to Do What Matters* (Atlanta: Chalice Press), 2006.

5. Ministry Opportunities for Lifestyle Segments

1. I have collaborated most with www.MissionInsite.com in the United States. This research engine gives church leaders direct access to a multilevel search tool that allows users to track pure demographic, lifestyle segment, and psychographic variables. I wrote *Mission Impact* for the website to highlight the

filter for ministry applications for lifestyle segments described here. It is designed to interface with two other tools available from sister website www.ChurchInsite. com. *The Church Life Survey* offers a quick analysis of your church and automatically provides an overview of your stage in church growth and makes recommendations for strategic development. *Accelerate Your Church: Out of the Box and Beyond* is a six-week strategic planning process that guides church planners to initiate new ministries, perfect ongoing ministries, and terminate ineffective ministries. Use these tools along with the lifestyle segment filters found here. The spiritual hunger of the public has never been more urgent, and the opportunities for ministry have never been greater. Now you can design ministries that are relevant and engaging. You can accelerate church growth and maximize mission impact.

2. See www.MissionInsite.com.

7. Hospitality Alternatives

1. One of the best books for training hospitality leaders is *Multicultural Manners* by Norine Dresser (Hoboken, NJ: John Wiley & Sons, 2005).

9. Education Alternatives

1. I provide a chart in my book *Mission Mover* (Nashville: Abingdon Press, 2004), 88–89.

10. Small-Group Alternatives

1. I discuss these kinds of groups more fully in my book *Christian Chaos* (Nashville: Abingdon Press, 1999), 196–201.

11. Outreach Alternatives

1. See my strategic planning book *Accelerate Your Church: Out of the Box and Beyond,* available as an e-book from www.ChurchInsite.com. I discuss the principles of strategic planning and how church planners use lifestyle segment information to set priorities.

13. Stewardship and Financial Management Alternatives

1. I discuss the seven "cost centers" more fully in two of my books: *Spirited Leadership: Empowering People to Do What Matters* (Atlanta: Chalice Press, 2006), 117 and *Accelerate Your Church* (www.MissionInsite.com, 2010), 90–100.

15. Synthesis: Two Contrasting Examples

1. *See Mosaic USA, Group and Segment Descriptions,* by Experian Marketing Services (www.Experian.com).

2. See *Mission Impact,* by Tom Bandy, www.MissionInsite.com.

3. These descriptions are excerpts from my larger study that is accessed through www.MissionInsite.com, which are in turn based on descriptions found in *Experian* lifestyle group and lifestyle segment commentaries. I provide similar and richer insights for each of the 19 lifestyle groups and 71 lifestyle segments developed by *Experian* in the United States today.

4. See *Mosaic USA*, 121–24.

5. See *Mission Impact*.

6. See *Mosaic USA*, 125–28.

7. See *Mission Impact*.

CPSIA information can be obtained at www.ICGtesting.com
Printed in the USA
LVOW12s1244260713

344675LV00005B/10/P